HAVE YOU SEEN MY COUNTRY LATELY?

America's Wake-Up Call

JERRY DOYLE

THRESHOLD
EDITIONS

New York   London   Toronto   Sydney

Threshold Editions
A Division of Simon & Schuster, Inc.
1230 Avenue of the Americas
New York, NY 10020

First Threshold Editions hardcover edition January 2010

THRESHOLD EDITIONS and colophon are
trademarks of Simon & Schuster, Inc.

For information about special discounts for bulk purchases,
please contact Simon & Schuster Special Sales at
1-866-506-1949 or business@simonandschuster.com.

The Simon & Schuster Speakers Bureau can bring authors to
your live event. For more information or to book an event contact
the Simon & Schuster Speakers Bureau at 1-866-248-3049
or visit our website at www.simonspeakers.com.

Designed by C. Elliott Beard

Manufactured in the United States of America

10   9   8   7   6   5   4   3   2   1

Library of Congress Cataloging-in-Publication Data

Doyle, Jerry, 1956–
    Have you seen my country lately? : America's wake-up call / Jerry Doyle. — 1st
Threshold editions.
        p.   c.m.
    1. United States—Politics and government—21st century—Anecdotes.   I. Title.
    JK275.D69   2010
973.932—dc22   2009040641

ISBN 978-1-4391-6801-1
ISBN 978-1-4391-6815-8 (pbk)
ISBN 978-1-4391-6863-9 (eBook)

CONTENTS

INTRODUCTION

Have You Seen My Country Lately?

As I survey the political, economic, moral, and social landscape of America, I'm left wondering where my country, the country I knew, has gone. Many of our biggest private companies are now owned by the federal government. Our banking system has been bailed out by taxpayers and, for the most part, nationalized. Our government is inflating the currency, running up unsustainable deficits that will surely burden future generations, taxing us at record rates, and promising to confiscate even more personal wealth on behalf of the village idiots. Our politicians are hand-in-glove with financial criminals, deadbeats, special interests, lobbyists, and leeches. Our media is asleep at the wheel, more concerned about the death of a washed-up singer, a missing blonde, a runaway bride, or an overboard groom than the destruction of our capitalist economy. Our military heroes have been torn down with accusations of murder, torture, and abuse, while bottom-feeders are held up as champions.

Have You Seen My Country Lately?

If you have, please let me know where it is—I'd like to go there. I'd like to go back to a country where equality of opportunity is the rule, not equality of result. I'd like to return to a country where property rights mean something. I'd like to find a country where parents can let their children walk the streets without fear, where cops, firefighters, and members of the military are treasured, and where the freedom and entrepreneurial spirit that bring prosperity are still the standard.

We're at a defining moment in our nation's history. Our government, along with its cronies on Wall Street, in Hollywood, and in the media, is seeking to crack down on every area of American life, destroying our liberties in the name of the collective: mortgage cheats, tax frauds, and bribe-minded officials are the suit-and-tie radicals, taking through government force what they haven't rightly earned. And our government officials are the benevolent dictators who see fit to pay off the political mobs with our hard-earned cash. Their allies in the media cover up their robbery with words like "social justice" and "fairer distribution of wealth." Everyone suffers—even the economic gangbangers and their enablers—because soon there will be no more money left to steal.

Have You Seen My Country Lately? is the story of that robbery. It's the story of government overseers who use government-sponsored entities to underwrite bad loans in order to pay off political allies—the Fannie Mae and Freddie Mac scandals. It's the story of elected officials who use inside information to pad their personal portfolios and politicians who rake in millions of campaign dollars from the tobacco industry in order to push nationalized health care, then treat smokers like lepers. It's the story of "public servants" who help their banker friends out with huge sums of taxpayer money, and blackmail their banker enemies when they don't get what they want. It's the story of the 1960s radical roots of today's liberal movement; the fascist roots of today's Obamanomics; the entitlement mentality that now dominates American youth. It's the story of the race baiters, poverty pimps, and leftist extremists who undermine the military and the police.

Mostly, it's the story of the new America—the America of "hope and change." And it's a very unsettling story.

But *Have You Seen My Country Lately?* is more than that. It's the information you need to help stand up and say "Not Today." It isn't economic double-talk or elitist mumbo jumbo. It's the bare facts, the hard facts, and the facts we need to absorb in order to fight back. Everyone can understand it. Everyone *must* understand it.

Most of all, *Have You Seen My Country Lately?* is a call to arms.

This is still our country. This is still the greatest nation on earth. We still have the world's most powerful economy, boosted by the world's most entrepreneurial people. We still have the world's best military, boosted by the world's bravest and most committed young people. We still have the world's best philosophy: freedom and liberty and personal responsibility, as laid out in our Declaration of Independence and the Constitution.

But too many of the principles that make the United States the greatest country on earth are beginning to crack at their foundations.

Have You Seen My Country Lately?

I've seen my country lately. Frankly I don't like what I see. Nevertheless, it's not too late to restore the great and unique wonder that is the United States. It's never too late. The moment we think it's too late and give up, darkness enshrouds us. Too many people have become feeble, weak, compliant, and dependent on government. We are the beacon of hope for the world, and we will remain so as long as we stay true to our principles—and that means standing up for our principles. As the old saying goes, if you don't stand for something, you'll fall for anything.

Let's stand for something. Something beyond our own petty wants and needs. Something beyond the things we think the government owes us. Something beyond the false security blanket of federal safety nets and regulatory authority.

Let's stand for what America was, what America is, and what America can be. As Abraham Lincoln put it, "We shall nobly save, or meanly lose, the last best hope of earth."

Let's find our country and restore her to glory.

Let's welcome a new morning in America.

Let's begin now.

HAVE YOU
SEEN MY COUNTRY
LATELY?

CHAPTER 1

SMOKE FOR
THE CHILDREN

I smoke cigarettes because I love kids.

Seriously.

Think about it: with every drag on a cigarette, I am doing my part to help support all the needy children in America forced to grow up in a world without health insurance.

Sound preposterous? Let's look at the facts.

The tax on the cigarettes that I smoke funds the State Children's Health Insurance Program (SCHIP) and provides health care for children of the working poor—and for children of the not-so-poor.

On February 4, 2009, President Obama signed into law a $0.62 increase in the federal cigarette tax, along with increases in other tobacco taxes. The total federal tax on cigarettes is now $1.01 per pack. That, by the way, is on top of state, city, and local taxes. In states like Massachusetts, where smokers are basically on par with terrorists, the total tax on a pack of smokes is now $3.52. And that doesn't even put them in the top ten. Barrow, Alaska, came in seventh place with $4.01 per pack.

Chicago, Illinois, clocked in second at $4.67 per pack. And crossing the tobacco finish line in first place is New York City, at $5.26 per pack—and remember, that's just for the taxes.[1]

I can almost hear the Smoke Nazis cheering, "More! More! More! Higher! Higher! Higher!" After all, it's "all for the children." Revenue produced by the increased tax will not only allow the federal government to expand the budget of SCHIP, it will also bring our nation closer to a government-controlled program for universal health care. All "for the children." All funded by my nicotine addiction. It makes a man proud.

That's what House Speaker Nancy Pelosi (D-CA) said at the signing of the SCHIP bill: "When people ask me the three most important issues facing the Congress, I always say the same thing: our children, our children, our children. When the SCHIP bill passed the House of Representatives, we were on the floor, and it was the end of the day, and I quoted the poem by Henry Wadsworth Longfellow, 'The Children's Hour.' And I said that when we passed that bill, it would be the children's hour for the Congress of the United States. As many of you know, when I took the gavel as first woman Speaker of the House, I took it surrounded by children. This is a comfortable environment for me. It reminds us constantly of our responsibility to the future. But when I took that gavel, I said, 'I take this gavel on behalf of all America's children.' And let's hear it for the children!"[2] For those of you who buy into Pelosi's sincerity, the same Nancy Pelosi, at her swearing-in as speaker of the house, said this: "After years of historic deficits, this new Congress will commit itself to a higher standard: pay as you go, no new deficit spending. Our new America will provide unlimited opportunity for future generations, not burden them with mountains of debt."[3] So much for the children.

Taxing cigarettes on behalf of the children is only one symptom of a broader governmental effort to control our lives. Whether it's driving an SUV, eating a burger, watering the lawn, or chugging a soda, government wants you to cut it out or pay through the nose. And when government says something, you'd better listen. It's easy to increase "sin taxes" when it's "for the children." But I warn you, it's only a matter of time before they come after something you enjoy.

Government has become the Pleasure Police.

And the administration of Barack Obama and the do-gooders in Congress are looking into every nook and cranny of our lives—as Pelosi put it, "every aspect of our lives must be subjected to an inventory."[4]

When they came for the smokers, you did nothing because you weren't a smoker. When they came for the beer drinkers, you did nothing because you weren't a beer drinker. When they came for the gamblers, you did nothing because you weren't a gambler. When they come for something you enjoy, who will be left to stand up for your rights?

I will.

LOVING THE SIN, HATING THE SINNER

Let's start with a case study: SCHIP.

After the Clinton universal health care plan failed in 1993—and after that failure led to the Republican Revolution of 1994—Democrats were looking under every rock for an alternative plan. One that would be less expensive and easier to sneak by the eyes of Congress. In particular, First Lady Hillary Rodham Clinton discovered that it was far easier to con Americans into supporting health care for tots than universal health care.[5] After all, it takes a village to pay for a kid's vaccinations.

So Hillary and Co. put together an action team, led by Senator Ted Kennedy (D-MA). Kennedy spearheaded the initiative to provide medical insurance to children—and he suggested that the bills be footed by dastardly smokers. Senator Orrin Hatch (R-UT) joined on, happy as a clam to be linked with any cause that could "help the children"—as Hatch said, "Children are being terribly hurt and perhaps scarred for the rest of their lives" by living without health insurance.[6]

Now, this "all for the children" move was terrific. After all, who doesn't want to give poor, innocent kids medical insurance? Especially when smokers are paying for it. How can anyone argue with that?

Obviously Congress couldn't. Hence the U.S. Senate was able to muster enough bipartisan support to pass the bill in August 1997.[7]

The only controversy surrounding SCHIP at its creation was its attempt to raise federal taxes on tobacco. Ironically enough, many states *opposed* this rise in taxes because it would cut into the revenue *they* were getting from taxing tobacco. The Republican Policy Committee, for example, called the bill "admirable" but misguided, stating that smokers would stop buying cigarettes due to high prices, and that such a market drop-off would cost states and localities $6.5 billion over five years. Kennedy's predictable response: "If we can keep people healthy and stop them from dying, I think most Americans would say 'Amen; isn't that a great result?'"[8]

Of course, that wasn't exactly Kennedy's true feeling on the matter. While Pleasure Police legislators across the partisan divide despise smokers—even President Obama, who likes to light up, won't do it in front of the cameras—the same Pleasure Police rely on smokers to keep buying to fund their socialist health care schemes. After all, as President Bill Clinton put it while signing the bill, "Because we have acted, millions of children all across this country will be able to get medicine, and have their sight and hearing tested and see dentists for the first time."[9] Would Teddy want to deny those millions of children their sight if all of us smokers decided to go cold turkey?

That's the schizophrenic attitude of the government on smoking— we need you to smoke, but you're bad people for smoking. Or, as I put it, love the sin, hate the sinner.

So we get two conflicting policies: as SCHIP grows toward universal health care, the government has to increase the taxes on cigarettes. In short, the government needs smokers. At the same time, the Pleasure Police hate smokers, so they try to stop them from smoking. This is somewhat like wearing a scuba suit while trying to drown yourself.

But there's one thing that unifies these two conflicting ideas— universal health care and the war on smoking—and that's control over Americans' lives. Your life and my life.

SCHIP: THE GOVERNMENT
DOCTOR WILL SEE YOU NOW

When SCHIP began, it was slated to provide a whopping $24 billion to provide health care to uninsured children (remember those quaint days when $24 billion was a lot of money?). That hefty chunk of change wasn't nearly enough, though. Not when the government could use Helping the Children™ as an excuse to control everybody's health care.

During his administration, George W. Bush twice vetoed bills to increase SCHIP funding by raising tobacco taxes.[10] As soon as the CEO of America, Barack Obama, was elected, he and his overwhelmingly Democratic Congress pushed through a measure to expand the program, moving closer to their goal of nationalized health care. On February 5, 2009, Obama signed the Children's Health Insurance Program Reauthorization Act of 2009, which was designed to increase the program's coverage to four million kids and adults—yes, I said adults—in addition to the seven million it already covers. Naturally, the new funding was going to come directly from smokers. Not only did the bill raise tobacco taxes, it loosened requirements for SCHIP eligibility—now newly legal immigrants, particularly pregnant women and people under twenty-one, could receive benefits right away, without spending one day paying taxes (previously, a five-year waiting period was required to receive benefits). *No waiting period required.*

And citizenship documentation was loosened, too—instead of requiring a passport or birth certificate to demonstrate citizenship, states are now allowed to verify citizenship by matching an applicant's name and Social Security number with federal records. Basically, steal somebody's Social Security number and you're in the pink—or, rather, the green. Said Congressman Henry Waxman (D-CA): "While this bill is short of our *ultimate goal* . . . it is a down payment, and it is an essential start." The key words: "ultimate goal." You can already see the Democrats' creeping incrementalism, which we will discuss in detail shortly.

And Nancy Pelosi seconded the motion: "This is the beginning of the change that the American people voted for in the last election, and that we will achieve with President Barack Obama." [11]

What's the problem with expanding government-covered health care, you ask? Actually, there are two problems. Number one: you don't get to choose your doctor anymore. The government chooses where, when, and why you'll see a doctor. Two, at the very least, you're going to be paying for someone else's health care. And now that Congress has begun expanding SCHIP to cover even those who aren't poor, you're probably paying for your next-door neighbor's health care. You know— the schlub who owns the Bentley.

Here's how it works. Individual states determine the eligibility requirements for SCHIP based on the federal poverty guidelines. State governments are allowed to broaden the scope of eligibility to families making as much as *300 percent* more than the federal poverty level. You read that right. *Three hundred percent.* That means middle-class children, even kids of the semirich, are now covered under the public health care system. For example, in New Jersey a family of four making over $66,000 who may already have insurance is eligible for SCHIP. [12]

It's even worse in New York, where the state legislature attempted to pass a bill promoted by former Governor Eliot "Client #9" Spitzer to expand the eligibility for SCHIP to more than *400 percent* over the poverty level. That would have meant that children in a family of four making $82,600 would have been covered. [13] I know New York City is expensive, but do you think it's possible that a family of four could eke out an existence on an annual income of $82,600?

That's quite a "limit." By allowing states to subjectively define poverty, more and more kids who are covered by private health insurance paid for by parents will be dumped off private rolls and signed onto government-issued universal health care. In turn, these families are beholden to the politicians and dependent on government programs. It is not likely that a person who depends on the government to pay for their medical insurance, food stamps, school lunches, education, and numerous other subsidies will vote against the congressman who protects and expands these programs.

This means the beginning of the end of private health care—the best health care system in the world. I'm not exaggerating. Listen to the Democrats on this score. When Senator Roger Wicker (R-MS) asked whether it was "the real intent of this legislation to replace the private health care system with a government-run health care system," Senate Democratic whip Dick Durbin (D-IL) quickly responded that he did not want to "trap people into private health insurance." [14]

This is government "care" we just don't need. In 2007, 12.5 percent of the population was living in poverty as defined by the federal government, and most of these people were in metropolitan areas.[15] That sounds like a lot of people. But that's much lower than the 18.5 percent of the population that was living in poverty in 1959, when this information was first recorded.[16] We *are* doing better, despite President Obama telling us that American families are barely scraping by and can't survive without the government's help.

But Obama and his political pals have a stake in telling us how rough we have it—after all, that's how they get us to vote for them. That's the payoff. They tell us the world is an awful place, they provide us the comfortable safety net of substandard services, and then we vote for them. That's why Obama and the other politicians who are pushing for nationalized health care cite misleading statistics with unnerving ease.

Sally Pipes, president and CEO of Pacific Research Institute in San Francisco and author of *The Top Ten Myths of American Health Care: A Citizen's Guide* and *Miracle Cure: How to Solve America's Health Care Crisis and Why Canada Isn't the Answer,* addressed some of the false facts on my syndicated radio program. For example, Pipes explained that Obama and his cronies like to say that preventive care, weight loss programs, and antismoking programs will save health care dollars. There is no solid evidence to show that those initiatives have any positive effect on medical spending in the long run. In actuality, after

Congress mandated nutritional information posted on food labels, the "percentage of obese Americans increased by two-thirds." [17]

Supporters of the Food and Drug Administration's regulation of tobacco cite figures from the Centers for Disease Control and Prevention that smokers cost the country $96 billion per year in direct health care costs, and an additional $97 billion in lost productivity. But as Sally Pipes pointed out, smokers die earlier than nonsmokers, and actually provide a savings to Medicare, Social Security, pensions, and other government programs. The average smoker dies at age seventy-seven; the average nonsmoker dies at age eighty-four. Those extra seven years cost about $100,000 more in medical costs. A Dutch study published in 2008 in the *Public Library of Science Medicine Journal* backs her up— the study found that health care costs for smokers were about $326,000 from age twenty on, compared with $417,000 for thin and healthy people. The reason? Thin, healthy people live longer. According to the Associated Press, the CDC refuses to put a health tag on the price savings from smoking—they think it's ghoulish, even though it's accurate.[18] Smoking not only helps the children, it saves the whole health care system money!

The most important myth propagated by liberals all across America is that 45 million Americans have no health insurance, and therefore no access to health care. That's a phony statistic. What politicians fail to mention is that the "48 million uninsured" figure includes about ten million illegal immigrants. Over nine million of the "uninsured" live in households with incomes above $75,000. About 30 percent of those "uninsured" lack insurance for only six months or less. And according to Pipes, "as many as 12 million uninsured Americans are eligible for Medicaid and the State Children's Health Insurance Program—but they haven't signed up." [19] When you subtract all the people who are in this country illegally, voluntarily do not have insurance, or just haven't applied for it, the total number of uninsured Americans is a fraction of the 45 million that we hear repeated over and over again.

With this administration, branding is the key, whether that branding is the truth or not. The reality is that we have eight to nine million chronically uninsured people that we should be focused on helping. What we don't need is a program designed to save the other 37 million people who don't need it.

Then there's the lie that uninsured people have no access to health care. This is absolutely false. The federal government passed a law in 1986 that requires any hospital that participates in Medicare to accept any patient that comes through the emergency room door and to provide care regardless of the patient's ability to pay.[20] Do not believe politicians who blather that America must be ashamed because "people in this country do not have access to medical care"; it's a flat-out lie. Everyone in this country has access to medical care, and most hospitals are required to provide it.

But lies matter less than ramming through policies that give government control over your life. The expansion of SCHIP is a perfect example of creeping incrementalism. Little by little the government takes control and intrudes into our private lives. You don't see it happening, but it's happening right in front of your eyes. I first began to think about creeping incrementalism while I was living in Florida. Each morning, I would go down to the Jupiter Inlet jetty and chat up the local fishheads. Every day, I would watch the relentless pounding of the waves on the jagged edges of the rocks, and with every wave, those edges were being slowly eroded, worn away. But unless you watched it as I did, day after day, year after year, you never saw that it was happening.

It's the same thing with the government's creeping incrementalism, intruding into our lives under the guise of government programs we can't live without. They start with a small step and use an emotional symbol like a poor sick child to get support for their health care program, or a seemingly starving and stranded polar bear to convince us that global warming is going to destroy the planet. A bill is passed. Taxes are raised. Then slowly, over time, the program is expanded. The regulations and programs keep growing. The jagged edges of the rock are worn away.

The more dependent private citizens are on the government, the more powerful the government becomes, and the less freedom we have to make decisions in our lives. Sooner or later, somebody becomes the scapegoat—somebody has to pay. Lately, it's been the smokers. Congressman Jack Kingston, a Republican from Georgia, was on my radio show, and estimates that we need 22 million additional smokers in this country to pay for the expansion of SCHIP.

The tax revenue from my pack of cigarettes is paying for your kid's health care. I choose to smoke, but I do not choose to pay for someone else's medical insurance. You had the kid. You pay the freight. Unless I was invited to the conception and birth, I don't want to be responsible for paying for your kid's medical coverage.

But in the liberal worldview, everybody is responsible for everybody's medical coverage. Which means that everybody gets to decide whether you *really* need that new hip, or whether you're just whining about it. It means that everybody gets to decide whether you or poor sick little Billy deserves chemo. Here's the problem with "it takes a village" medical care—medical care is inherently about the individual, and socialistic medicine is inherently about the community. When you've got a broken leg, you're not concerned about the rest of the folks in the hospital—you want your damn leg fixed this very instant. In a socialized system, your broken leg might have to wait for Bentley Boy's sprained ankle.

Liberals love it. They believe that they're the brightest, smartest folks who ever lived. And they believe that they should be in control of idiots like me and you.

THE ASSAULT ON SMOKERS

As we just saw, smoking pays for children's health care. So the next time you see someone who's *not* smoking, ask them, "Why do you hate children so much?"

In fact, ask a liberal. Here's why: while liberals are constantly encouraging people to smoke so they can tax the sales, they're also treating smokers like they have the plague. In Las Vegas, you can't smoke in the airport, but as soon as you get off the plane you can gamble away your kid's college tuition, hire a prostitute (so I've been told), or play video blackjack until you are broke. Or as people in the industry say, "play to extinction." In Nevada the state and federal tax per pack of cigarettes is targeted to be $2.[21] That means a carton of cigarettes costs about $50. Every time you buy a carton, you're paying the equivalent of your phone bill. In New York, a single pack of cigarettes may cost you upward of $8.[22]

On the federal level, the largest tax hikes have been on bulk tobacco and small cigars. Bulk tobacco was previously taxed at $1.10 per pound. That was raised to $24.78 per pound, a 2,259 percent increase.[23] Small cigars were taxed at $1.828 per 1,000 and are now $50.33 per 1,000, an increase of over 2,700 percent.[24]

Worse than the tax hikes are the numerous laws seeking to turn smokers into social outcasts. Around the country, smoking bans have been put in place to protect the innocent public from cigarette smoke. It is illegal to smoke on the beach in San Diego; we wouldn't want smokers tossing their butts on the beach, don't you know. (By the way, I'm all for courteous behavior—people should throw their butts in the garbage. But by the same token, I don't want to watch some fat slob toss his Big Mac wrapper on the sand.)

At Torrey Pines Golf Course, which is a municipal course, smoking is not allowed at all. You can't smoke a cigar on the course even if the others in your group all want to smoke cigars and the only offendable people are hundreds of yards away. Torrey Pines is located on a cliff near the ocean. The winds are so strong at Torrey Pines that hanggliders use the air currents to fly along the coast. But apparently, the winds aren't strong enough to carry away the stench of cigarette smoke or cigar smoke.

It isn't just restricted to golf courses and beaches. The entire state of California treats smoking as though it's the bubonic plague: "Stay away, you diseased bastard, and keep your cancer sticks to yourself!" If California treated illegal immigration the same way it treats smokers, the illegal population would be cut in half within the year.

California started its attack on smokers in 1994 when smoking in the workplace, including restaurants, was made illegal.[25] Four years later, smoking was banned in bars. The bar ban included $100 fines for bar owners allowing smoking for a first offense. The second time around, the fine jumps to $7,000.[26]

In October 2007, California went even further, making it illegal to smoke in a car with another person seventeen years old or younger. "I am so proud that my fellow legislators and the governor agree that our children must be protected from the toxins in secondhand smoke. I will continue to help lead California in eliminating pollutants that hurt our kids' health," said State Senator Jenny Oropeza (D).[27] It's all "for the children." Anything "for the children." And hey, just to help the children, how about lighting up with me, Senator Oropeza?

In October 2007, Belmont, California, passed one of the most ridiculous smoking restrictions—they made it illegal to smoke in your own apartment or condominium. In fact, under applicable local and state rules, residents of Belmont can't smoke anywhere except in detached homes and yards, streets and some sidewalks, and certain outdoor "designated smoking areas."[28] The rationale? If your home has a shared wall with another residence, your smoke could seep through the wall or out a window and into your neighbor's home. The noxious fumes could magically creep through solid steel and tainted Chinese drywall and poison you to death.

This is a massive violation of property rights. If you own a condo and want to allow your tenants to smoke in Belmont—well, tough for you, bud. If the Pleasure Police catch your tenant lighting up, they'll fine you $100.[29]

Belmont isn't alone. El Cajon, a town in San Diego County, California, made it illegal to smoke in most public spaces—including on sidewalks. The city outlawed smoking in parks, and required businesses selling tobacco to acquire a license. The City Council vote in favor of the measure was unanimous. "It's a health issue," said city spokeswoman Monica Zech. "It is not taking away rights."[30] What, exactly, would "taking away rights" constitute? Locking smokers into public stocks? Summary execution? Branding with the scarlet "S" of smoking?

They're moving in that direction in Calabasas, California. In March 2006, the Calabasas City Council prohibited smoking in all public places where anyone—anyone!—might be exposed to secondhand smoke. The ban encompasses bus stops, soccer fields, parks, sidewalks, and outdoor cafés. You can smoke in your car—but not if the windows are open and someone is nearby.[31]

Barry Groveman, mayor of Calabasas and an environmental lawyer, crows that the regulations "push the envelope," and celebrates the "ground breaking public health law." "This is the right time and the right place to take this step," says Groveman. "We hope it will be the way things are done all over the country and all over the world." First offenders, reportedly, will be given a warning and a breath mint.[32] Second offenders may get a caning.

It's not just smokers the government hates—it's the tobacco sellers. In April 2009, Teddy Kennedy and Henry Waxman passed a bill through Congress to have tobacco regulated by the Food and Drug Administration. Never mind that the bill actually benefits Big Tobacco— companies like Philip Morris backed the bill, since it effectively shuts down smaller competitors. Congressman Waxman couldn't be prouder: "Today is truly a historic day in the fight against tobacco, and I am proud that we have taken such decisive action . . . now we all can breathe a little easier."[33] With all the crappy food we eat in this country, doesn't the FDA have enough to worry about?

It doesn't end there. The SCHIP expansion bill, which relies on nicotine addiction for its income, requires any manufacturer or importer of tobacco to apply for a permit from the Tobacco Trade Bureau, which is part of Timothy "Son of Shifty" Geithner's Department of the Treasury. The TTB states on its Web site that "as a result of the [Children's Health Insurance Program Reauthorization Act of 2009], any person who manufactures or imports processed tobacco will now be required to qualify for and obtain a permit from TTB, and take inventories, submit reports, and keep records as required by regulation." The government now requires you to qualify for the business you are already in, and submit reports to them.

It's even worse. The TTB can put any importer or manufacturer out of business, or tie up the permit application with bureaucratic nonsense for so long that it is impossible to survive. According to the TTB's Web site, "As a result of the Act, the basis for denial, suspension, or revocation of permits has been broadened." In other words, the government gives itself the authority to deny you a permit to make tobacco products, and suspend or even revoke the permit once they've given it to you.

Here are my questions: Where's the bailout? Is the government now going into the tobacco business? If you are a tobacco manufacturer and the government denies your permit, what will they do for those laid-off employees? Will they take over your business and make you a government employee like they have with executives at General Motors and AIG?

This hurts consumers and business at the same time it sucks the lifeblood for children's health care from those very folks. It's a radical 1960s agenda packaged as a nice way to pay for kids' doctor's appointments.

But here's the real question: How far will the government go? If smoke is so damn dangerous, how about outlawing backyard barbecues on the Fourth of July? Or how about buying carbon offsets before dumping on the lighter fluid?

And here's an even bigger question: Why not just make it illegal to smoke tobacco? The government wants us to stop smoking—we just spent $75 million in Obama's stimulus behemoth in order to create programs to get people to quit smoking[34] (perhaps Obama can be the first beneficiary). Yet they won't just ban cigarettes. That would be the easiest way of stopping people from smoking. We could have a modern-day Tobacco Prohibition. We could stand up for health. We could stop lung cancer right in its tracks. We could do it "for the children." And the Democrats and Republicans have the votes to do it. So why not?

The answer is simple: they don't want to make it illegal. First off, they want to milk the tobacco companies for all they're worth. The same Democrats who say they just want to "help the children" are taking boatloads of greenbacks from companies in the tobacco industry.

Over the last decade, Democrats from New York have gotten rich from the tobacco folks: former Senator Hillary Clinton and Senator Charles Schumer took $5,000 each; Rep Gregory Meeks took $17,000; Rep. Joseph Crowley took $17,000; Rep. Edolphus Towns took $15,450; and Rep. Charlie "I'm Investigating Myself" Rangel took a whopping $44,000. Only one Republican took more money than Rangel—Rep. Thomas Reynolds, who pocketed $48,000. In California, it's the same story: Democratic Rep. Mike Thompson took $26,000; Rep. Dennis Cardoza took $26,500; and Rep. Joe Baca led the Democratic pack with $28,310. The only Republican who received more money than the Democrats was Rep. Devin Nunes at $44,500. Even in Nevada, Senate Majority Leader Harry Reid (D) took $23,000 from the evil tobacco industry.[35]

They want the tobacco industry to stay in business, and they want smokers to smoke. All so they can pocket everyone's money, control your life, and do it "for the children." And they want you to smoke "for the children" so that they can expand their control even further, by taking over the health care system.

It's a big cycle of control. And it doesn't stop at cigarettes.

THE FIGHT AGAINST FAT

So now you can't smoke. "Okay," you figure, "at least I can still go down to the McDonald's and have a burger and fries." Not so fast there, buddy. The government is coming after your food, too.

In December 2006, in a regulative move that shocked the nation, the New York Board of Health banned the use of trans fats from all restaurants in New York. Of course, the FDA had already approved the use of trans fats, but that didn't stop those brave New York legislators. Trans fats are hydrogenated oils—products like Crisco are trans fats. They're cheap and they have a long shelf life. They're used in everything from pizza to hot chocolate mix to French fries. According to the FDA, the average American eats 4.7 pounds of trans fats every year. And yet, somehow, the country has been functioning for years.

And the legislators went even further: restaurants that included certain health info on menus were forced to start listing calorie counts on their menus, too. Just in case that dude at Dunkin' Donuts thinks the chocolate éclair is good for him, of course.

Some might call this fascistic control over everyday life. After all, if you want to chow down on some greasy fries, that's your business. But the government calls it a step forward. "Nobody wants to take away your french fries and hamburgers," says New York mayor Michael Bloomberg. "I love those things, too. But if you can make them with something that is less damaging to your health, we should do that."[36]

Now, contrary to popular elitist opinion, Americans are not total morons. We know that French fries aren't good for us. But we like 'em anyway. We know they're fried in oil. We know they're instant heart attacks. That's our business. If I'm out at Yankee Stadium for the afternoon, I don't need to know the calorie count on a Bud Lite in a souvenir $10 cup. And I certainly don't need to know how many ounces of fat an order of KFC chicken tenders has. If I want to find out, that's my business. But who put Little Lord Bloomberg in charge of the food industry? Who said that just because Mikey Likes It, we all have to like it? Or, conversely, just because Mikey Hates It, we can't eat it? Isn't this a free country? Or does the Constitution no longer apply to those who enjoy pork rinds?

Here's the dumbest part: this government regulation, like virtually all other government regulation, is designed to take effect quickly. And this government regulation, like virtually all other government regulation, hasn't properly considered what will happen because of this rush to action. The bill gave restaurants six months to replace cooking oils and shortening, and eighteen months to phase out trans fats altogether. So what did many restaurants do? They simply switched over to palm oil—which, says the American Heart Association, is high in saturated fat.[37] Well done, New York!

So now you can't smoke and you can't eat fatty foods. All that craving and hunger is making you thirsty. What you could really go for at this point is a nice, cool Coke.

Not so fast, Soda Boy. Soda's another no-no.

According to the health commissioner of New York, Dr. Thomas Frieden, "Sugar-sweetened beverages (soda sweetened with sugar, corn syrup, or other caloric sweeteners and other carbonated and non-carbonated drinks, such as sports and energy drinks) may be the single largest driver of the obesity epidemic."[38] We could tell people to use their best judgment and get some exercise, of course. Or, Dr. Frieden suggests, we could tax the hell out of these things.

Frieden notes that such taxes are not unheard of. Sadly, they're quite popular. According to Frieden, forty states already have "small taxes on sugared beverages and snack foods. . . . Because excess consumption of unhealthful foods underlies many leading causes of death, food taxes at local, state, and national levels are likely to remain part of political and public health discourse."[39]

Predictably, Frieden is using his position as New York City's health commissioner to push for such taxes. Frieden says that a penny-per-ounce tax could decrease consumption by 10 percent and raise over $1.2 billion per year in the state. "Only heftier taxes," says the unelected New York Food Czar, "will significantly reduce consumption."[40] Frieden even suggests how the tax should be levied: an excise tax, he says, will make consumers aware that they're paying extra for the sin of soda, whereas a per-ounce tax simply raises the price without informing the consumer why. And Frieden suggests, unsurprisingly, that the money raised be used to prevent obesity "for the children."

New York governor David Paterson, the profligate womanizer and political charlatan, originally embraced this sort of nonsense. He proposed an 18 percent tax on nondiet soda, stating that it would raise hundreds of millions for the state. But he dropped the proposal in March 2009 after the public rejected the idea as idiotic. Even Little Lord Bloomberg has rejected the proposal—for the moment.[41] But don't expect that opposition to last long. It's a recession, and the government wants cash. What better way to get it than to do something "for the children" while penalizing those who simply want a Mountain Dew?

PICKING ON THE MINORITIES
"FOR THE CHILDREN"

The simple fact is that the government isn't interested in stopping smoking, or hamburgers, or Gatorade. They want people to continue consuming those products in order to fund their massive and growing control over the health care program in this country.

Well, I'm sick of subsidizing Big Government spending programs with my smoking. Why don't some of these liberals help out? They need to sacrifice, pitch in, and do their share. That's why I invite Mayor Bloomberg and Speaker of the House Nancy Pelosi—the woman who saccharinely and sickeningly opened her speakership by stating that she was accepting her post "for the children. . . . For these children, our children, and for all Americans' children"[42]—to come out to Nevada, sit down with me, chug some Red Bulls, and gag down a few Camel Lights. In fact, let's have a smoke-a-thon. Whoever can wrap and smoke the most small cigars in a day will be given the honorary title "America's Biggest Patriot." As Joe Biden has said, paying taxes is patriotic.

Now that I think about it, smokers and drinkers really are "America's Biggest Patriots." So I think we're entitled to some long overdue respect.

And here's the thing: targeting a minority group in the United States is un-American. Perhaps the only thing liberals understand better than gibberish is legalese, so here's some legalese for them: under *United States v. Carolene Products Co.* (1938), it is unconstitutional to legislate against "discrete and insular minorities." Now I know that normally the Supreme Court thinks discriminating against economic minorities is okay—that's why the rich minority pays all the taxes in this country.

But what I'm saying is this: you liberals acknowledge that we smokers are addicts. You know that we're driven by our biology to smoke up. And you liberals know that we who enjoy soda are driven to enjoy soda by our bodies' desire for glucose. So why is my desire for a cigarette, a burger, or sugary soda any less constitutionally protected than a woman's right to choose (*Roe v. Wade*)? After all, it's my body, isn't it?

In fact, in many ways, my rights should be *more* protected. After all, women—who are hardly a "discrete and insular minority"—get the protections of the ever-changing Constitution. Why not those of us who constitute a vast minority of the voting public? Why don't we get protection? Don't we deserve the freedom to choose?

I like smoking. I know it's not good for me. I know it's killing me. And yet I choose to do it anyway. I like eating greasy chili-cheese fries. I know it's not good for me. I know it's killing me. And yet I choose to do it anyway. I like lots of things that Little Lord Bloomberg, Henry Waxman, Ted Kennedy, and the Pleasure Police don't like. But why do they get to treat me as though I'm public enemy number one while profiting from my purchases? If they don't like my cigarettes, let them come take them from my cold, tobacco-stained fingers.

What's more, if they're going to use my Pleasure Tax dollars for something, it better not be to control my health care. If I can choose to smoke, I sure as hell can choose which doctor I want to see about my respiratory demise.

THE DOWNHILL ROAD TO PERDITION

Cigarettes, soda, and trans fats are the low-hanging fruit. It's easy to institute popular "sin taxes," especially in a crappy economy—you know, the "worst economy since the Great Depression." But let's pretend, for just one moment, that the government decided to raise taxes on red meat. Burgers. Steaks. Sausage. Hot dogs. Anything and everything with meat. (Okay, maybe that doesn't include hot dogs.)

It isn't that far-fetched. The "nanny staters" are constantly harping on the horrific effects of red meat. They act like the stuff is made of cyanide. And they say that red meat eating causes the production of baby cows—and baby cows are like Kryptonite to the earth's Superman, since they produce tons of methane, which contributes to global warming. The sleazeballs at the United Nations are already calling for decreased consumption of red meat to help stop global warming. "Give up meat for one day (per week) initially, and decrease it from there," says Dr. Rajendra Pachauri, chair of the United Nations Intergovernmental Panel on Climate Change (IPCC). And Joyce D'Silva, ambassador for compassion in world farming, says, "If we continue to consume meat and dairy at the current rate both animals and the planet will suffer."

So let's assume the Democrats take the U.N.'s lead and decide to start taxing red meat at a higher rate. Will Americans stand up then? Or will we continue to sleep?

How about when the liberals come for your water? I live in a desert in Nevada, where my water use is regulated. The local Water Police come to my house, evaluate my landscaping, and regulate how much water I can use to irrigate my backyard. I am allowed certain days a week when I can water my lawn and plants. Local officials drive around the neighborhood with a sensor to listen for running water on days that it is not permitted—the Water Police.

Now, I understand that if everyone in Las Vegas ran their irrigation systems all the time, Lake Mead could potentially dry up. But there's a solution to that: privatize the water industry! If water usage started to run out of control, prices would rise—and that would lower water usage. Instead, the government wants to control who gets water how, and how much water each person gets.

A few months ago, I was chastised by the Water Police for having forty-one palm trees and some grass in my backyard.

"You live in the desert, you know," they told me.

Yes, Sherlock, I know. I sort of figured that one out when I looked around and I was in the *middle of a desert*. And the temperature was 116 degrees in the shade. But if I wanted to *live in a desert*, with all that implies, I'd set up a tent in the dirt surrounded by brown dusty rocks. The whole point of using water is to make my house look *less* like a desert, and more like a tropical paradise. I'm willing to pay to do that. What business is it of the government whether I want to pay a few hundred dollars more to keep that forty-first palm tree alive? (I'm coming up with a solution to my landscaping problem, actually—I'll just kidnap some spotted owls, plant them in the trees, and tell the Water Police that federal law requires that I keep their habitat unharmed. Take that, all you regulatory morons!)

Whether it's red meat or water, whether it's soda or French fries, whether it's health care or tobacco, the government is creeping incrementally toward total control over Americans' lives. It starts with the Pleasure Police, who use their power not to ban pleasure, but to severely circumscribe it with fines; they then use that confiscated cash to increase their control in other areas of American life like health care, in the name of the children. Soon they'll be coming after your air conditioning and the size of your toilet (again).

And they're not making any secret of their desire to control every aspect of your life. Barack Obama spoke in Portland, Oregon, on May 18, 2008. "We can't drive our SUVs and eat as much as we want and keep our homes on 72 degrees at all times . . . and then just expect that other countries are going to say OK," said the future president. "That's not leadership. That's not going to happen."

I don't want to ask the government whether I can turn up my thermostat. Apparently, neither does Obama. According to senior advisor David Axelrod, Obama "likes it warm" in the Oval Office during winter—so warm that "you could grow orchids in there."[43]

Maybe the government is right that eating less red meat and drinking less Coke and slurping down less Crisco will make me live longer. Maybe they're right that smoking will be the death of me. But that isn't theirs to decide, it's mine. If I don't want to live my life that way, it's none of their business. It is thoroughly disturbing that Americans' freedom to make the most basic choices, right or wrong, is being eroded by our own elected officials.

Slowly our freedoms and liberties are being eroded like the rocks on the jetty. Texas governor Rick Perry came on the program recently. He used the analogy of a frog in a pot. The government, he said, gets the frog in the pot and slowly turns up the heat. Before the frog knows it, he's done.[44]

This is what the liberal Congress and the president are doing to the American public. They're slowly turning up the heat. It makes us feel all nice and toasty warm. But before we know it, we're all beholden to the government, and our personal freedoms have been deep-fried. Too late to escape the slow government boil.

The freedom to choose how to live our lives is the basis of the entrepreneurial spirit that makes this country great. And that spirit is being eroded. Choices we make in our daily lives—choices like what to eat, what car to drive, and at what temperature we keep our homes—are being co-opted by our elected officials. We're becoming dependent on government, enslaved to government, utterly reliant on government. If we don't defend our liberties now—and that means liberty for fat people and red meat eaters and, yes, smokers—there won't be any liberty left to save.

CHAPTER 2

FORKS IN THE ROAD

If you don't know where you're going,
you might wind up someplace else.
Yogi Berra

I was lucky enough to be born at a time in America that I believe was the sweet spot, the 1950s. Everything seemed possible and nothing was impossible. It was a time of relative peace and prosperity for starting out on the path to living and achieving the American dream. Your imagination, determination, and optimism could open up any door.

Over the course of my life, I've reached many forks in the road. Each one of those forks existed only because I live in a country that offers us the ability to choose. In countries like North Korea and Iran there aren't many forks in the road. There, someone chooses for you.

It's when the forks in the road become barricades to our free will that we have to stand up for our right to self-determination. In the past decade and a half, I've watched as choices diminished for many Americans, as the government intruded into our private lives, exercising control over nearly everything we do: what we drive, how much of our money we get to keep, when we are eligible for retirement benefits, and even over our eating, drinking, and smoking habits. I've watched our ability to choose get narrower and narrower.

And I've watched as the value of personal responsibility—the essence of human behavior that makes the freedom to choose worthwhile—has diminished also. With the government promising us the moon and giving away our cash and our neighbor's cash to pay for it, the value of choice disappears. We're trading our liberties for a false sense of security.

But it's not too late. It's never too late to reassess the path and decide that perhaps there's a better way of doing things. It's never too late to change our path or that of our nation.

WE'LL TAKE THAT ONE

The first fork in the road of my life was when I was born on July 16, 1956. I don't know my birth mother nor do I have any desire to know who my biological parents are. She was probably some Catholic high school girl who wasn't married, got pregnant with me, was sent away for the summer, and came back to school the same weight she left. Sans baby, of course. This baby headed straight to the Angel Guardian Adoption Home in Brooklyn, New York.

The Angel Guardian Home was an imposing brick building located on the corner of 12th Avenue and 63rd Street. It was filled with kids of varying ages, all of whom were cared for by the staff. In those days, hopeful adoptive parents would walk through the facility as if it were some sort of a delicatessen serving up their familial future. And then after all the background checks and legalese, they'd come to the fateful decision and say, "We'll take that one."

One day, Al and Eleanor Doyle entered the Angel Guardian Home. I was about six months old at the time. Al was a rookie New York City cop; Eleanor had just stopped work to be a full-time mom. Of all the kids they had to choose from, they picked me, the big fat baby, and took me home to 1328 East 34th Street in Brooklyn. I was home. I had a family.

It was really a small miracle. It could have been anybody who walked through those doors. It could have been Malcolm Forbes (but who needs that kind of money headache anyway?). It could have been Cindy Sheehan (perish the thought). But Al and Eleanor Doyle picked me, and I was the luckiest kid on earth.

I had the perfect childhood in Flatbush. Our house was a traditional skinny and long two-story attached home with a brick front stoop, perfect for stoopball. It had a big picture window in the front facing the street. A picture window was a big thing back then. Not only did it let you see the comings and goings outside, you could put the Christmas tree in the window for all the neighbors to see and enjoy. We had a small front and back yard with one tree, a wisteria. There was a swing set that always seemed to pull out of the ground. We even sprang one year for a twenty-seven-inch, eight-foot-diameter aboveground pool. We were living the good life. To me it was a wonderful life.

The house always seemed big to me, even though it was rather small. The lawn seemed huge, particularly when Dad told me to mow it—we had one of those old push mowers with the metal wheels, and I always dreaded moving that hunk of junk around the spacious knoll. When I visited the house as an adult, the lawn looked like a postage stamp. I could have cut it with a pair of scissors. One of those tricks of memory and perspective, I guess.

Our block was loaded with families of different nationalities and religions and ethnicities. There were tons of kids my age. During the summers, we'd play stoopball (a combination of handball and baseball) and stickball (street baseball with a broom-handle bat). Watering the lawn after dinner routinely turned into a neighborhood hose fight.

On Friday nights, our parents, aunts, uncles, and grandparents would get together at O'Halloran's bar a few blocks over, the bar where my mom and dad met. Just like Cheers and everybody knew your name. Lindy dancing, smokes, beer, highballs, and laughter were always served up and in whatever quantity you wanted. It was all about family, neighbors, and friends new and old.

Every summer the entire extended family would head to the Glendella in Yulan, New York, for two glorious weeks in the country. The Glendella was an old property with a wrap-around porch, comfortable rocking chairs, screened windows, and no air conditioning. It also had horseshoes and—my favorite—shuffleboard. (I'm still obsessed with shuffleboard. On cruises, people will tell me that I should try the wave pool or the rock-climbing wall. I always head straight for the shuffleboard.) It was run by a German couple, who served up family-style meals, with seventy or eighty people piled into an oversized dining room. At mealtime, they would run around the property ringing a bell announcing that it was time to chow down.

As the sun began to set we'd pile into Dad's 1963 Mercury Comet to go deer hunting. Not Robert De Niro–style *Deer Hunter* deer hunting, but a different kind: we'd drive around trying to spot deer in the woods, trying desperately to beat the count from the night before.

After the kids went to bed, the parents would head up the hill to the "Rec Room," a euphemism for the bar. I would fall asleep listening to them in the distance joking, drinking, playing the piano, singing and dancing.

As we spent year after year at the Glendella, I started feeling grown up—after all, I was already ten. All the adults were sitting around after dinner one night, smoking cigars. Yes—cigars, indoors in front of the children. (We all survived.) My dad noticed me eyeing his cigar.

"You want to try this?" he asked.

I nodded eagerly.

"Do you know how to smoke?" he asked.

I shook my head no but I had watched my mom and dad smoke every day of my life.

How hard could it be?

"Well," he said, "you breathe out, then you put the cigar in your mouth, and you suck in as much as you can. Then you blow it out."

With that, he handed me the cigar. With the entire dining room looking on, I exhaled as hard as I could and then stuck the stogie between my teeth, just like in the movies. I inhaled as much as I could and for a split second I had pulled it off.

Then I turned green, started coughing and spitting, and the entire room cracked up. Funny funny ha ha.

That was Dad teaching me the responsibility that comes with choice. I wasn't ready for a cigar much less a cigarette, and he knew it—but he also knew that I'd find a way to try it unless he showed me why I wasn't ready for it. Nowadays, they'd probably drag him down to the courthouse for that lesson. Then, it was seen for what it was: a good teaching tool and a laugh or two.

The only thing better than counting deer was snagging fish from the Delaware River. We released all the fish we caught not out of some environmental concern but because the German cooking at the hotel was out of this world.

Whether it was the Delaware River or back in New York, my dad taught me the love of fishing and a love of the sea. He would take me to Sheepshead Bay, where we'd get on the *Elaine B*, a well-worn boat piloted by Captain Izzie, a tooth-challenged old salt who never followed the crowd. He'd take us to spots where no one else was fishing. I can't remember a single time we got skunked. The last time I went fishing with my dad I remember exactly what he was wearing and the sandwiches we ate. He had on khaki pants and a white T-shirt and we ate Swiss cheese sandwiches on white bread with yellow mustard. I remember his smile as I landed another flounder. I was happy.

THE DAY THE MUSIC DIED

Eventually, the Glendella was sold, and it was never quite the same. The new owners decided to line the entryway with plant-filled sinks! That mood setter was a turn-off even for city folk fond of a country getaway.

So my aunt Joan decided that we needed another way to escape the summertime city heat. In the early months of 1968, she bought a two-bedroom, one-bath, screened-porch summer house with no heat and no insulation in the mountains of northern New Jersey. Ten of us and my grandfather Connie's dog Peppy would cram into 1,100 square feet. My grandmother Bubbie would cook all day. My dad, my grandpa, my uncle Bob, my cousin Neil, and I would spend two or three hours a day digging out the crawl space beneath the house that Aunt Joan wanted to turn into a basement. There are a lot of boulders in the mountains of New Jersey. I can't think of a better way to describe the "fun" we had. Remember the chain gang in *Cool Hand Luke*?

When we weren't digging we were painting. Nothing a twelve-year-old loves more than climbing a rickety ladder with a gallon of barnyard-red paint. My dad, my uncle Bob, and my cousin Neil joined in the fun. It was a Thursday, and it was hot, the sun beating down on us in the humidity. After a few hours my dad wasn't feeling right—he was starting to have trouble breathing.

Aunt Joan and my mom put Dad in the car and took him to St. Anthony's Hospital in Warwick, New York. Over the next four days his condition got much worse. The doctors thought it would be better to transfer him to a bigger hospital in Middletown. It was better set up to treat him. Mom and Joan followed the ambulance and spent the night in a motel near the hospital.

The next morning, Mom came back with Aunt Joan. I remember it was a drizzly day, a Tuesday. Dad and I were supposed to go fishing that Saturday. The gravel in the driveway crunched under the tires as Joan pulled the '63 Comet into the driveway. I came bursting out the door.

"Mom!" I yelled. "Where's Dad? When's he coming home?"

"Go inside," she said quietly.

"What's going on?" I asked.

"Go inside," she repeated.

I went inside. She and Joan followed me through the door. The family gathered together in the living room. That's when we learned that my dad had died at three that morning. That was the day my world changed.

We went back to Brooklyn for the wake and funeral. Dad was a Korean War Navy veteran, a radioman, and was buried at Pine Lawn, the military cemetery on Long Island. They gave him full military honors, including the folding of the flag. I keep that flag in my home studio along with his dog tags and three of the shells they fired at the funeral, each representing Duty, Honor, and Country.

After the wake, everyone came back to our house, where there was plenty of food, booze, and stories. The old joke goes that the only difference between an Irish funeral and an Irish wedding is one less drunk. I didn't want to be around anyone, so I stayed in the basement. I flipped on the TV and remember watching the series *Dark Shadows*.

When the sun started to set and everything got cleaned up and put away, we all went to bed. I had the front bedroom and my mom and dad had the back bedroom, my one-year-old brother, John, in the middle room. Grandma stayed over to be there for my mom.

The house was eerily silent. I remember how quiet it was outside, which was very strange for a summer night in Brooklyn. No kids playing, no car horns, no distant laughter. Nothing. After a while the silence was broken with sobs coming from my mom's room as she cried to her mother, "Oh, Mama, he's gone, Oh, Mama, he's gone. . . ."

As I lay there trying to process what was happening all I knew was that everything was going to be a lot different from now on.

WORKING FOR A LIVING

We didn't have very much money after Dad died; my mom had given up her job at Pan Am after I arrived on the scene, so I tried to help out wherever I could. I worked my high school lunch line and for that I got a free lunch. After school and on weekends I worked and hung out at a local deli, Al's Luncheonette. There my duties were making tuna sandwiches, serving up hard rolls and fountain drinks, and on occasion running a craps game in the back room. This is the part of the book where my mom learns that I lost my Pea coat in a crap game. Long hours with no pay to get my coat out of hock taught me a very valuable lesson: don't gamble your jacket when you're out of money—especially in the dead of winter!

The neighborhood was changing, though.

The truth is that things had started to change a long time before that. Dad used to occasionally take me to school in the squad car, wearing his stiffly pressed blue uniform. I don't remember the 1964 riots in Bedford-Stuyvesant, which started after an NYPD cop shot a fifteen-year-old black kid. The cop was in the right, incidentally—the kid had attacked him with a knife and actually cut his arm. But that didn't prevent the riots from starting. I remember Dad heading out to work the 4 P.M. to 12 A.M. shift carrying his riot gear.

"What's that for, Dad?" I asked. I was young. Dad was a cop. I had always thought the uniform was a symbol of respect. Now it was becoming a target.

After Dad's death, the neighborhood started getting run-down, with higher crime rates. So in the summer before my junior year of high school, Mom packed up and moved us to Jersey. I transferred from Xavier High School to Pope John XXIII Regional High School.

When I finished high school, I took a look at my life and I knew I needed to make a choice. It was another fork in the road. I could get a job—I knew that. But Dad had always worked hard, and he had always told me his dream: to move to Florida and buy a boat. He'd never gotten to fulfill that dream. He'd told me, "Jerry, if you can—if the good Lord blesses you with another day and you have the option of making it good or bad—make it a good day." Dad hadn't gotten enough good days.

I decided that life was too short not to try to make every day a good day.

I decided to become a pilot.

FLYING HIGH

I had always been interested in flying. I thought the military flyboys were tops, the coolest cats in the room.

See, while I lived in Jersey, I started working at the Playboy Club—yes, that Playboy Club—which had certain perks. No, not what you're thinking. All the great acts went through the Playboy Club: Johnny Mathis, Redd Foxx, David Brenner, Bill Cosby, Frankie Valli and the Four Seasons. More than that, there were girls. I was underage at the time to be working around alcohol, but with a fake ID, I managed to score a job as a busboy in the main showroom, the Penthouse. I would have done that for free, because every so often, as the doors closed to the elevators heading up to the Penthouse, twenty-six fantastic-looking girls in Playboy bunny outfits would cram into the elevator with me. Do you need any more proof that there is a God!

While working at the Playboy Club, I met a guy who knew how to fly. I'd skip school and he'd take me flying. The towering heights and high speeds left me excited—and after high school, the possibility of getting paid to fly stuck with me.

So I enrolled at Embry-Riddle Aeronautical University in Daytona Beach, Florida, where I got my degree and pilot ratings. After graduation and turning down an opportunity to work for Fred Smith of FedEx—telling him his business plan would never work out—I got hired on at Falcon Jet in Teterboro, New Jersey. I managed to work my way into a job on "Mahogany Row" thanks to a very kind senior VP of sales, Don Sterling. What a job! Private jets, limos, and a company credit card. I was set. Nothing but blue skies and life's tail winds! Or so I thought.

In December 1980, I was hanging out back at the Playboy Club when I ran into a group of stockbrokers having their Christmas party at the hotel. I struck up a conversation with one of the branch managers and the conversation inevitably turned to what kind of money you can make on Wall Street. He asked me what kind of money you can make pushing iron and I proudly stated my yearly figure.

His response: "How would you like to make that in a month?"

I was sold. Six months later, I was heading to Wall Street.

WALL STREET DAYS

My early days were spent trying to build what they called "a book of business" the old-fashioned way, cold-calling. That was long before the do-not-call lists. We'd use Thomas Guides, targeting certain zip codes. We'd use business directories. We'd use the Forbes 400, the Fortune 500, and the Inc. 100 lists. We even did a little Dumpster diving to get brokerage runs. That was before paper shredders.

We'd go after individual accounts, IRAs, pensions, endowments, and trusts. I quickly learned that when you start off, you can't target only the whales. Being paid on commission, hunger had a way of helping you adjust your strategy. So we went after the squirrels, with a little whale hunting on the side. We'd cold-call all day long, day after day. Think *Pursuit of Happyness* with Will Smith. That was us.

All you needed was a name, a phone number, a title, and a company. Armed with that information, you could start to build your book of business. You'd call up a company and say, "Jerry Doyle from Drexel calling for John So-and-So." The job was to get through the gatekeepers. Keep it polite, compelling, and to the point. "Is he expecting your call?" "If he's interested in an exceptional investment opportunity he is." Time is money and there was no time to waste. He *was* interested. *Everyone* was interested. It was the 1980s and while the "greed is good" movie *Wall Street* wasn't out yet, the sentiment was taking hold.

One place to find leads was the fishbowls at the front of restaurants, where businessmen and women would drop their cards hoping to win the free lunch or dinner. When you're looking for information, that was a gold mine: names, titles, businesses, phone numbers. We'd cut a deal with the restaurant that after the contest there was no sense in throwing the cards away. Why not recycle. Information in hand, it was back to the office to hit the phones.

Sometimes we ran into total jerks. It was fine to turn us down, say you weren't interested. But every so often, you'd run up against a doozy: "Where'd you get this phone number? Who the hell are you? Why are you wasting my time?" You know the type. We'd apologize and then hang up: "Sorry, sorry, didn't mean to bother you."

But sometimes a real jerk deserved special treatment. We could play it one of three ways. First, we could send his information to everyone in the office—so he'd be cold-called ten times in a single day. Second, we could send his information to everyone in the office and all the guys in other offices. Then everyone would cold-call him: fifty calls in a day.

The third strategy was the "Free Lunch Winner" strategy. Here's how it would play out. Every month or so, the guys would get together in a bar and we'd have a stack of cards belonging to the biggest jerks. We'd discuss them and finally pick the worst of the lot. Then we'd go back to the office and call him. "Bill? This is Scott, the maître d' at the La Tee Da Room." (We'd find out the actual name of the maître d'. You'll see why.) "You ate at our restaurant last week, right? Well, congratulations, you've been selected as the winner of a free lunch (or free dinner)." Then we'd up the ante: "Bill, it's not just for you and a friend. You're not just this week's winner, you're our one hundredth winner! And that means we're going to do something really special. Dinner for you and five friends. What date and time works best for you? Just call us back if that changes at this number, 555-555-5555. We look forward to seeing you!" When he called back to confirm, somebody would pick up and be Scott, maître d' at the La Tee Da Room. "Yes, Bill, this is Scott. Sure we can change your reservation. We'll see you Thursday night at seven."

On Thursday at seven, we'd all go to the La Tee Da Room and sit at the bar. And we'd watch as Bill came in with five friends, acting the big shot.

"Scott," he'd say, "I'm Bill, I spoke with you on the phone. I'm the one hundredth winner."

"I have no idea who you are, sir. Do you have a reservation?"

"Do I have a reservation?" Bill would yell. "I'm your free dinner winner! You told me tonight at seven, five of my friends and I and it was all on the house!"

"We have no such promotion, Bill," Scott would tell him.

You should have seen the fireworks. We'd sit back and clink glasses and tell one another "Mission accomplished."

Sure, it was a game, although when I first entered the business, it was a game where we'd help people make money. In fact, I worked with the SEC to help expose a securities firm that was cheating its clients with "pump and dump": taking a thinly traded, obscure security, hyping it in one part of the country and raising the price, then selling it at the inflated price to unknowing buyers on the other side of the country. The takedown was profiled on *60 Minutes*.

It was becoming a dirtier and dirtier business. There was one trader who was prospecting at church or wherever he prayed. When the market crashed in 1986, he brought his entire investment/church group into his office and they all got down on their knees to pray for their stocks. He was screwing them every day, all the time, and they never knew it. He was loading them up with closed-end funds, secondary and tertiary products that really had no place in people's portfolios unless they were true speculators.

In the late 1980s, federal prosecutors began looking at Drexel. By the time the dust settled, they had cut their employees from ten thousand to forty. I moved over to retail at Prudential Securities.

But I was getting disillusioned. Things were changing, just as they had in my old neighborhood. There was crime. There was too much speculation, too much pump and dump and churn and burn. At one point, I was having a big run-in with my boss at Prudential, who was telling me what to sell to my clients.

"You're sitting on a lot of client cash. You should put that money to work," he told me.

"Screw you," I told him. "I'll sit on the cash. I'm not going to flush their money down one of your financial toilets."

After the meeting, my assistant, a wonderful woman in the business for twenty-five years, came into my office and shut the door. "Jerry," she said, "you're not going to be as good and successful at this as you're capable of being. Because you have a conscience."

She was right. And I was facing another fork in the road: what was I going to do now?

LIGHTS, CAMERA, ACTION

In 1991, I quit Wall Street. I had a few bucks, which provided me with some choices. Dad had always wanted to be a tugboat captain, and I thought about being a fishing boat captain in Florida as a sort of tribute to him. I also thought about medical school. I also contemplated an acting career.

A few years before I quit slinging stocks, I had been approached by a friend. "You look like Bruce Willis," she said, "and you could make some decent money as a double for Bruce."

On a whim, I flew out to Los Angeles and auditioned for the television series *Moonlighting*. Bruce Willis was having major run-ins with Cybill Shepherd at the time, and there was talk of bringing in a brother or relative of Willis's character. The episode was a show about the show. I had no head shot, no résumé, and no acting experience. Amazingly, I got a callback and after auditioning for the producers and director, I booked the job. I filmed the episode on location in L.A. and with my cast-and-crew *Moonlighting* hat I headed back to the joys of Wall Street.

When I finally quit the Street, I began seriously thinking about acting. How hard could this acting thing be? From what I could gather, you got paid (stupid money), didn't have to do it right the first time, and got to make out with smoking-hot women onscreen. What possibly was the downside?

I packed up and went to Hollywood.

If there was one thing I knew how to do from my days on Wall Street, it was cold-call. So I put that to good use. I didn't know anything about acting but I knew how to get someone on the phone or get a meeting. I called anyone who had name ID in the industry. I simply bulldogged my way into casting sessions and talent agencies.

I learned that I needed a résumé. There was only one problem: I'd never acted before, other than that bit part in *Moonlighting*. So I faked one. I figured that if I got busted, I'd better have a good excuse, so I came up with one: you should have known. They should have known because on my résumé I listed the Dance Theatre of Harlem. Nobody ever caught it. This meant to me that most everyone in Hollywood was as big a phony as my résumé was or so PC they were afraid to call me on it. (I was technically onstage once with the Dance Theatre of Harlem. A friend of mine received an award as a benefactor, and I was the wingman. Not a lot of white guys can say they were onstage with the Dance Theatre of Harlem.)

Within months, I got my first regular gig. It started with an audition for *The Bold and the Beautiful*, a daytime soap. I am neither bold nor beautiful. It didn't matter—I got cast as a day player, a "one-and-done" actor.

The first day I went to shoot, I arrived at 9 A.M., and I actually got to act at two o'clock the following morning. I had about five lines. Everyone was staring at me. "Don't screw it up," I could hear them thinking. "Just hit your marks and we can go home. We want to get the hell out of here."

I hit the marks. The director said, "We're moving on." And the cast cheered. It was terrific.

The next day, the casting director, Christy Dooley, got a call from Brad Bell, creator of the show. "Who the hell is Jerry Doyle?" he asked Christy. Christy, afraid that I had screwed something up royally, immediately began to apologize for casting me. "No," said Bell. "Doyle has the best 'screw you' look I've seen in a long time. Bring him back." So I became a recurring character on *The Bold and the Beautiful*.

I was excited. This was a soap opera, and pretty soon I'd get my onscreen love scene! Except that they promptly cast me opposite Susan Flannery, a sixty-year-old Rubinesque blonde. I was her attorney, with a potential love interest story line. Susan was wonderful—when the producers tried to push me around, Susan would tell me to tell them to take a flying leap.

I was making it in Hollywood. I was a working actor!

BABYLON 5

A few months later, I got a call from my agent that I had an audition for a TV pilot: *Babylon 5*.

"What's a *Babylon 5* and what happened to the first four?" I asked.

"A new sci-fi show Warner Brothers is producing."

I didn't know anything about science fiction. "What's the role?" I asked.

"Mars-born Security Chief Michael Alfredo Garibaldi."

"Oh, this is going to work out," I thought. "A mick from Brooklyn playing a wop from Mars."

I walked into the audition and everyone was there: executive producer and head writer Joe Straczynski; Richard Compton, the director; executive producer Doug Netter; the casting director—everyone. This was a big deal. The shot at playing one of the leads in a studio series.

"What character are you here to read for?" they asked.

"The part I'm going to get," I confidently replied.

"*Garibaldi*," said the director.

"That's *Mr. Garibaldi* to you," I said.

The director smiled.

"I knew if you could string together more than two words and come close to hitting your marks, you would be the guy," he later told me.

And so I was cast in *Babylon 5*.

Another small miracle. What are the odds of a guy with no real acting chops, never going to acting school, never working on Broadway, off-Broadway, off-off-Broadway, getting cast in a pilot, a two-hour movie for a potential series?

Slim to none. But there I was.

And there I stayed. Through luck, timing, and a certain degree of talent, I stayed on the series after pickup. I ran the complete five seasons that we were supposed to be on the air.

It was phenomenal. I was actually getting paid for saying someone else's lines, standing on sets that someone else built, wearing uniforms that someone else made, and having production assistants who would get you just about anything you wanted whenever you wanted it—plus residuals. To this day, I'm still getting paid for *Babylon 5*, getting money for stuff I did a decade ago, not necessarily well or right the first time. Acting is a tremendous job—you get do-overs. When you're a doctor, an astronaut, fighter pilot, or other edge-of-the-seater, there's no take two.

But when you're an actor, you can screw up and still get paid. Here's a note to anyone out there who listens to these actors talking about the long days and the hours they have to put in on the set: if someone offers you a TV series, take it. The actors have the cushy jobs. The people who really put in the long hours are the crew. They're there every day, for every scene, for every setup, for every screwup by an actor who just can't seem to remember his lines, hit his marks, or for that matter—act.

Science fiction is a hard genre to act in, harder than most others. You have to suspend your disbelief. I would stack the *Babylon 5* cast against the cast of *ER* or any drama series anyday. If we swapped roles, the *Babylon 5* cast could do what the *ER* cast does, but the *ER* folks would have a tough time doing what we did. Can anyone really picture Noah Wyle as a Narn or Klingon?

Celebrity opens a lot of doors previously welded shut. I didn't realize what a stud I was until I was on the cover of *TV Guide* and women who wouldn't let me buy them a drink the previous week were suddenly giving me their phone numbers. Hollywood can make Drew Carey a sex symbol.

And once you're on a series, the jobs and perks just keep coming. In a way you're sort of made. The logic in Hollywood says if you can get a series you must be talented. I'll leave that for the critics, but the doors do swing open. Showtime and TNT films, personal appearances, voice-overs (I was the voice of TGI Friday's, John Deere, and AT&T, among others). I was cast as the lead voice in *Captain Simian and the Space Monkeys*. I would have paid to go to work to do that cartoon series every day—it was that much fun.

Celebrity opened up other doors, too. Doors that wouldn't be open if you weren't flying a plywood spaceship on a Warner Brothers soundstage. I got to fly and hang out with the 416 FLTS F-16 test squadron

at Edwards Air Force Base. I got to fly the space shuttle motion simulator at Johnson Space Center. I attended at least a dozen launches, half
a dozen landings, and hung out with astronauts who walked on the
moon. I got to do a cat-and-trap on the aircraft carrier USS *Constella-
tion* (CV-64) while they were at sea doing night carrier qualifications. I
got to travel all around the world to talk about a TV show.

With that celebrity, I always believed, came responsibility. If Kathy
Griffin is the D-List, I was the Z-List, but I always felt I had to use my
opportunity to highlight what other people are doing, really important
people: the military, the police, NASA. I never hung out with actors—
I hung out with the crew. It was an amazing gift, to be able to do things
like that just because I stood in front of a camera.

SMOKE ALARMS

That isn't to say I completely avoided getting sucked into the cult of celebrity. I did. Later on my radio show I asked a famous Hollywood pub-
licist, Michael Levine, how people like Michael Jackson or Mike Tyson
could make and lose half a billion dollars and end up with messed-up
lives.

"I've got two words," said Levine. "Smoke alarms. We need smoke
alarms in our lives. We need people that will tell us stop. No. Don't do
that. And a lot of time people disable the smoke alarms because they
don't want to hear what people are saying."

It's true. When you're in Hollywood, you can start to think you're
a big shot. One week, I had a run-in with the head writer and producers on *Babylon 5*. I started calling all the people I was paying—all the
yes-men—and ranting to them about the horrors I was facing. I called
my manager (who gets a 10 percent cut), my agent (10 percent), my publi-
cist, and my attorney, basically anybody who had to listen to me because
I was paying them. "This story line stinks!" I'd yell. "This script stinks!
My character isn't getting enough screen time." And they'd "yes" me.
Every time I had a break in the shooting schedule, I'd call up my entire

Rolodex (old-school) and scream about the injustices being perpetrated against me. And I started believing my own garbage.

One day, I called up one of my buddies, Jesse Iglesias, to continue my rant. Jesse is a Hell's Kitchen guy, a former Marine, an executive at Merrill Lynch—the kind of guy you'd want your sister to marry. I started into my rant, and as I went on, I realized he wasn't saying anything. I wasn't hearing "Yes, Jerry, that's right, Jerry." Eventually I stopped.

"You done?" he finally said.

"Not really," I said.

"Here's what you do," he said. "Put on your little space suit. Shoot your little ray gun. And send me your big fat paychecks."

That was the end of that. He hung up. Jesse was my smoke alarm.

GETTING INTO POLITICS

I have always loved politics. When I was shooting a 2002 movie called *Devious Beings*, I was heavily into talk radio. During breaks, I'd watch the stock market ticker and listen to the radio hosts and watch the news. I would read only nonfiction.

Then, one day, I heard that the Republican Party couldn't find a credible candidate to run against my congressman, Brad Sherman. I was up in San Luis Obispo, and I began making some phone calls, finding out about the possibility of running. "After all," I thought, "if nobody else will run, I will."

Then I seriously began thinking about the trade-offs. "Your quote is $120,000 for ten days of shooting on a made-for-cable movie. Do you want to walk away from that and jump into politics in lovable liberal Hollywood as a Republican? It's easier to come out in Hollywood as a heroin addict than as a Republican. Burn your bridges? Kill your career?"

I decided that the answer was yes: After watching heroes do heroic work day in and day out without recognition—and after experiencing fame and fortune without doing anything heroic—I wanted to do something. I wanted to try to restore the best elements of America from my childhood while preserving the great changes that had come about since then. I wanted to make a difference.

And so I went to the movie's writer-producer, P. J. Haarsma. P.J. was a friend, and he was also a hard-core liberal hailing from Canada. We'd discussed a little politics in the past, but there hadn't been any need to defend my Republican roots.

"P.J.," I said, "I really need to take a day."

"Why? We have this little thing called a shooting schedule."

"I need to get down to L.A. to register to run for Congress."

"Jerry," he said, "you're an actor."

"P.J.," I replied, "I know. But there are a lot of things going on in this country I just don't like, and I want to do something about them. It's something I need to do."

After a few hours of some schedule juggling he finally conceded.

Then, a thought occurred to him. "You are a Democrat, right?"

"No, P.J., I'm a Republican," I said as I walked away.

"You can't have the day off!" he yelled, sickened at the thought of aiding the dreaded Republican Party.

"Fine, P.J.," I said. "Then I'll just have to take a sick day, and it'll cost you twice as much money."

The next day, I drove down to the Los Angeles County Recorder's Office and got in line. I was wearing jeans and a baseball cap and a sweatshirt, everyone else a suit and tie.

Finally, I reached the window. "Miss," I asked the attendant, "can you tell me how I go about running for Congress?"

CHAPTER 3

RIP THAT SINK OUT

In the Oscar-winning movie *One Flew Over the Cuckoo's Nest*, the lead character, R. P. McMurphy, was played brilliantly by Jack Nicholson. McMurphy is a hothead with assault convictions who finds himself heading back to prison. He thinks he can do his time on easy street by convincing the judge and the doctors he's certifiably nuts. He's so convincing they confine him to a mental institution to serve out his sentence. Inside the institution he becomes more convinced not only of his own sanity, but that his fellow lunatics are saner than the sane people in charge of the nuthouse. Their spirit and individuality have been destroyed by the authoritarian rule of Nurse Ratched (Oscar winner Louise Fletcher).

In a pivotal scene, McMurphy decides he's had enough and it's time to push back. He tells his colorful cast of loons that he's going to rip this hulking marble sink out of the floor, throw it through the steel-barred bathroom window, and go see a baseball game. They follow him to the bathroom, where he positions himself in front of this monstrosity of marble and metal that five men couldn't lift much less dislodge from the floor.

He grasps the sink by the metal faucets and pulls up with all his might. Nothing. He tries again. Nothing. He pulls harder and harder, his face red, his veins popping. Still nothing. The weight of the sink is too much for him. With sweat pouring from his forehead and blood trickling from his hands, McMurphy finally submits to reality and slumps against the wall.

He looks over to the skeptical bunch with some snickering at his failure and says, "But I tried. G**dammit, I sure as hell did that much. Didn't I?"

THE POLITICAL NUTHOUSE

Everyone who runs for Congress has to be somewhat of a McMurphy at heart. It's too much work and too much strain and too much ass-kissing and hand-holding to do it just for fun. But at some level I believe they go to Washington to be the sanest nut in the political institution.

I decided to give up my career in film and television to join the lunatics on Capitol Hill. Maybe I had watched Jimmy Stewart in *Mr. Smith Goes to Washington* one too many times. I was laboring under the delusion that I could actually go to Washington, D.C., get something done, help to change the status quo, and remain personally unchanged.

It seemed to me that common sense was all too uncommon, and that there was still a place in government for logic, reason, and accountability. I thought that what I saw happening in D.C.—the stupid decisions, the recklessness, the lack of responsibility—all of it could be altered in some way. I just had to throw my hat in the ring and stand for certain principles and deliver that to the halls of power. It might to some sound egotistical, naive, and altruistic, I admit, but I think there's a place for that in our representative government. In the words of Jefferson Smith (Jimmy Stewart), I was either dead right, or I was crazy.

Turns out I was crazy.

I registered to run for Congress in the heavily Democratic California District 24 in 2000. My opponent was Brad Sherman, the Democrat incumbent. Someone once said that "timing is everything in politics." That year, my timing couldn't have been worse. Fully 98 percent of federal politicians across the country were reelected, and all 125-plus federal and state officials in California remained in office. Not one incumbent lost his election. Not one. It was the year of the incumbent, and I was a challenger.

I was also an actor. To my surprise, Sherman never made an issue of it. Perhaps it's because he knew that I was well versed on the issues and my background was more than that of a thespian. When people liken me to Al Franken or Janeane Garofalo or Michael Moore or Sean Penn or Matt Damon or Whoopi Goldberg, it makes my stomach churn. Put me on a debating stage with any of them, and you'll be wiping them off the floor. Logic and facts trump emotion and feelings every time.

The CA-24 district, consisting of about 600,000 people, was racially diverse, about 65 percent white, 20 percent Hispanic, 10 percent Asian, and a couple of percent black. It was religiously diverse, with Catholics and Protestants and Jews and Muslims.

I had no sense of what the constituency of my district would respond to, and more important, how they would respond to me. I thought that all I would have to do was speak the truth about the issues as I saw them, and people would flock to me with votes and the mother's milk of politics: cash.

I ran on a platform that was ahead of its time in certain ways. I ran on fiscal responsibility, pledging limited government. I wanted to eliminate the Departments of Redundancy Departments. I wanted to shrink the size and scope of government. I wanted to mandate a balanced budget. I wanted to build up our infrastructure. I wanted to constrain the Department of Education. I wanted to address our growing deficits.

On national security, I felt strongly that we had to build up the military and that Clinton had cut too much and wasted too much. I felt that even though the Cold War had ended, we still had to face the ever-present threat of terrorism. Yes, I talked about it during the campaign. It was right after the bombing of the USS *Cole* and the bombings of our embassies in Kenya and Tanzania. And even though we hadn't yet been hit at home, those embassies were our sovereign territory, which meant that, technically, we *had* been attacked on our own soil. Our military men and women needed the weaponry and equipment and logistical and financial support necessary to undertake an assault on our enemies. We needed to train them to fight unconventional wars. As the 9/11 Commission report later pointed out, Congress was slow to adapt to the rising threat of global terrorism. I could see it while running for Congress. Why couldn't Congress see it while they were running Congress?

I also talked a good deal about infrastructure. In California, we had experienced somewhere in the neighborhood of a 125 percent increase in infrastructure usage over the past decade, but just a 16 percent increase in spending for that infrastructure. Eventually, our roads, bridges, and water and sewage systems were going to start breaking down, having a negative effect on industry and commerce. I was talking shovel-ready before there was shovel-ready, but not simply to create jobs. It was designed to fix the problems for my district and the state.

I talked, too, about securing our borders. I pointed out that we couldn't have an unsustainable illegal immigrant population swamping our schools and hospitals; it was destroying both the educational and health care systems. Of course, since I spoke those words, millions more illegal immigrants have crossed the border into California, and California has gone virtually bankrupt.

Those were my big issues: national security, the economy, illegal immigration, and infrastructure. The press tried to drag me into discussions of hot-button issues, particularly abortion. I said: "Here's my view on abortion. I'm glad my mom didn't have one. I'm glad I was given the choice to have the choice about choice." That ended the discussion of abortion.

I assumed that voters in my district wouldn't care that I wasn't "crafting" a message to meet the party line. They wanted straight talk, I thought, and I thought, too, that we all had a common interest in some of the principles I ran on. In other words, I thought they just had to be told the truth, and they'd recognize it.

My campaign slogan was "Doyle for Congress: No BS." It was

actually a play on words, since my opponent's initials were "BS." The mailers and walk pieces featured the letters "BS" with a red circle and line through them. (My original campaign slogan was "Doyle for Congress: Why Not?" My campaign manager talked me out of it.)

My opponent's campaign strategy was simple: ignore Jerry Doyle. It worked to perfection. I underestimated the game. I thought it was about right and wrong and common sense and policy.

I quickly learned that it was about money.

THE MONEY GAME

It would take money to win. Politics is all about money. Without money, politics wouldn't be possible, but it's certainly a shame that our politicians have to spend the vast majority of their time looking for handouts. It's a part of the job I never got used to.

The first time I visited the California congressional delegation in Washington, I sat down to lunch with some of the bigwigs. Their first question: "How much of your own money are you going to commit to this campaign?"

My answer: $100,000.

That got their attention.

Working the D.C. rounds was basically going from the National Republican Congressional Committee (NRCC) to congressional office after congressional office asking for help. That part was actually a lot of fun. My D.C. contact was a fellow named Jim Kaplan, who was also the associate director of the American Israel Public Affairs Committee. He had some good relationships on the Hill and was a *Babylon 5* fan, which meant he did a lot for free. Thanks, Jim!

We met with numerous congressmen and senators trying to drum up interest for my campaign, to secure commitments from some of them to do fund-raisers in the district and write checks to help the Federal Election Commission reports look like we had momentum within the party.

Rep. J. C. Watts (R-OK) became one of my biggest supporters, traveling to my district to be the featured speaker at my first major fundraiser. He opened his remarks by recalling a conversation he and I had weeks earlier. He said, "J.D. called me up and asked if I believe in free speech. When I told him I did, J.D. said good, now fly to California and give one." J.C. made numerous visits to the district and helped me out in ways that can never be repaid. He is an asset to the Republican Party and I hope he gets back in the game.

Rep. J. D. Hayworth (AZ) was also very helpful, along with Rep. Ken Calvert (CA), Rep. Buck McKeon (CA), and Rep. Ed Royce (CA). There were a lot of people who liked the fact that I had a certain degree of celebrity, a pretty good-sized wallet, and actually knew what I was talking about without having to refer to a script or TelePrompTer.

What astounded me the most was the amount of time they put into raising money to run for reelection. They'd go to the floor of the House, vote on a bill or amendment, and then head back to their offices for a grueling schedule of meetings. Whenever they weren't conducting official business they'd have out their donor lists, and they'd be dialing for dollars. In the car, in the phone bank at the NRCC, at their district office, waiting at the airport, meeting with political action committees or lobbyists, attending fund-raisers for themselves or the Republican Party. It was an endless process of filling the campaign coffers. It was something I had a problem with. A problem of asking for money. I thought if you had a good message and you built the political *Field of Dreams* they would come. I forgot my Wall Street training: ask for the order.

Months later I had an opportunity to address the entire Republican Conference, courtesy of a little arm-twisting by the conference chair, J. C. Watts. I had a rare opportunity to make my pitch as to why they should get onboard and help fund my campaign. I was also learning that if there's no Buck, there's no Buck Rogers. J. C. brought me up, introduced me, then turned to me and said, "Three minutes." I did my little spiel about how competitive the district was, how we were starting to get some good press. All the things I wished were really happening.

I ended by telling the assembled crowd that I'd be at the back of the room afterward with a vacuum cleaner, sucking up their money. Then I took questions. The first question was about the poll numbers in my district.

"Well," I said, "the current *L.A. Times* poll has me down 27 or 28 points. But it also has Al Gore up on Governor Bush by 37½ points. If you believe that, then you also believe that one day there will be a Richard Simmons, Jr." When in doubt bring the comedy out!

JC was impressed that it got a laugh out of the room although it seemed to trouble House Speaker Dennis Hastert (R-IL) a wee bit. More importantly, it didn't translate into very much money.

The bottom line was that the bigwigs thought my race was a lost cause. They had a stash of *mea culpa* money they'd give me if I won; they'd apologize, tell me that they had underestimated my cachet, and help pay off my campaign debts. But they wouldn't actively fund-raise nor do much to help monetarily.

It showed. I was doing all my own organizing. I stapled signs, handled the logistics of campaign events, coordinated fund-raisers, designed and approved campaign material and newspaper ads. I had a wonderful group of volunteers, great people who knocked on doors and put up signs, and they worked ceaselessly and tirelessly. I got John McCain to endorse me in a television commercial. Congressman Jim Rogan took time out of his $10 million campaign to speak at an event with me. But the powers that be weren't going to pour cash into my race.

Along with the fact that I was outspent, incumbents have tremendous advantages. They've got frank mail—free mailing privileges from D.C. to their constituents, which is worth tens of thousands of dollars. They've also got the facial recognition and the power of having handed out political patronage over the past few years. They know the "secret handshake."

All in all, I invested about $70,000 of my own cash and a total of $126,148 in the race. Congressman Sherman spent $539,122. Sherman got 155,395 votes; I got 70,169. On a dollar-per-vote basis, I could make the case that I won the race. (How's that for rationalizing a good old-fashioned political ass-kicking?) I conceded the race to Congressman Sherman in a truly classy way, on the radio with three and a half million listeners to my radio show—six years later in 2006. No sore loser here! Actually Congressman Sherman has done a pretty good job of meeting the needs of his constituents. I have him on the show occasionally and while we don't agree in a lot of areas we found important areas where we do. That's how politics *should* work.

ON THE TRAIL

Being out on the trail was the fun part of the campaign. I enjoyed meeting people, hearing their concerns, pitching my ideas, and coming to understand the monumental responsibility elected officials have. People are giving you their trust by giving you their support and ultimately their vote. But running for such an important position also had its downsides.

One of them was wearing suits.

I hate wearing suits. They're constrictive and annoying and boring and uncomfortable. I swore to myself after I left Wall Street that never again would I wear a suit and tie. When I ran, I had a single suit, four shirts, three ties, five pairs of socks, and two pairs of shoes. Having such a limited wardrobe while doing multiple events in one day can present unexpected challenges.

One day, I was campaigning with soon-to-be President George W. Bush at a whistle stop in Ventura. We met on the platform, talked for a bit, and shared a photo op. Then it was time for the introductions and GWB's speech; four thousand people had gathered near the rear of the train to hear him speak.

It was an unusually hot day but the crowd, which had been waiting for over four hours, was fired up. I worked my way to a shaded spot with a great up-close view of Governor Bush. I had a perfect angle, and I was right where he'd be working the rope line. As I stood there, waiting for him to be introduced, I heard a voice behind me.

"Excuse me, Mr. Doyle, you might want to move to a different position."

I turned around and saw that the guy was wearing an earpiece and was someone who would talk into his cuff (i.e., Secret Service). I thought to myself how the hell does this guy know my name? Answer: meeting with the Republican nominee for president of the United States. Check.

"I'm fine," I said.

"You might want to reconsider," he said.

"Do I need to move, or can I stay here?"

"You can stay there," he said, "but I wouldn't recommend it."

I stayed.

Bush gave a rousing speech and the crowd was whipped into a frenzy. Electricity was in the air. Bush was finishing strong. With a rousing finale, the event organizers began firing off the confetti bombs and streamers. The victory music began blaring away. It was awesome.

Except for one thing. The event coordinators had coordinated a cage full of doves right behind me. And in all the noise and mayhem they released those doves. About fifty of them.

The doves came flying out of their cage, and they began attacking me like it was a remake of Alfred Hitchcock's *The Birds*. They stuck to my back, clawed at me. Then they started crapping on me and my only suit.

So now my one and only suit jacket was totally covered in bird crap. I took it off under the all-knowing watch of the Secret Service guy, who was now moving over to the rope line. I can only imagine what he was thinking.

Bush started working the rope line. As I said it was a hot day. An elderly woman near the rope line fainted onto the blacktop. Gentleman that I am, I turned my coat inside out, clean lining out, and wrapped it up in a bundle and put it under her head. The paramedics came rushing over and started working on her. That's when she turned her head to the side and yakked on my jacket. Now I have dove bombs and puke on my only jacket—and another campaign dinner scheduled in two hours.

Some days are better than others on the campaign trail.

ELECTION POSTPARTUM

In the aftermath of the election, everybody was telling me I did a great job under very trying circumstances and that I needed to run again in 2002. A few months after my defeat, I sat down with Congressman Buck McKeon in his D.C. office, looked around, and said, "So this is what it looks like when you win."

He laughed, told me to forget about the last election, that I ran a very respectable campaign and should focus on the next one. "Start running your '02 campaign right now," he said.

Even though a lot of people wanted me to give it another shot, frankly I was tired of it. Maybe it was election postpartum. I had the classic postpartum symptoms: mood swings, irritability, loss of appetite, and a general sense of wanting to withdraw. I was tired of hearing myself talk. I had turned into Mr. Sound Bite. I needed time to decompress. So I packed up some of my stuff and drove cross-country to my house in Jupiter, Florida.

On the drive, I had one of the most valuable political discussions of my life. As I was cruising across East Texas, my cell phone rang. It was Jim Rogan, and he was calling to check in on me—even though he had just lost the first $10 million congressional race in the history of American politics.

"How are you doing?" he asked.

"I'm beat up," I said. Then I realized what I was saying. Rogan was far more beat up than I was.

"You were great," he said. "It's unfortunate you didn't win. But a lot of people don't win the first time out."

"Are you okay?" I asked.

"I'm fine," he said. "I fought the good race, and I lost the race. I'll live to fight another day."

We got to chatting about why he had lost. "Do you think you lost because of your involvement in the Clinton impeachment?" I asked him. Rogan had led the charge to impeach Clinton after Clinton's perjury in the Paula Jones case regarding Monica Lewinsky.

"Maybe," he said.

"Would you do it the same way if you had to do it again?"

"Yes," he said. "I had a responsibility to impeach President Clinton. He perjured himself."

"Why did you get all the heat?" I asked.

"Here's the story," he told me. "I was approached by the Senate majority leader, Trent Lott of Mississippi. He told me that the polls weren't looking good on the Clinton impeachment and that it was unpopular. He told me that I had to make the issue disappear, or I had to take the fall. I had a duty to impeach Clinton, and I took the fall."

That was politics in a nutshell. "Principles need not apply," I thought. "It's all about political posturing."

"Jerry," he finally said, "I applaud you. You walked away from a very lucrative career, and you probably damaged your appeal in Hollywood because you stood up as a proud conservative. I can't imagine your return will be an open-armed embrace." We talked for over an hour and a half as the Texas landscape passed by. We left each other with the hope of one day joining up again on the political trail. Jim Rogan is a stand-up guy. He didn't have to call me. I was the new guy. I was the challenger. I lost. But I will always remember what he told me about my race: "Jerry, you can always say you were the Republican nominee from California's 24th Congressional District, and that's saying something."

FROM HOLLYWOOD TO TALK RADIO

When I got to Florida, I crashed for a while. After about six months of fishing, going out on the boat, snorkeling, and partying I was bored with my *Groundhog Day* life and decided to get back into the Hollywood game. I told my agent I'd be heading back to Hollywood, and that I wanted to start auditioning again. Alert the media, J.D.'s back.

Only when I did return to L.A., things weren't the same. There was a different vibe. When I was on *Babylon 5*, if I had the flu and was filming, my agents or manager would call and ask if I wanted them to bring me some chicken soup to the set. Now they were slow to return phone calls if at all. Auditions, forget about it.

I quickly went from a guy who had starred for five seasons in an Emmy-winning series, Showtime and TNT movies, done film work, countless national voice-over campaigns, animation voice-overs, was featured in numerous national and international magazines and recently on the cover of *TV Guide,* to a guy who was basically shut out of getting any new work. I remember speaking to John Zogby's Arab American Institute when I ran for Congress. Zogby talked about the dangers of flying while Arab and driving in Beverly Hills while black. I said to the group, "Driving while black in Beverly Hills and flying while Arab can be a problem. Try running as a Republican actor in Hollywood if you want to understand what profiling is really all about."

Hollywood for me became the land of the long, slow "no." I wasn't the only one who experienced this soft discrimination. Dwight Schultz, star of *The A-Team*, has written about the death of his film and TV career after coming out conservative: "Hollywood is now a liberal Bastille. . . . The atmosphere is intimidating and oppressive, but that's not an official blacklist. . . . During the last 8 years, I have rarely been to an audition waiting room where I have not been assaulted with anti-Bush, anti-Reagan, anti-Republican outbursts. . . . So, what about that blacklist? If it exists, in my opinion it's social, not institutional. But the social aspect of this business is, to a large degree, everything there is.[1]

Once you come out as a conservative, you're in the actors' witness protection program.

I recently spoke to Ben Shapiro, a nationally syndicated columnist and Harvard Law grad who was writing a book on political bias in Hollywood. He's had a chance to speak with dozens of Hollywood big shots—everyone from programming executives at the alphabet networks, Comedy Central, and the Hallmark Channel to the creators, producers, and writers of shows like *The Honeymooners, M*A*S*H, Roseanne, The Cosby Show, Friends, ER, House*, and *Lost*, among others. "There's no doubt Hollywood is a liberal town," says Shapiro. "People there will feel completely comfortable handing out Obama T-shirts at work, and they'll rip people like you on a regular basis. It's not a conscious effort on most of their parts to exclude conservatives—it's just that conservatives are so *wrongheaded* all the time. And why would they give a job to someone who is so *wrongheaded* when they could give a job to someone who's more 'politically and socially aware'?

"I've talked to Emmy-nominated conservative writers who can't get work because producers think conservatives are incapable of writing empathetic works of art," Shapiro continues. "I've talked to actors who can't get an audition because conservatives supposedly have no capacity for true feeling onscreen. Not everyone has to know somebody to get ahead in Hollywood—you're the perfect example, Jerry—but everyone has to *get along with everyone*. Unless you're a big star, that is—a Bruce Willis or a Gary Sinise. The problem is that if you're not, you're best off keeping your political opinions to yourself, even if others on the set are talking about how President Obama is the Second Coming."

That's certainly how it was for me. I was reaching another fork in the road.

That's when I decided to retire. I was no longer ready for my close-up. I was grateful to Hollywood—I still am. It made me a lot of money and took me all over the world. I made great friends on the set and still to this day enjoy watching some of the people I worked with go on to bigger and better careers. But I was done with Hollywood or so I thought. That's when I met a guy by the name of Mark Masters.

3, 2, 1, YOU'RE LIVE

One of my good friends is a radio host named Mancow Muller (Mancow has his own syndicated show through Mark Masters and Talk Radio Network). Mancow introduced me to Mark, and we hit it off immediately. Mark was a huge *Babylon 5* fan, and he thought the series had ended too soon. Mark is the founder of Talk Radio Network, the syndicator for Michael Savage, Laura Ingraham, Rusty Humphries, Phil Hendrie, *America's Morning News*, and many other programs.

Soon Mark and I were talking about putting *Babylon 5* back on the air. I reached out to some of the *Babylon 5* actors, writers, and producers to see what their interest level was. To make a long story short, all that ended when the show's creator and I had a bit of a tiff. He felt that he should control everything and I thought his ego deserved a much bigger person.

Mark and I had struck up a really good relationship and I had always been fascinated with talk radio. When I was filming and I wasn't shooting a scene, I'd rush back to my trailer and watch the CNBC ticker while listening to talk radio. I love staying up on trends, trivia, politics, current events, and the economy. I was reading three or four newspapers a day. For me, talk radio was the perfect outlet for all of that. Besides, when you're an actor a therapist is standard-issue. Pay a lot of money for an hour to talk to a stranger about your problems and concerns. Talk radio was the perfect reverse of that: talk to strangers about your problems and concerns and get paid every hour. Brilliant!

After a few months of informal coaching, Mark finally hit on the idea of having me guest-host Rusty Humphries's syndicated *Saturday Night America*, broadcast on over two hundred stations. "Would you like to fill in?" he asked. I couldn't believe it. I was going to be on the radio for three glorious hours.

"Learn the show clock," said Mark. He meant that I should know what I want to say in each segment between commercials. And by all means don't be in the middle of a keen insight or witty dissertation only to have the clock sneak up on you and cut you short. Learn the topics.

Study the material. He coached me on topic management, on breaking open a topic, on asking questions of callers. He taught me the secret of "teasing the giant squid." What he meant by that was something cable news often uses. Prior to commercial break, the talent will attempt to keep the audience tuned in by teasing with something like "Coming up—a giant squid attacks family dog." You've seen it; the water-skiing-squirrel tease or the shark-swarm-off-the-coast-of-Florida tease or the fourteen-foot-alligator-in-the-family-swimming-pool tease.

On the day of the show, I arrived at the studio at 3 P.M. for the 5 P.M. show. The studio engineer laughed. "You're here two hours before your show," he said. I later learned that's not exactly how radio flows. I just wanted to have time to set up all my ducks in a row, review the material, lay out my stuff, and settle in.

They linked my studio in with the main Talk Radio Network studios in Oregon. Mark went over my material and sounded happy. At 5:05 P.M. Pacific Time, I went live. At 5:16, I went to break. At that point, I looked at the clock and realized that I had two hours and forty-four minutes left of live programming, and I had already said everything I ever wanted to say in my life on the radio. I had emptied my cranial clip. Click. Click. I was out of ammo. That's when sheer panic set in. Help!

Mark calmly coached me through the rest of the show. With a little help from my buddy Mancow as an on-air guest I somehow made it through. When the show was over, I felt like the first puppy pulled from the litter and put in the basement without the alarm clock. I was destroyed, absolutely wrung out.

The next day, Mark called. "So, what do you think?" he said.

"It was like sex for the first time," I said. "You can't wait for it to happen, it was over way too soon, and you can't wait to do it again."

Then Mark told me that he had been sitting with all of the Talk Radio Network suits, listening to the show. One of them turned to Mark halfway through the show and said, "If you don't syndicate this guy, I'll quit and do it myself."

"So," said Mark, "how'd you like to do this for a living?"

In December 2003, Mark gave me a development deal for a weekend show, with an option for a weekday show. The weekday show finally premiered on April 5, 2004. And gradually, we grew. We started at 10 P.M. and ended at 1 A.M. originally. Then the program directors at various stations asked if I could move earlier. My slot became 7–10 P.M., then 4–7 P.M., then 1–4 P.M. Finally, I went to the 12–3 P.M. PST slot, where I am today.

After five years, the show is now the seventh biggest in the country, with 230 affiliates and over four million listeners per week. Talk Radio Network is a fantastic syndicator with a great sales department and a great affiliate team. My producer, Jesse Edwards, is a total pro and at times I'm not too bad a host.

I thank my lucky stars every day that I have this job. I've been blessed. I've been fortunate to have had some degree of success in aviation, on Wall Street, in Hollywood, and now on talk radio. I know a lot of people who have worked for years in Hollywood waiting tables and desperately trying to get a script produced or land a steady acting gig. I know lots of talk show hosts who have done the overnights, the morning shows, and moved from market to market just waiting for their big break in radio. I know I'm a very lucky guy.

I think that it's also because I took Yogi Berra's advice: "When you come to a fork in the road, take it." Sounds simple but it's really not if you analyze where you are and where you want to be. Passion has overcome talent more times than not. Let your passion be your guide.

It's easy to overlook opportunities because you have bills to pay, a family to feed, fears of what if I fail or what if I succeed. But I think it's worthwhile to look at all your opportunities, weigh them against what you've got right now, and make plans to see how far that opportunity, your passion, and your dreams can take you. Life's too short not to.

CHAPTER 4

ECONOMIC FASCISM: THE ORIGINS

F ascism" has become a throwaway word nowadays.

The left claimed that President George W. Bush was a fascist. Militant atheists baptized the Reverend Billy Graham as a fascist. Socialists say that tax cutting is fascist. Hell, people label me a fascist for merely introducing the concept of Economic Fascism.

Watering down the term "fascism" is an exercise in stupidity but that's not what I'm doing.

I'm using the term "Economic Fascism" to denote a very specific set of policies that lead to government domination of the economy. Economic Fascism has a precisely defined meaning. And Barack Obama's economic policy fulfills that meaning in every conceivable way.

My definition of Economic Fascism is simple and direct: Economic Fascism embraces the underlying logic of socialism while cloaking it in the terminology of capitalism. The Economic Fascist takes control of private industries, not through open nationalization, but through indirect means: he controls the company without owning it.

But Economic Fascism means something even more specific and dangerous than that. It means that the government has control over what I call the Four Ps: Product, Price, Profit Margin, and People.

PRODUCT: The government gets to control what gets made and what gets put into the marketplace. If the government doesn't like SUVs, SUVs don't get made. If the government likes Segways, Segways get made.

PRICE: The government controls the price of both labor and product. That means the government gets to decide which workers get paid and how much is charged for the product.

PROFIT MARGIN: As you can imagine, if the government is controlling the cost of labor and the price of products, the government also gets to decide profit margins. If the government thinks you're making too much money, the government can simply step in and take away your profits, citing fairness.

PEOPLE: The government gets to decide who runs companies, who works at companies, who must be hired and fired.

Sound familiar? It should. You and I are living under the reign of Economic Fascism. And the Big Man, the Head Honcho, the Grand Leader of the Economic Fascist Movement is our beloved president, Barack Obama.

Now, Obama likes to pretend that he still thinks highly of capitalism. He shies away from labels like "socialist." In fact, he gets downright defensive about such labels. "We've actually been operating in a way that has been entirely consistent with free-market principles . . ." Obama told the press on March 8, 2009. "Some of the same folks who are throwing around the word 'socialist' around can't say the same."

If, Obama said, "the market was doing fine, nobody would be happier than me to stay out of it. I have more than enough to do without having to worry about the financial system. The fact that we've had to take these extraordinary measures and intervene is not an indication of my ideological preference, but an indication of the degree to which lax regulation and extravagant risk taking has precipitated a crisis."[1]

Right. And Lenin just stumbled into that whole communist revolution in Russia.

Obama and his cronies, in the words of chief of staff Rahm Emanuel, "never allow a crisis to go to waste."[2] And Obama got his wish—he got a wonderful crisis. He took office in the wake of George W. Bush, a fiscal quasi-socialist, and Bush deputies like Treasury Secretary Henry "Shifty" Paulson. And he got his big opportunity to enforce his vision of how economics should work. And just how should economics work according to Obama? Taxes should be raised, Obama said back during the campaign, "for purposes of fairness."[3] We're all better off, he told Joe the Plumber, "when you spread the wealth around."[4] Obama's vice president, Joe Biden, thinks that paying higher taxes is "patriotic."[5]

Economic ideologues like Obama have no compunction about using every means at their disposal to increase "fairness." Hence their Economic Fascism. It doesn't take brown shirts and black shirts to destroy a capitalist economy. All it takes is a smooth-tallking politician willing to throw entrepreneurs under the bus.

And it's already started.

A BRIEF HISTORY OF ECONOMIC FASCISM

Political fascism is defined by Merriam-Webster's dictionary as "a political philosophy, movement, or regime that exalts nation and often race above the individual and that stands for a centralized autocratic government headed by a dictatorial leader, severe economic and social regimentation, and forcible suppression of opposition."[6] Remember those elements, folks: nation above individual, centralized government led by a charismatic leader, and economic regimentation. We'll hear more about those later.

Back to our story: The fascist movement arose in Italy in the 1920s under Benito Mussolini. Mussolini began as an ardent socialist, a member of the party. During World War I, however, he refused to adhere to the Socialist Party's line of absolute neutrality, arguing instead in favor of Italian involvement in the war on behalf of the Allies. For that failure to bow to the party, he was expelled. While his estrangement from the Socialist Party drove him to fight the party as he formed his Fasci for Revolutionary Action,[7] Mussolini never abandoned his core beliefs in socialism. Once he solidified his grip on power, Mussolini undertook massive government control of industry. First, he inflated the currency in order to destroy the power of private business. Then he enacted protectionist measures. By the end of 1934, one-third of capital capacity was out of commission, and over a million workers were out of jobs. Mussolini's response? He "bailed out big businesses and banks, fostered mergers and acquisitions, cartelized the remaining, now larger enterprises, and renewed spending . . . appointed a majority of the boards of . . . new credit institutions and provided them with their funds by direct subsidies and by guaranteeing their industrial investments with state bonds. . . . By 1935, Mussolini boasted that fully three-fourths of Italian businesses rested on the shoulders of the state."[8]

All of this fit with Mussolini's fascist worldview. "The Fascist conception of life," wrote Mussolini, "stresses the importance of the State and accepts the individual only in so far as his interests coincide with the State. It is opposed to classical liberalism [which] denied the State in the name of the individual." More briefly, "If classical liberalism spells individual, Fascism spells government."[9]

Almost a century later, the Obama administration is repeating the same failed strategies: enormous bailouts at taxpayer expense; gargantuan government projects; inflation of the currency; government buy-ins.

Obama and Mussolini have something else in common: the use of skilled oratory to destroy independent industry. Mussolini consistently utilized propaganda to champion his "achievements" in working for the people. Most famously, he spread the myth that he had fixed Italy's ever-misfiring train system—he claimed that he had made "the trains run on time." It was a myth so pervasive that as late as 1970, *Time* magazine was still repeating it—and praising Il Duce for building "1,534 miles of railroads . . . 620 miles of waterway, 1,075 miles of highway and 400 major bridges." [10] There's only one problem: it wasn't true. The train system ran no less badly under Mussolini than it had under his predecessors. [11]

Adolf Hitler saw Il Duce's National Socialism as a model—hence his National Socialist German Workers' Party. Hitler's economic policy was closely related to Mussolini's. The Nazi Party platform called for nationalization of trusts, profit sharing, "communalization of department stores," land reform, and the abolition of interest on mortgages. According to William Shirer in his *The Rise and Fall of the Third Reich*, Hitler's economic policy was devoted "largely to putting the unemployed back to work by means of greatly expanded public works"; manipulating the currency "with such legerdemain that at one time it was estimated by foreign economists to have 237 different values"; massive restriction on imports; and tremendous restrictions and regulations on private industry. "Buried under mountains of red tape," Shirer writes, "directed by the State as to what they could produce, how much and at what price, burdened by increasing taxation and milked by steep and never ending 'special contributions' to the party, the businessmen, who had welcomed Hitler's regime so enthusiastically . . . became greatly disillusioned." However, notes Shirer, "In the beginning . . . the businessmen fooled themselves into believing that the Nazi rule was the answer to all their prayers." [12]

These foolish businessmen sound familiar because they *are* familiar. They are the executives at places like General Motors and Chrysler. And they are currently meeting the same fate as their German and Italian predecessors.

GM AND CHRYSLER: THE SETUP

The government-induced destruction of GM and Chrysler is ripped straight from the headlines—of 1935. Back then, Mussolini and Hitler were busy controlling the Four Ps: Product, Price, Profit Margin, and People. Now it's Barack Obama doing it, and doing it well.

Why did Obama start with the auto industry? It simply appeared the easiest industry to take down. The industry was reeling from declining sales, high union wages and benefits, exploding legacy costs for retirees—and all this in the "worst economy since the Great Depression."

Those problems grew as Hillary Clinton and Barack Obama crisscrossed the nation on their Great American Misery Tour: Big Government in Search of Bad News. Convincing the American people that the end of the American way of life was in sight, telling them over and over again that the economy was on the brink of collapse, explaining that every single American was one paycheck from the bread line and one medical diagnosis away from total bankruptcy, the Democratic contenders told battered Americans that the market was the problem, and that government was the answer. They persuaded Americans that the American Dream was no longer a reality, or even a possibility.

It was a self-fulfilling prophecy. By the middle of 2008, Ford, GM, and Chrysler were all reportedly teetering on the edge of bankruptcy. Ford posted a record quarterly loss of $8.7 billion and, undoubtedly in order to satisfy Democrats in Congress, pushed hard to convert its fleet to fuel-efficient compacts instead of trucks.[13] GM, too, was in steep decline—it had not shown an annual profit since 2005.[14]

But Chrysler was in the worst position. In 2006, Chrysler posted a net loss of $1.5 billion. In February 2007, Chrysler cut 16 percent of its workforce—13,000 jobs—in a restructuring plan. In May 2007, DaimlerChrysler sold 80 percent of Chrysler to Cerberus Capital Management for $7.4 billion.[15] During the third quarter of 2008, Chrysler reportedly posted a loss of $400 million.[16] And by November 26, 2008,

Cerberus was pursuing DaimlerChrysler to get back $7 billion, claiming that Daimler had not fully disclosed the possibilities of losses.[17]

On October 27, 2008, the *Wall Street Journal* reported that Chrysler and GM would seek federal aid. Chrysler in particular was in trouble; Cerberus was hoping against hope that GM would buy its stake in Chrysler, even though GM had severe cash flow issues of its own. "Bankruptcy is not an option for Chrysler," said spokeswoman Lori McTavish, even as Chrysler cut five thousand white-collar jobs.[18] And Chrysler's lenders, the biggest of whom—Goldman Sachs, JPMorgan, Citigroup, and Morgan Stanley—owned 70 percent of Chrysler and took government bailout cash themselves,[19] weren't going to sink more money into the company.[20]

In short, the Big Three were in trouble. Their sales were down. Their workers were overpaid. Their product was too pricey. Their lenders, who were largely controlled by the government, were balking. And so they figured it was time to visit the lender of last resort: the federal government. In a sign of solidarity, the CEOs of the Big Three automakers headed to Washington, to plead their case.

STEP ONE: VILIFICATION

The heads of the Big Three traveled to D.C. ready to present evidence as to their collective plight. Instead, their travel methods made the case against them.

In what consitutes one of the biggest PR blunders of all time, Rick Wagoner of GM, Robert Nardelli of Chrysler, and Alan Mulally of Ford flew in not one but *three* separate corporate jets to grovel before Congress claiming they were desperately in need of cash, and asking for $25 billion in taxpayer money to stave off bankruptcy. While GM was losing $181,000 a minute in the third quarter of 2008, Wagoner flew in a $36 million G4 jet, costing an estimated $20,000 round-trip, while requesting a $10 to $12 billion bailout for GM alone. Mulally flew in on one of eight private jets in the Ford fleet, a perk that is part of his employment contract along with a 2007 salary of $28 million. Mulally loves that jet, and used it to travel from Detroit to his Seattle home on weekends. To make matters worse, GM and Ford testified before Congress that the decision to have CEOs fly in on private jets was a corporate one, and not negotiable.[21]

Congress pounced. One of the more memorable moments of the House Financial Services Committee Hearing on November 18, 2008, came courtesy of Gary Ackerman (D-NY), who straightened the carnation in his lapel and said, "There is a delicious irony in seeing private luxury jets flying into Washington, D.C., and the people coming off of them with tin cups in their hand saying that they're going to be trimming down and streamlining their businesses. It's almost like seeing a guy show up at the soup kitchen in a high hat and tuxedo. It kind of makes you a little suspicious. Couldn't you all have downgraded to first class or jet-pooled or something to get here? It would have at least sent a message that you get it."[22]

This is a bit hypocritical, to say the least. While Congressman Ackerman was inquiring about whether the CEOs "got it" with regard to fiscal responsibility at shareholder expense, Democratic Speaker of the House Nancy Pelosi was planning a one-week trip to Italy on a government-owned 737 at taxpayer expense. The price tag for the flight alone: $200,000, ten times the price tag for Wagoner's flight.[23] Seven fellow Democrats accompanied Pelosi on the trip. One of them was Gary Ackerman of New York, carnation blazing in his lapel.[24] So much for "getting it."

Such perks are not uncommon for members of Congress. While Congress was lecturing these greedy, Gordon Gekko goliaths for flying around in luxurious private jets, congressmen and women flew these same jets around the country until the recent "ethics reform." Here's how it worked: Congress would contact a Fortune 500 company's travel department through a "friend" and inquire as to the availability of the company's aircraft. The company—which of course felt no pressure to accommodate the powerful federal legislator who regulates that company's industry—would, just coincidentally, find an available jet precisely when the congressperson needed it. By law, Congress had to pay for travel on that corporate jet—but not at the rate it cost to operate or charter that aircraft. Some of the more luxurious jets Congress used would cost folks like you and me anywhere from $2,500 to $5,000 an hour. But Congress merely had to reimburse the corporation for the equivalent of a coach ticket for their route. So while Congress was busy maligning Wagoner's $20,000 round-trip between Detroit and D.C., someone in Congress who took that very same trip on a jet would need to reimburse the company for only $288, the going rate for a coach ticket on Northwest Flight 2364 from Detroit to Washington.[25] While GM actually pays for its flights, you and I pay for Gary Ackerman's flights.

In January 2007, the House passed rules aimed at demonstrating the Democrats' commitment to cleaning up Congress. By a vote of 430–1, the House bill banned congressional use of corporate jets.[26] The Senate passed similar ethics legislation—but with the provision that senators could still fly on corporate jets if they paid charter rates.[27] Congress's version of ethics reform is like a prostitute with a new business card that says "escort." You're still doing the same thing, you just feel a little classier.

So Congress had no business lecturing the Big Three CEOs—after all, the same members of Congress could have been hitting up Wagoner, Mulally, and Nardelli to use the jets hours before. But reality doesn't matter nearly as much as image. The CEOs didn't understand that, but Congress did. They understood that it was important for Congress to vilify the excesses of the evil corporate executive; when you are trying to undermine and dismantle the free markets and the capitalist system, you have to find a way to turn the tide of public opinion against corporate America. You need a symbol. And that symbol was the corporate jet.

What better way to point out the disconnect between corporate America and the common man? These out-of-touch executives were flying in jets other Americans can't afford. They were taking the quick security line—you know, the one where you don't have to take off your shoes, put your laptop in a filthy plastic bin, and get wanded by some TSA Luke Skywalker wannabe. They have champagne wishes and caviar dreams, while we get free Sprite—if we're lucky. And they were asking for taxpayer money. It was perfect.

The vilification stage of the setup had begun—the first step in any company takedown. With the vilification well underway, the auto executives returned to Detroit with their tails between their legs. The fate of the Big Three was in jeopardy. And everyone reliant on the Big Three cranked up their own PR machine. Suppliers, unions, mayors, and executives launched massive PR campaigns to "save jobs," "save our towns," "save our families." Now Congress could swoop in and play the hero.

GM: THE TAKEDOWN

In early December the executives returned to DC—this time driving in a happy hybrid caravan to prove that they "got it." Wagoner of GM and Mulally of Ford agreed to take a salary of $1 a year if they took any government money; Nardelli was already taking just $1 per year. Both Wagoner and Mulally said that they would sell their corporate jets.[28]

This seemed to satisfy Congress, and after much posturing and hand-wringing, the Bush administration gave GM and Chrysler an early Christmas present: GM was given $9.4 billion and Chrysler got $4 billion. They had ninety days to put together a viable plan that would demonstrate the long-term ability of their companies to be competitive and profitable—Bush expected the unions and the automakers to get down to business to hash out a better business model. If they wanted any more taxpayer money in the future, they needed to come back to Washington with a plan. If they had no such plan by March 31, the automakers would have to repay the cash.[29]

But Bush wasn't president by the time the deadline hit. President and CEO in Chief Barack Obama was in the House. With Obama entering office, the unions refused to make concessions, and the companies had no successful business plan.

That was all the excuse Obama needed to put Economic Fascism into full-fledged practice with GM. Remember: controlling Product, Price, Profit Margin, and People is Economic Fascism.

First, Obama decided to axe GM CEO Rick Wagoner—controlling the People. On March 29, Obama made any more bailouts for GM conditional on Wagoner's resignation. Despite Wagoner's pioneering moves in "green technology"—Wagoner was a big proponent of the Chevy Volt, due out in 2010—Obama thought he was a symptom of the Age of the SUVs. He refused to bow to the gods of global warming, and so his head had to roll. Obama replaced Wagoner with GM COO Frederick "Fritz" Henderson, Obama's handpicked man.[30] Henderson vowed to "offer consumers alternatives and [assure them] that we have the right technologies ready for the future."[31]

Wagoner wasn't the only one who headed for the career graveyard. Obama cleaned out GM's board, too, and stacked it with his friends. Obama called the Michigan congressional delegation on a Sunday night to let them know about his decision to essentially take control of GM's executive structure. They weren't happy about it. But that didn't stop Obama. Said Senator Carl Levin (D-MI), "[Obama] had made the decision that this kind of change was necessary to kind of signal to the public that there was going to be a real effort to make a fresh start. There wasn't much point in arguing whether or not it was fair or unfair, wise or unwise. It was a decision that he didn't ask us about, he informed us of."[32] Michigan governor Jennifer Granholm called Wagoner a "sacrificial lamb."[33]

Wagoner wasn't the solution—he was part of the problem. But he wasn't the whole problem. And by scapegoating Wagoner, Obama had something more ambitious in mind: scaring the living hell out of any CEO who dared get in his way. Wagoner's firing sent the message to every executive in the country: do what we say or you're out.

Once Wagoner was gone—and once Obama controlled this first factor in Economic Fascism—Obama moved on to the next stage of his plan: total control. After replacing the management of GM with his own appointees, GM returned to Capitol Hill with a plan for its rescue. The plan: the Treasury Department (i.e., the taxpayer) would provide an additional $11.6 billion in loans, and the government would own at least half of the company. Meanwhile, GM would use stock instead of cash to pay off the United Auto Workers, leaving the UAW in control of 39 percent of GM. In order to make the plan work, GM pledged to blackmail its bondholders—the bondholders would either swap their $27 billion in unsecured debt for a 10 percent company stake, or GM would file for bankruptcy.[34] The bondholders would lose nearly 100 percent of their investment, and would come away with a mere 5 cents on the dollar. By contrast, the Treasury Department would receive 87 cents on the dollar.[35]

Obama had what he wanted: total government control of one of the biggest auto companies in the world, and an enormous payoff to one of his biggest supporters, the UAW.

CHRYSLER: THE TAKEDOWN

If GM's takedown was an egregious example of Economic Fascism in action, Chrysler's was textbook. Despite Chrysler's claims that it wanted to avoid bankruptcy and avoid merging with Italian car company Fiat, Obama decided that Chrysler was not a viable stand-alone company. On March 30, Obama told Chrysler that it had until April 30 to complete the Fiat merger, or it would face a total cutoff of federal funding.[36] It was nothing less than an offer the company could not refuse. Chrysler's brains, or its signature, would be on the merger contract.

On April 29, 2009, Obama announced that he had no intention of running auto companies.[37] The next day, Obama reversed himself. He announced that Chrysler, America's third-largest auto company, would seek bankruptcy protection and enter into a merger with Fiat. The feds would provide debtor-in-possession financing of up to $3.5 billion to keep the company operating; once the company was reorganized,

Chrysler would receive another government infusion of $4.5 billion. As with Wagoner, Obama decided Nardelli had to go, as well as Chrysler's board.[38]

There was only one holdup: the bankruptcy restructuring. Obama was pushing for a plan that would give the UAW 55 percent of Chrysler—the union would effectively control two of the three largest auto companies in the United States. Fiat would get 35 percent. The government would get 10 percent, along with various other secured lenders.[39] In practice, this would mean that secured lenders holding $6.9 billion in debt would get just 29 cents on the dollar.[40] Liquidation of Chrysler, by contrast, would pay them 65 cents on the dollar. Chrysler's four biggest lenders—JPMorgan Chase, Citigroup, Morgan Stanley, and Goldman Sachs—all paid off with TARP money, were encouraging the secured lenders to accept the 29 cent deal.[41]

The secured lenders rightly refused.

And Obama went into action. In order to make the trains run on time, he would have to destroy these investors. In order to control Chrysler, he would have to make lenders look like Lionel Barrymore's character Potter in the 1947 classic *It's a Wonderful Life*.

This is what Obama does best. He is an incredibly skilled orator, and he's wonderful at selling Economic Fascism to the American people.

His masterpiece in the art of twenty-first-century hucksterism was his April 30 speech on Chrysler's bankruptcy. He began by stating some basic claims: Chrysler was becoming less and less competitive, failing to produce more fuel-efficient and reliable vehicles. He argued that taxpayer dollars could not keep the company afloat if it was behind the times and unable to adapt to a changing marketplace. Instead, Obama suggested "investing" tax money in restructuring the company. The restructure would include partnership with Italian carmaker Fiat—even though Obama was encouraging Americans to buy American cars. And Fiat, Obama said, would share "cutting-edge," environmentally friendly technology to build better vehicles.

Next, Obama praised those who made "unprecedented sacrifices" so that the company and its workers could "see a better day." Those do-gooders were the UAW and certain stakeholders—stakeholders like JPMorgan Chase, Citigroup, Morgan Stanley, and Goldman Sachs, who had "agreed to reduce their debt to less than one-third of its face value to help free Chrysler from its crushing obligations." The way Obama talked about these institutions made you want a cup of cocoa and a warm fire. It was warm and fuzzy "let's get together" sweetness.

That was all a setup. Finally, Obama got to his point: demagogically attacking the evil investors who wouldn't kowtow and sell out. After convincing Americans how wonderful it would be to save Chrysler *his* way, he demonizes the debt holders who have thrown a wrench into his plan. After surrounding himself with the workers, communities, unions, their families, apple pie, and the American flag, Obama turns to the greedy folks who just won't take one for the team.

"While many stakeholders made sacrifices and worked construc- tively," Obama somberly intoned, "I have to tell you some did not. In particular, a group of investment firms and hedge funds decided to hold out for the prospect of an unjustified taxpayer-funded bailout. They were hoping that everybody else would make sacrifices, and they would have to make none. Some demanded twice the return that other lenders were getting. I don't stand with them. I stand with Chrysler's employees and their families and communities. I stand with Chrysler's manage- ment, its dealers, and its suppliers. I stand with the millions of Ameri- cans who own and want to buy Chrysler cars."

Then Obama delivered the coup de grâce: "It was unacceptable to let a small group of speculators endanger Chrysler's future by refusing to sacrifice like everyone else." [42]

Obama's use of the Marxist buzzword "speculators" was a direct attack on the American system of economics. Those "speculators" are the people who allow companies to begin and grow—without investors, Chrysler would still be two guys in a garage somewhere. Dictators from Lenin to Hitler have used the word "speculator" in order to promote their goals of Economic Fascism. [43]

Obama's speech was a string of lies topped with a whopper. Those who "sacrificed" in the proposed deal *benefited* from the deal; those who refused to go along with Obama's plan did so for entirely rational reasons. The UAW would control Chrysler—how tough would the new union negotiations be when the union ran the company? Fiat would get a huge stake in the company; the government would get a chunk, too, and would be able to control the Four Ps. But the investors were expected to take a bath.

This wasn't just unfair—it ran contrary to established law during bankruptcies. Senior creditors always get paid off first. Those senior creditors—firms like Perella Weinberg Partners, Oppenheimer Funds, Stairway Capital Management, Elliott Management, the Indiana State Teachers Retirement Fund, and the Indiana State Police Pension Fund (you know, those speculators who respond to 911 calls and handle drug dealers every day—those speculators)—were being shifted to second-tier status, while the UAW, which owned lesser forms of Chrysler debt, was being shifted to the forefront due to their loyalty to the Obama administration. Even Fiat, which didn't take on any risk and had no investment in Chrysler, would receive a better deal.

The next day in the *Wall Street Journal*, the slandered investors of Chrysler responded to Obama's complaints. Attempting to set the record straight, they explained that they represented teachers unions, major pension and retirement plans, and school endowments with loans to Chrysler topping $1 billion. None of them had taken "a dime in TARP money."

And they had been screwed by Obama. "Under long recognized legal and business principles," the companies wrote, "junior creditors are ordinarily not entitled to anything until senior secured creditors like our investors are repaid in full. Nevertheless, to facilitate Chrysler's rehabilitation, we offered to take a 40% haircut even though some groups lower down in the legal priority chain in Chrysler debt were being given recoveries of up to 50% or more and being allowed to take out billions of dollars. . . . Our offer has been flatly rejected or ignored."[44]

Basically, the investors were stating, Obama tried to use banks that are partially government-owned to negotiate the takeover of a car company that has already taken billions in federal funds, with billions more pledged; and Obama tried to pass over senior creditors in order to pay off his union buddies. Did Obama and his auto task force truly believe that no one would spot the conflict of interest?

It was even worse than that. According to Thomas Lauria, lawyer for the non-TARP Chrysler lenders, Steve Rattner, the leader of the Obama administration's Auto Industry Task Force, actually threatened one of the investment banks with ruinous press coverage if it refused to kowtow. Perella Weinberg Partners, said Lauria, "was directly threatened by the White House and in essence compelled to withdraw its opposition to the deal under the threat that the full force of the White House press corps would destroy its reputation if it continued to fight. That's how hard it is to stand on this side of the fence." [45] Obama wasn't just implementing Economic Fascist policies; he was now attempting fascist tactics.

It worked. On May 8, 2009, the group of Chrysler creditors opposing the reorganization announced that they would disband after several of the lenders dropped out of the group under government pressure. "After a great deal of soul-searching and quite frankly agony, Chrysler's non-TARP lenders concluded they just don't have the critical mass to withstand the enormous pressure and machinery of the US government," announced Lauria. "As a result, they have collectively withdrawn their participation in the court case."

Obama was now in total control of the Chrysler reorganization. The takedown was complete.

ECONOMIC FASCISM: THE TAKEDOWNS IN REVIEW

Remember the Four Ps of Economic Fascism? Product, Price, Profit Margin, and People. Each of those elements of both GM and Chrysler is now within the control of the federal government of the United States.

PRODUCT: "I'm not an auto engineer," Obama said on April 29. "I don't know how to create an affordable, well-designed plug-in hybrid.

But I know that, if the Japanese can design an affordable, well-designed hybrid, then, doggone it, the American people should be able to do the same thing. So my job is to ask the auto industry: Why is it that you can't do this?"

No, sir. That's not your job. Obama certainly isn't an auto engineer—under his tutelage, one of GM's first moves was to team up with Segway to create a two-wheeled idiotmobile "designed to move easily through congested urban streets." The green machine would run on batteries and use wireless technology to avoid traffic.[46]

Obama has never run so much as a Popsicle stand, and now he's deigning to decide whether Fiat makes superior cars to Chrysler, and whether a Fiat-Chrysler partnership will create the kind of light, green cars he likes. For the record, the Fiat-Chrysler deal will not move the company toward electric cars, in all likelihood—it's far more likely that Fiat will use its "4-cylinder diesel engines instead to meet future fuel mileage standards," according to J. D. Power and Associates power train analyst Mike Omotoso. In fact, says Reuters, "By the time Chrysler and Fiat are able to invest in new technology, today's startups could be some of the more established players" in the battery industry—meaning that it will take years for Chrysler to go green.[47]

But that won't stop Obama from setting new fuel-efficiency standards. On May 19, he announced that he would require all cars manufactured by American companies to get 35 miles per gallon by 2016. This will add at least $1,300 to the average price of a car.[48]

PRICE: Now that Obama has ensured that American automobile manufacturers will make cars no one wants to buy, he has to ensure that Americans will be forced to buy them. By kowtowing to the unions and forcing fuel-efficient technology onto an unwilling market, he has made certain that car prices will rise. By pushing his "cash for clunkers" policy, he hoped to use tax dollars to spur Americans to buy Obama-mobiles. This appeared to have worked in the short term, with post-incentive sales questionable. We know however that foreign automobile manufacturers were a bigger beneficiary of the program than were GM, Ford, and Chrysler.

On March 30, Obama endorsed a "trade-in program" encouraging Americans to dump their old gas-guzzlers and to embrace the Prius-laden future.[49] On May 5, Congress came up with a bill that would give consumers up to $4,500 to buy a new, more fuel-efficient vehicle. "By stimulating consumer demand for new vehicles, this proposal will directly benefit domestic autoworkers and automotive manufacturers, which have arguably been hardest hit by the current economic downturn," explained Representative John Dingell (D-MI), cosponsor of the bill. The total cost of the bill: $4 billion for one year.[50]

From where is that money going to come? You know the answer to that one: from me and from you.

PROFIT MARGIN: Chrysler and GM are now owned lock, stock, and barrel by the UAW. That means that the UAW will be negotiating with the UAW to set wages. And they don't have to worry about selling cars—after all, the federal government has shown its willingness to force Americans to buy green, and its willingness to bail out ailing automakers, so long as those automakers are focused on making cheap, light, fuel-efficient cars nobody wants to buy. It's no wonder Obama turned both GM and Chrysler over to the UAW—by the way, UAW leadership spent $5 million to get Obama elected[51] and unanimously endorsed him for president, and the AFL-CIO spent $53.4 million to get him elected.[52]

Meanwhile, auto executives tread lightly, lest Obama cut their pay and bonuses as he did with AIG.

PEOPLE: Wagoner—out. Nardelli—out. How long before Mulally joins his colleagues on the sidelines? Obama has shifted his buddies into power at America's major automobile companies, and he has summarily dismissed those he does not control. He has purposefully bullied investors into giving up their stakes in favor of government ownership, and he has blackmailed stockholders into selling out. This spells the death of American industry. When loans become unprofitable, no one will lend. And Obama is focused on making loans unprofitable by refusing lenders the knowledge that they will be repaid in case of a bankruptcy.

And so the government steps in to grant loans. Only government loans aren't the same as private loans—they're designed not to profit both the borrower and the lender but to allow the government to exercise control over industry. It is easy for the administration to hand out billions in bailouts, because it's not their money—it's ours. For most people, including investors, there are two kinds of money: your money, and my money. It's my job to protect my money and not to steal your money. For the government, there's only one kind of money: the government's money. And your money is the government's money.

THE REIGN OF ECONOMIC FASCISM

Economic Fascism is clearly at hand under Obama. By tapping into public ire at automakers and banks, Obama sold the bailouts and the takeovers. He convinced us that the greedy Wall Street bankers deserved to lose their jobs and bonuses because the terrible economy is *their* fault. He convinced us that heads needed to roll at the automakers, and that lenders were greedy "speculators" who deserved to lose their investments.

And he gradually expanded his power, and the power of his allies. With the financial system quasi-nationalized, and with the precedent of the auto takeover in place, all American industry must live in fear of government intervention.

Obama is likable. That is his strength. Most people can relate to him; he has a nice family, a swing set on the lawn of the White House, and an organic vegetable garden. I personally like Obama—he seems like a great guy. But politically and economically, he is destroying much of what makes America great. The Obama administration is far too cavalier toward the rule of law, the overabundance of regulation, and the division between the public and private sectors. Under Hitler and Mussolini, Economic Fascism went under the name corporatism. Today's Economic Fascism goes under the name Obamanomics. But whether you call it corporatism or Obamanomics, Economic Fascism is Economic Fascism.

And the goal of Economic Fascism isn't merely control over daily life—it's the "Beijing" of America. Obama wants to dismantle our free market system in order to reengineer the country into a perfect, fair, classless society in which the government controls industry. Obama wants a monochromatic America, where everyone owns the same house, the same car, eats the same food—and votes for the same president. The Obama administration wants to dictate what we consume, how much we consume, and how it will be produced. Instituting government control over an individual's behavior and choices like what car you drive; what foods you eat; what health care your family uses—all of it leads us down a dangerous and potentially irreversible path. The government's tentacles are reaching further and further into the private sector. The tighter the grip, the harder it will be to return to a free market system.

We are living in momentous times. There are many who question whether American capitalism will survive Obama. The verdict is in: It *has* not. It *will* not, if we continue these ruinous government policies.

We are already living under the rule of Economic Fascism. The economic jackboots are already in charge of Washington, D.C. Obama's dictatorial command and control of the economy spells disaster for our principles and our prosperity. Freedom, liberty, and capitalism require constant faith in the power of the individual, not the power of government. We began to rely on the government instead of ourselves.

We've gotten what we deserve. Now what do we do?

CHAPTER 5

FINANCIAL INCEST

When you get in bed with the federal government, expect to get screwed. And don't expect to be respected in the morning.

That truism applies especially if you're unfortunate enough to be involved with a program known as the Troubled Asset Relief Program, better known as TARP.

It's a story that began with corporate greed, corruption, regulatory incompetence, and deceit. It grew into a regulatory monster that has so undermined the foundation of American capitalism that it will take decades for America to recover.

But it's a much more complex story than that. On September 19, 2008, President Bush stepped to the podium in the White House Rose Garden to announce the beginning of the end of American economic freedom: the $700 billion TARP. "This is a pivotal moment for America's economy," Bush said. "Problems that originated in the credit markets—and first showed up in the area of subprime mortgages—have spread throughout our financial system. This has led to an erosion of confidence that has frozen many financial transactions, including loans to consumers and to businesses seeking to expand and create jobs. As a result, we must act now to protect our nation's economic health from serious risk. . . .

"Our system of free enterprise rests on the conviction that the federal government should interfere in the marketplace only when necessary. Given the precarious state of today's financial markets—and their vital importance to the daily lives of the American people—government intervention is not only warranted, it is essential. . . .

"This action," Bush continued, "does entail risk. But we expect that this money will eventually be paid back. The vast majority of assets the government is planning to purchase have good value over time, because the vast majority of homeowners continue to pay their mortgages. And the risk of not acting would be far higher." [1]

As Bush reassured the American people that doing nothing was worse than doing something, his wingman, Treasury Secretary and former CEO of Goldman Sachs Henry Paulson, standing by Bush's side, shifted from side to side like a second-grader with a bladder problem. As I watched him uncomfortably shifting his weight from foot to foot and watched his eyes darting left and right, I knew there was something very wrong with this picture. We were being lied to, and he knew it. From that day forward, he earned my nickname: Henry "Shifty" Paulson.

His body language told us much more than Bush's reassuring words. He knew that the taxpayers were embarking on an unending set of bailouts designed to rescue his Wall Street friends and former cronies at Goldman Sachs. What he didn't know—or did he?—was that the bailouts would open the door for the Economic Fascism of the Obama administration to dismantle the very system he and Bush were feverishly and foolishly trying to "rescue."

The Bush administration's massive $700 billion bailout proposal marked the culmination of a years-long process of systematic malfeasance by federal regulators, corrupt congressmen, and the Good Ol' Boy and Gal Network.

The original bailout program got underway on Sunday, March

16, 2008, when JPMorgan announced plans to buy Bear Stearns in a government-brokered deal for $2 per share, the same stock that was trading at $171 per share just fourteen months earlier. The Federal Reserve agreed to provide special financing, "backstopping" up to $30 billion of Bear Stearns's bad assets.[2] "Given the exceptional pressures on the global economy and financial system, the damage caused by a default by Bear Stearns could have been severe and extremely difficult to contain," said Federal Reserve Chairman Ben "I'm Just a College Professor" Bernanke, justifying the deal.[3]

Tim Geithner, at the time president of the Fed's New York regional bank, soon to be the next treasury secretary—or as I like to refer to him, "Son of Shifty"—also signed off on the deal.[4] Eventually, JPMorgan Chase gobbled up Bear Stearns for a whopping $10 per share.[5]

According to Treasury Department undersecretary Robert Steel, the Federal Reserve had no idea that Bear Stearns was in danger of collapse until March 13, when the firm supposedly told Shifty Paulson and Fed Chair Bernanke that it was twenty-four hours from having to file for bankruptcy protection. On March 12, 2008, the day before Bear Stearns supposedly informed the Fed of its liquidity crisis, the chief executive officer of Bear Stearns told CNBC that he was not aware of any threat to Bear Stearns's liquidity. Securities and Exchange Commission chairman Chris Cox said that same week that the SEC was comfortable with Bear's "capital cushions."[6] When Geithner was asked whether he should have foreseen Bear's collapse, he punted: "Very hard to know . . . these things can happen incredibly quickly in markets like this."[7] Here's the reality, folks: Stevie Wonder could have seen this one coming. (No offense, Stevie—I still enjoy listening to *Songs in the Key of Life*.)

The financial insiders knew that these problems were on their way for years. Take, for example, the World Economic Forum (WEF), held in Davos, Switzerland. The WEF is an annual gathering of 2,500 "global leaders" in world finance. It's a Fantasy Island for the global insiders, where the cover charge is $750,000 per firm, and these financial gurus for the most part spend their time skiing, partying, and cutting deals.

And when they're not shushing the slopes or sipping champagne, they find time to design the new World Economic Order. The preparation process for this glitzy event says it all: "In the days leading up to the conference, volunteers in lederhosen draped the village with hundreds of white and blue banners that declared the 38-year-old conclave's purpose: 'Committed to Improving the State of the World.'"

Now let's take a look at some of the names of the attendees of this Crock Pot of Capitalism: Richard Fuld, Jr., CEO of the now defunct Lehman Brothers; former Freddie Mac CEO Richard Syron; former treasury secretary and current Obama chief economic advisor Larry Summers; Citigroup Inc.'s copresident of investment banking Michael Klein; David Rubenstein, managing director of the Carlyle Group; Goldman Sachs CEO Lloyd Blankfein; Congressman Barney Frank (D-MA);[8] Bill Clinton, who was a "Davos regular";[9] and, you guessed it, Shifty Paulson.[10] That's just a small sampling of the familial financial incest that headed to Davos year after year. Between snow-polo matches (seriously!) the Financial Jet Set found time to hold seminars on the state of the international economy. Remember, folks, we were told nobody could see this coming.

In 2005, Goldman Sachs and Freddie Mac held a session entitled "Spotting the Next Bubble Before It Bursts." In 2006, another breakout session targeted the real estate market and its systematic risk to the international financial system. That meeting was chaired by Morgan Stanley chief economist Stephen Roach, who went on to become chairman of Morgan Stanley Asia Limited. Mr. Roach said this: "A sharp decline in housing prices could have a tremendous impact on the global economy; in the U.S. alone, 40 percent of new jobs since 2001 have been related to the housing sector. With low interest rates and excess liquidity, other bubbles may follow."[11]

Founder of the WEF Klaus Schwab seconded the motion, repeatedly warning about the risks of asset price bubbles in real estate and stocks. As early as 2003, the WEF issued warnings to investment banks, insurance companies, and hedge funds about the tremendous amount of risk they were taking on. In addition, WEF CEO Kevin Steinberg said there were intelligent people raising red flags in Davos for at least five years. "The financial community didn't listen," says Schwab. "They were told that any serious look at the economic fundamentals showed that we were in an unstable situation. It was denial, total psychological denial." [12]

So there you have a sliver of an insight into the goings-on at Davos. But now, kids, it's time to jump off the snow-polo ponies, put down those champagne glasses, slip on your Ugg boots, jump into that private jet, and head back to America, where those greedy "predatory lenders" were writing 100 percent financing loans on two-and-a-half-bath, 1,400-square-foot houses in Peoria, Illinois, attempting to "Dr. Evil" the entire international financial structure.

It was more than Swiss Alp yodeling about systemic risks that should have alerted the government to the downfall of institutions like Bear Stearns. According to a report requested by Senator Charles Grassley (R-IA) and written by Inspector General H. David Kotz, SEC chairman Cox stood by as Bear's capital ratios shrank and subprime holdings exploded, leading to the firm's collapse. Before the report was released to the public, however, Kotz deleted 136 references, many dealing with SEC memos, meetings, and comments, at the SEC's request. "People can judge for themselves," wrote Grassley, "but it sure looks like the SEC didn't want the public to know about the red flags it apparently ignored in allowing Bear Stearns and other investment banks to engage in excessively risky behavior." [13]

It was even worse than that. In 2005, an SEC branch office launched an investigation into Bear Stearns, suspecting that the Wall Street firm had fraudulently valued mortgage-related securities, the very same securities that eventually brought down the firm. According to the *Wall Street Journal* in December 2007, the SEC branch office stated that it "intended to recommend that Bear Stearns be charged for improperly pricing about $63 million of mortgage securities it sold to a bank." Bear Stearns was valuing those mortgage securities—the highly risky collateralized debt obligations (CDOs)—at 90 percent of face value for purposes of selling them, then buying them from clients at 30 percent of face value.

Meanwhile, New York attorney general Eliot Spitzer was looking into prosecuting Bear Stearns over mispricing $16 million of mortgage securities.[14] He was also coming down hard on Wall Street and the moneyed interests didn't like anyone screwing with their cash cow. Of course, we all know what eventually happened to Spitzer, when he came to be known as Governor Eliot "Client #9" Spitzer.

While everyone seemed to ignore the red flags in Davos, while they ignored the red flags in the growth of the credit default swap market from $100 billion to $62 trillion in just ten years, the regulators some-how managed to stumble across the $5,000 Suspicious Activity Report (SAR) red flag that took down Spitzer for hiring a prostitute. While I certainly don't condone a married man hiring a prostitute, is it just me, or is this more than just a coincidence?

In the end, predictably, the Washington, D.C.–headquartered SEC dropped the cases. Grassley, who sat on the Senate Finance Commit-tee, sent an inquiry to the SEC. "Given the later collapse and federally-backed bail-out of Bear Stearns," wrote Grassley, "Congress needs to understand more about this case and why the SEC ultimately sought no enforcement action." SEC chair Chris Cox rejected Senator Grassley's request for information on April 16, 2008. "The Commission does not disclose the existence or nonexistence of an investigation or information generated in any investigation unless made a matter of public record in proceedings brought before the Commission or the courts," Cox wrote to Grassley.[15]

It is impossible not to surmise that there were decisions made behind the scenes to cover up problems at Bear. I spent ten years on Wall Street in the 1980s, and I know a thing or two about where the bodies are buried, how they get there, and more importantly, who wants to make sure they stay there. There's no way to convince me that Shifty Paulson and Company weren't fully aware of what was going on. They knew there were serious violations of investment law going on at America's biggest financial institutions. Instead of investigating, they chose to keep their shareholders, employees, and the taxpayers completely in the dark. The predictable result: trillions of your tax money spent to bail out these institutions that were improperly valuing assets—institutions that should have been disciplined by the SEC long ago. The problem wasn't "predatory lenders" who tricked people into buying dream homes with adjustable-rate mortgages; it wasn't feckless homeowners buying into bad deals. The problem was corruption on Wall Street's Mahogany Row and even deeper corruption on Capitol Hill.

FROM FANNIE AND FREDDIE TO AIG

Three of the biggest companies on the face of the earth, American International Group (AIG), Fannie Mae, and Freddie Mac, eventually followed the same pattern as Bear Stearns: horrific internal risk management, interventionist government policies, and failed regulatory oversight. As government-sponsored entities (GSEs), Fannie and Freddie knew they could take on massive risks knowing that the government would ultimately bail them out. Urged on by congressional lobbyists and a compliant Federal Reserve, these firms financed subprime mortgages to bad credit risks like candy to Overeaters Anonymous. Certain Republicans, "for their part," repeatedly attempted to regulate Fannie Mae and Freddie Mac, and they were systematically stonewalled. In 2003, the Bush administration attempted to create an agency to oversee Fannie and Freddie, but Rep. Barney Frank and friends protested and assured us that Fannie and Freddie weren't "facing any kind of financial crisis." [16] In 2005, the Federal Housing Enterprise Regulatory Reform Act, sponsored by Senators Chuck Hagel (R-NE), Elizabeth Dole (R-NC), John McCain (R-AZ), and John Sununu (R-NH), was rejected. [17]

Meanwhile, those risky loans flowed like water, in particular to unqualified minorities. In 1992, Democrats required that Fannie and Freddie increase loans to low-income ("victims!") and medium-income borrowers ("victims!"), particularly racial minorities ("victims!"). Andrew Cuomo, President Clinton's secretary of housing and urban development, suggested that Fannie and Freddie give 50 percent of its loans to low- and moderate-income borrowers.[18] Under intense pressure from congressional Democrats, Freddie Mac watered down its underwriting standards an incredible twenty-eight times, and allowed applicants with no credit history to receive loans. Even more amazing, Democrats forced Freddie Mac to allow applicants to claim income from seasonal jobs and public assistance, including *food stamps*, toward loan-qualifying income minimums.[19] It wasn't only Democrats who were covering for Fannie Mae and Freddie Mac, by the way—Shifty Paulson similarly assured us that Fannie and Freddie were "adequately capitalized." [20] In the year leading up to Fannie Mae's and Freddie Mac's nationalization, they ran up a debt of $1.6 trillion.[21] Then, for all intents and purposes, they were nationalized. All at taxpayer expense! And what did this get us? In the fourth quarter of 2008 alone, Fannie Mae reported a staggering loss of $25.2 billion, and turned to the taxpayer for another $15.2 billion, which they received.[22]

While Fannie and Freddie were fiddling away the taxpayers' money, American International Group was building its business on diversification and borderline accounting. The former CEO of AIG, Maurice Greenberg, was ousted from AIG by Eliot Spitzer in 2005 for shady business practices. Back in November 2004, the Bush Justice Department and SEC agreed not to prosecute AIG for cooking clients' books; instead, they settled for an AIG agreement to host a government auditor in meetings.[23]

Once again, the auditor apparently didn't see any of the red flags. Much of AIG's asset portfolio was tied to subprime mortgages via credit default swaps (CDSs)—basically, a form of noninsurance insurance bought by investment groups in case the subprime mortgages started going bad. The only problem was that it wasn't really insurance. Insurance requires that you set aside a certain amount of capital to meet current and future obligations. CDSs were noninsurance insurance, which means there was little to no money set aside to meet these obligations.

When and if things went bad the house of financial cards would come crashing down. And bad they went. This meant that AIG had to pay up. And AIG didn't have that kind of cash. It was a scam.

Time for government, i.e., the taxpayer, to come to the rescue on the notion of "too big to fail." AIG became a government-owned and government-operated company for the bargain basement price of $85 billion. Corporate executives are normally ousted by their boards or their shareholders. But under Shifty Paulson, the roots of Economic Fascism began to grow. With the AIG bailout, Robert Willumstad was forced to step aside by Shifty Paulson.[24]

Fannie and Freddie, too, joined the newly increasing government portfolio. But that was no surprise—Fannie Mae and Freddie Mac spent $170 million lobbying Congress over the past decade.[25] "Fannie Mae and Freddie Mac are so large and so interwoven in our financial system that a failure of either of them would cause great turmoil in our financial markets at home and across the globe," said Shifty. And suddenly the taxpayers owned the world's biggest mortgage issuer. And as with AIG, the leadership was dumped and replaced with two Paulson cronies— Herb Allison of Merrill Lynch, and David Moffett of U.S. Bancorp.[26]

So corporate America as we knew it began to wither and die on the vine. But why did the Bush administration willingly lay the foundation for Obama's Economic Fascism?

THE CURSE OF
COMPASSIONATE CONSERVATISM

George W. Bush's presidency was animated by a single overarching ideal: Compassionate Conservatism. He described that philosophy in a speech in San Jose, California, in 2002. "Government cannot solve every problem," Bush said, "but it can encourage people and communities to help themselves and to help one another. Often the truest kind of compassion is to help citizens build lives of their own. I call my philosophy and approach 'Compassionate Conservatism.' *It is compassionate to actively help our fellow citizens in need.* It is conservative to insist on responsibility and on results." [27]

There's a basic problem with this philosophy. Conservatism by its very nature *is* compassionate and doesn't need to be tempered with compassion. Conservatism relies on the judgment and integrity of the individual, and demands that individual freedom and liberty should be protected by the Constitution. I want to protect compassion *from* the government the same way I want to protect the separation of church and state: it's not that I want to protect government from religion; I want to protect religion from government.

But for Bush, compassion flowing from the government became necessary on a regular basis. That means that when there's a "crisis," government must step in to solve it. Bush is a "strong government conservative," a man who thinks along the lines described by George Will: "Today 'strong government conservatism'—'strong' is not synonymous with 'big'—is the only conservatism palatable to a public that expects government to assuage . . . life's largest fears." [28] When companies began to go under, Bush jumped in to save them. When he was notified by his "expert" advisors that a crisis was looming, Bush leveraged the power of government to fight the crisis. And so he suggested in the aftermath of his bailouts that "I've abandoned free-market principles to save the free-market system. . . . I am sorry we're having to do it. I feel a sense of obligation to my successor to make sure there is not a, you know, a huge economic crisis. Look, we're in a crisis now. I mean, this is—we're in a huge recession, but I don't want to make it even worse." [29] Well, George: you did.

Bush was compassionate. But he wasn't a conservative, and didn't have faith in the free market system. In using government to shore up bad corporations, Bush paved the way for the destruction of the free market he wanted so desperately to save. The precipitous slide from Compassionate Conservatism to Economic Fascism began with the Big Bank Bonanza.

THE BIG BANK BONANZA

With AIG, Bear Stearns, Fannie Mae, and Freddie Mac, the Bush administration stepped into the fray at the behest of the companies. With the first TARP program, Bush, Shifty Paulson, and the rest of the fiscally socialist crew finally stepped over the line from aid to coercion.

The government takeover of the entire financial system began with the $700 billion economic stimulus plan pushed by Bush in September 2008. The plan was originally designed, and sold, to Congress, to free up credit for lending by taking "toxic assets" off the banks' balance sheets. Soon, the public relations firm of Bush, Bernanke & Paulson was hard-selling the American people on the idea of the taxpayers' "investing" in the United States's major financial institutions. A little fear-mongering helped, too, when certain members of Congress were told of the threat of martial law if Congress didn't act quickly. Their public relations efforts paid off. Just one month later, on October 16, 2008, the government announced that it would be buying shares in the nation's largest banks. Bush, predictably, claimed that the intervention was "not intended to take over the free market but to preserve it." He explained that his first instinct "wasn't to lay out a huge government plan. My first instinct was to let the market work until I realized, upon being briefed by the experts, of how significant this problem became." Shifty Paulson sounded less broken up about the intervention: "Government owning a stake in any private US company is objectionable to most Americans—me included. Yet the alternative of leaving businesses and consumers without access to financing is totally unacceptable." Ben Bernanke was downright celebratory: "Our strategy will continue to evolve and be refined as we adapt to new developments and the inevitable setbacks. But we will not stand down until we have achieved our goals of repairing and reforming our financial system and thereby restoring prosperity to our economy."[30]

The banks weren't all happy about the buy-in. On October 13, 2008, the Treasury Department summoned the CEOs of Citigroup, JPMorgan, Wells Fargo, Merrill Lynch, Morgan Stanley, Goldman Sachs, Bank of New York, Bank of America, and State Street Bank to Washington and presented them with "CEO Talking Points." These talking points made clear that the banks would have no choice in the matter: "If a capital infusion is not appealing," they stated, "you should be aware your regulator will require it in any circumstance." Also present at the meeting: Treasury Secretary Tim Geithner, FDIC chair Sheila Bair, and Fed chair Ben Bernanke. Interestingly, Judicial Watch filed a Freedom of Information Act, FOIA, request to release all documents from the October 13, 2008, meeting. The Obama Treasury Department claimed on February 4, 2009, that it had no documents from the historic meeting. Pressure from Judicial Watch, however, forced Treasury to reevaluate its response, which resulted in the partial document release. Tim Geithner's input on the meeting was withheld by the Obama Treasury Department anyway. Such secrecy is unsurprising; the Treasury Department reportedly wanted to use Secret Service agents to keep the press away from the arriving CEOs.[31] What were they hiding?

Just weeks before, however, Shifty Paulson had stated that buying into the banks would be a sign of "failure." At the meeting, he wasn't hewing to that line. He wanted government control over banking, and he wasn't going to take no for an answer. "The system needs more money," he told the bankers, "and all of you will be better off if there's more capital in the system."[32] The tacit threat was obvious: if the banks didn't sign now, there would be no bailout money on the table in the future. There was also the bigger threat of firing—the Federal Reserve is the primary regulator for the banks of the country, and has the power to remove executives it feels are acting irresponsibly.

THE UNHAPPIEST MAN IN THE ROOM

The biggest force-feed—and the most egregious example of how a corrupt government can destroy a private company already hell-bent on destroying itself—was Bank of America. In September 2008, with rumors in the air that the government would be absorbing firms' toxic assets,

Ken Lewis, CEO of Bank of America, decided the timing was ripe for Bank of America to buy Merrill Lynch, a firm he had long coveted. On September 15, Bank of America made an offer to purchase Merrill Lynch for $50 billion. Lewis figured, "What's the worst-case scenario? If the deal doesn't work out, the government is there as a financial backstop." TARP to the rescue!

Not so fast, said the government. With the October 2008 decision by Shifty Paulson, Bush, and Bernanke to turn TARP into a stock buy-in program, all hope dissolved for Bank of America. By November, Shifty was telling the public that nine of the nation's largest banks would be accepting $125 million from the feds. By December, Merrill was reporting a pretax loss of $21 billion.[33]

A material adverse change clause could have allowed Bank of America to back out of the Merrill Lynch deal—Merrill had lost a whopping $15 billion in the last three months of 2008. Bank of America could have walked on the deal due to the deteriorating financial health of Merrill Lynch. But Shifty would have none of that. He informed Lewis that the deal with Merrill would go through. Washington had made up its mind that the financial system needed the deal. Any pullout, said Paulson, would "frazzle the market, spark a flurry of lawsuits against Bank of America and tarnish the bank for years . . . and any future requests for government assistance would cause government officials to consider taking a heavier hand in Bank of America's operations." And Shifty threatened Lewis that his job was on the line—if Bank of America needed cash in the future, Paulson said, they could expect regulators "to think hard about their confidence in management."[34] Shifty Paulson and Bernanke told Lewis he'd have government funds with which to wash down Merrill. But the two wizards would not put that in writing. "We do not want a disclosable event," said Shifty. "We do not want a public disclosure."[35]

The merger was completed on January 1, 2009—without Lewis informing stockholders of the material adverse change possibility. Shifty Paulson and Bernanke meanwhile kept quiet to both SEC chair Cox and the Financial Stability Oversight Board.[36] So much for oversight and transparency. And so much for Bank of America and Ken Lewis. On April 29, 2009, the Bank of America shareholders summarily fired Lewis as chairman. "I find it incredible you didn't have the guts to stand up to the U.S. government," railed one shareholder. Bank of America's stock finished at $8.68 the day of Lewis's dismissal.[37] One year earlier, the stock price had been almost $40.

It was an almost Shakespearean ending to a tragic tale. Everyone involved demonstrated horrific judgment throughout. Lewis kowtowed to the government to save his own neck—a fundamental breach of his duty to the shareholders. Bernanke and Paulson demonstrated their willingness to waterboard banks to get their way. The government demonized the banks in order to foist its agenda upon them—and the banks played the suckers in order to take the money.

More than that, the government played a dangerous game with the free market—it held itself to a different standard than it would the private sector. If someone had knowledge about Merrill's yet to be disclosed losses and taken financial action based upon it, that person would be prosecuted for insider trading. In this case, Bernanke, Paulson, and Lewis all knew how bad the losses were at Merrill—and all three kept quiet in order to force the deal through. Millions of Americans lost billions of dollars, both through bailouts and through declining stock prices. The market works based on the free, unfettered flow of accurate information. That's the only way for investors to determine what's worth buying, selling, holding, or hedging. Disclosure is the essence of the free market.

The deception of the Bank of America–Merrill Lynch merger turned the rules of the free market upside down. Paulson and Bernanke threatened Ken Lewis into silence just like they threatened and strong-armed banks into taking TARP money. How are we supposed to trust anything we are told about a company that we might invest in? We should be incredibly concerned when the chairman and CEO of this country's largest bank was forced by the government to lie to his shareholders on penalty of replacement. This is Economic Fascism. The government, together with its accomplices in the financial industry, erased the line between the public and private sectors. The Treasury Department and the Federal Reserve shouldn't have the authority to decide who runs a private company—their job is to enforce rules and regulations. Owners of the company, the shareholders, vote on the board of directors and have the authority to effect change when they don't like how the company is run. But the Bush administration in "rescuing" Wall Street opened the door for the partial ownership and control of literally every industry under the sun. Shareholders and investors had lost their power. Enter Barack Obama.

THE FINAL FRONTIER:
OBAMA CAPS SALARIES AND BONUSES

When Barack Obama was sworn in, corporate America had no idea just how much control government had or wanted and to what lengths it would go to get it. Citigroup is a classic example of a government stranglehold.

Citigroup received $25 billion in the first round of bailouts, and in November 2008, after the stock was pounded down to $2 a share, the government stepped in and invested another $20 billion in the bank and received preferred nonvoting shares. With the second rescue the terms of the bailout changed, and Citigroup was no longer able to pay out a dividend of more than a penny a share per quarter for the next three years.[38] In January 2009, the U.S. government became even more involved in Citigroup. The Treasury Department took control of 36 percent of Citigroup by transferring their preferred nonvoting shares into common stock, which allows them a vote. The Treasury Department took $25 billion in loans and turned that money into equity in the company, overnight becoming Citigroup's single largest voting shareholder.[39]

As the fallout from the bailouts continued to unfold, the rules kept changing. The original programs did not include any regulations on salary. Under Obama, however, accepting TARP money meant you had to cap executive pay at $500,000 per year. In setting the cap, Obama engaged in his usual bout of demagoguery against free markets: "For top executives to award themselves these kinds of compensation packages in the midst of this economic crisis isn't just bad taste," he said, "it's a bad strategy—and I will not tolerate it. We're going to be demanding some restraint in exchange for federal aid—so that when firms seek new federal dollars, we won't find them up to the same old tricks." [40] He went even further: "We all need to take responsibility. And this includes executives at major financial firms who turned to the American people, hat in hand, when they were in trouble, even as they paid themselves their customary lavish bonuses," Obama railed. "As I said last week, that's the height of irresponsibility. That's shameful. And that's exactly the kind of disregard for the costs and consequences of their actions that brought about this crisis: a culture of narrow self-interest and short-term gain at the expense of everything else." [41]

Obama clearly has no idea how salary works in the financial industry. He caps pay for "executives," but does not define executives. Are "executives" anybody making over $500,000? Anybody with "VP" next to their name? Anybody who gets a key to the executive washroom? Obama doesn't say, because he doesn't know. He just knows what *sounds* good.

There's a reason pay has been so high in the financial industry. With the general exception of retail brokers, executives, investment bankers, traders, those in mergers and acquisitions, and most everyone else on Wall Street are compensated with one large annual bonus and a decent base salary. The bonus is based on a pool for each division and the money allocated in the pool is based on that division's contribution to the firm that year. It's basically a commission-based system, a simple structure that in the past has allowed banks to correctly allocate salaries based on performance—you get a big bonus if you make a big profit for your division. Is the government going to cap the bonus that traders earn from actual deals they generate? What is the incentive to continue to do business if you know you've done enough to make that $500,000? You might as well take the rest of the year off.

A brief example demonstrates just how counterproductive government caps on salaries are. Citigroup, which is now another member of the government portfolio, has a division called Phibro, an energy-trading unit led by Andrew Hall. In April 2009, Citigroup approached the government to ask about increasing pay limits for Phibro workers, since those employees were producing hundreds of millions of dollars for the bank—Citigroup's $667 million in pretax revenue in commodities trading in 2008 was largely due to Phibro's work; in 2007, Phibro income was 10 percent of all Citigroup income. Because of that success, Hall was rewarded with a $100 million bonus in 2008, after taking in over $250 million the five years before that. Huge numbers, yes—but Hall had every reason to threaten to walk if his salary was capped at $500,000.[42] Hall and many members of this lucrative unit will simply leave and take their knowledge and talent to other firms that will compensate them for the revenue they produce. So while the public oohs and aahs at the number of zeroes in Hall's salary, they forget that he has brought in exponentially more money than that—he is a profit-making machine. It's not his fault Citigroup is in such lousy shape, but he is lumped in with all the other rejects who screwed up Citi.

And yet the public, led by President Obama's histrionic appeal to emotion, says to spin off Phibro and get rid of Hall. This, of course, leads only to more losses at Citigroup—seeing high-profile, valuable units spun off is only going to erode confidence and hurt the firm that has to let these employees go. Wouldn't it make more sense to compensate the people at Phibro for their work and allow them to continue to bring profits to the firm? Why not fire the five thousand useless employees and keep the profit-producing ones?

Because in the government's world, profit is a dirty word—it's public image that counts. Citigroup isn't an outlier—Morgan Stanley is also considering spinning off a profitable proprietary-trading unit to protect it from the feds and allow it to continue making money.[43] Profits are the goal of a bank; power is the goal of the government. Now that the federal government owns the banks, this fundamental difference will destroy these firms and hurt the economy even more.

And Obama and his lackeys *know that*. They just don't care enough to do anything about it—it's far more important to them to bash the bankers. Even Tim Geithner, Obama's secretary of the treasury, understands that executive pay caps are foolish and irresponsible. "I don't think our government should set caps on compensation," Geithner told *Newsweek*. Instead Geither proposed better supervision from federal regulators and corporate boards.[44] Unsurprisingly, Obama has not picked up on this suggestion. Despite all the hubbub over the salaries at institutions like Citigroup, Obama has yet to mention cutting federal salaries for the regulators who failed to stop Citigroup and other institutions from totally imploding; instead, he's focused his ire on the banks alone. That's because in Obamaland, private industry is the problem and government is the solution. Always. This means that private industry must be demonized and punished, and government workers must be praised and rewarded.

The vast majority of Americans—including me—agree that many people at the top of the food chain on Wall Street are overpaid. The compensation numbers are staggering. But unless I have a financial interest in that firm, i.e., a shareholder or debtholder, who am I to decide what is excessive? It's certainly not the government's place to decide minimum wage, maximum wage, and every wage in between. To act as though these numbers are only now becoming a problem, however, ignores the plain reality that these numbers have been published and discussed thoroughly in the media every year. Huge Wall Street bonuses are nothing new and have never been a secret. Shareholders are responsible for protesting executive salaries—after all, the money is coming out of their pocket. Sell your stock or don't buy stock in a company if you don't like their executive compensation packages—don't react with "outrage" when these compensation schemes become the hot news item of the week.

THE FINAL FRONTIER:
OBAMA PREVENTS COMPANIES
FROM PAYING BACK TARP CASH

On April 4, 2009, Stuart Varney of Fox Business Network published a stunning piece in the *Wall Street Journal*. According to Varney, a prominent bank that had taken under $1 billion in TARP funds from the Bush administration was now desperate to pay back the government—the company was sick and tired of watching the government defame and restrict it. "The chairman offers to write a check, now, with interest," relates Varney. "But the Obama team says no, since unlike smaller banks that gave their TARP money back, this bank is far more prominent. The bank has also been threatened with 'adverse' consequences if its chairman persists."[45]

The bottom line: Obama didn't want the money back. He didn't want to hear about getting the money back. He wanted to continue exercising massive control over the banks to work his way to his ultimate goal: getting control of health care.

This is frightening stuff. Remember that when Bush announced TARP, he stated, "we expect that this money will eventually be paid back." Now companies want to pay back the money—they feel they're solvent. And the government is telling them they can't.

Imagine this situation applied to your personal life. You take out a credit card and charge up a couple thousand dollars—you're short on money this month. You intend to pay off the card before the interest rates hit. You finally get your paycheck and approach the credit card company to pay off the debt. And the credit card company tells you no. "We know you're not fiscally viable if you pay back that money," says Al, the Indian dude, from customer service on the other end of the phone (the dot Indian, not the feather Indian). "So you're going to keep that money, and keep paying interest on it. And in return, we'll call you from time to time to do small favors for us. Thank you. Bye-bye. Call anytime." Click.

The credit card company would be prosecuted. But when the

Obama administration does precisely the same thing, its approval ratings skyrocket.

This isn't an isolated incident. Tim Geithner's Treasury Department has conducted "stress tests" on the banks that received bailout money. These tests, designed by the Treasury, will be used to determine the health of the banks and if they need to raise more capital. Should the government determine that a bank is not well capitalized, it could force the firm to convert the preferred shares the government owns into common shares; common shares, as opposed to preferred shares, carry voting privileges.[46] To summarize, then: the federal government forces banks to take TARP money. It then runs stress tests to determine if these banks have taken enough TARP money. If the federal government determines that they're not stressed enough, then more stress is applied until they get the results they want, allowing the federal government to put in more cash and essentially take over day-to-day decision making at the banks.

It's the same principle as John Kerry's misery index when he was running for the presidency in 2004. When Kerry's campaign looked at the misery index, they realized that Americans weren't miserable—quite the opposite, they were fairly happy and optimistic. So Kerry simply changed the standards for misery. Lo and behold, presto whammo! Americans were miserable and pessimistic. And he still wonders why he didn't get elected. (I have to say, I really miss Teresa Heinz Kerry. Or Teresa Heinz. Or whatever she's calling herself these days.)

The government designs the stress test and determines whether or not it should take over banks. There's a wee conflict of interest there. It seems pretty obvious that Treasury can manipulate the results of the stress tests and use them as a tool to justify taking larger and larger stakes in financial institutions. That is precisely what the feds attempted to do. The initial set of stress tests by the government reported Bank of America's initial "capital hole" at a ridiculous $50 billion; Citigroup and Wells Fargo were similarly shocked by the Fed's estimate of their capital shortfall. Wells Fargo was so adamant that the feds were playing games with the numbers that they threatened to file a lawsuit. Overall, half of the banks subjected to the stress tests rejected the government's initial findings, leading the government to change its numbers. Bank of America's final capital shortfall was $33.9 billion, down from that whopping $50 billion; Wells Fargo's was $13.7 billion, down from the initial estimate of $17.3 billion; at Fifth Third Bancorp, the number dropped from $2.6 billion to $1.1 billion; at Citigroup, the initial number was $35 billion—that number plummeted to $5.5 billion.[47] For "objective" stress tests, these sure are malleable.

The stress tests are a massive government power grab. Obama, Congress, and Treasury sell it to the American people by blaming Wall Street; they claim that Uncle Sam knows best. And, pathetically, Americans buy it—literally. After all, we're paying for that government stock.

THE FINAL FRONTIER:
TARP MONEY POLITICAL PAYOFFS

Government programs like TARP are giant bags of cash waiting to be stolen by elected officials. These legislators are supposed to bring home the bacon for their constituents—a shorthand way of saying that legislators are supposed to use your taxpayer dollars to bribe their voters to vote for them. TARP is no exception.

Barney "Pimp My Apartment" Frank is supposed to be the main oversight figure for TARP. Frank is, after all, the chair of the House Financial Services Committee. He is also the fellow who had an affair with a high-ranking member of the Fannie Mae board, Herb Moses. Frank also took $40,000 in Fannie Mae cash from 1989 to 2008, and, not coincidentally, he stood up over and over for Fannie Mae's fiscal health.[48]

Utilizing that high moral sense, Frank immediately jumped into the TARP cash and started funneling it to his friends. One UnitedBank in Boston was not near the top of the TARP list—the bank was capital-poor, under investigation by regulators for its lending practices and executive pay abuses (the company was using a 2008 Porsche to shuttle around its bosses)—but Frank somehow scored a $12 million bailout. He did it for a very simple reason: he cared. About the black vote, that is. OneUnited serves the black community in large part; Sidney Williams, a director at OneUnited, is married to Maxine Waters (D-CA), a black congresswoman, who chairs the House Financial Services subcommittee on housing. Said Frank: "We did say, yes, I thought it would have been a social tragedy if the one minority bank in Massachusetts that has been working so hard and had been overextended into housing was to be wiped out by a federal action . . . and that's why I think it was important to try to help them." [49] So now we've gone from "too big to fail" to "too black to fail."

Frank is more the rule than the exception. Lobbyists from Arizona have been hitting up the Treasury Department to bail out their banks; so have lobbyists from Wisconsin and Ohio. The process—banks apply for aid through federal regulators, which then make their decision quietly so as to avoid runs on nonapproved banks—has created chaos. "I think it's just a question of advocacy," says Arizona banking superintendent Felecia Rotellini. "It has to be a congressional voice."

It's a mess. As Tim Geithner put it, "there are serious concerns about transparency and accountability . . . confusion about the goals of the program, and a deep skepticism about whether we are using the taxpayers' money wisely." "It's totally arbitrary," agrees South Carolina governor Mark Sanford (R). "If you've got the right lobbyist and the right representative connected to Washington or the right ties to Washington, you get the golden tap on the shoulder."

Where there's government cash, there are government leeches looking to siphon off that cash. Whether it's the Obama administration or Barney Frank, friends get paid off first. By you.

THE END OF CAPITALISM

Bush burned the free market village in order to save it. And now Obama walks, Zen-like, over the hot embers. TARP, which was once designed to take bad assets off bank books, has been thrown away in favor of the more direct government buy-ins to banks—and the banks have no choice whether they want to take the money or pay it back. President Obama now uses TARP as a threat to turn private enterprises into socialist enterprises; government standards for lending programs, credit card programs, and mortgage programs must be accepted. Or else.

There is a direct line from Bush's Compassionate Conservatism to Obama's Economic Fascism. Once government is seen not as a protector of liberty but as a guarantor of financial security, there is no way to rein it in. The free market is not perfect. Far from it. But when the government runs businesses rather than ensuring that cheating, lying, and stealing are punished, the economy is sure to suffer.

But perhaps that's what Obama wants: the level playing field. Obama doesn't care whether the playing field is below or above economic sea level—he just wants to make sure the field itself is level. This means government-owned and government-operated.

The free market is the only way to ensure prosperity for every American. That means letting bad businesses go under, and allowing new businesses to take their place. That means no one is too big or too black to fail. True compassion is thinking of the bigger picture: rising standards of living, entrepreneurial liberty.

The moment that the government created TARP—and the moment that the free market bought into it or was forced into it—the death knell rang for the economic way of life we once knew.

CHAPTER 6

TIMOTHY LEARY
IS NOT DEAD

So how did an unknown junior senator from Illinois named Barack Hussein Obama, elected in 2004 to national office, virtually anonymous in the United States, let alone on the international stage, rise to the most powerful position in the world and occupy the White House as the forty-fourth president of the United States?

How did a man with no senatorial record to speak of hold off the powerful Clinton attack machine? How was he able to turn the entire Democratic establishment on its ear? How did he defeat Senator John McCain, a decorated war hero, in a time of war, and his running mate, Governor Sarah Palin?

He couldn't do it alone. No one is that good, or that lucky. Not even the Great One, Barack Hussein Obama.

Obama himself has acknowledged his bizarre path to power. "Barack is actually Swahili for 'that one,'" he joked at the annual Al Smith Dinner in 2008. "And I got my middle name from somebody who obviously didn't think I'd ever run for president." [1]

So how did Barack Hussein Obama do it?

He did it by becoming the culmination of the 1960s philosophy.

Sure, his rhetorical flair helped. So did his well-groomed appearance and smoothness on his feet. But most politicians who manage to fail upward have some rhetorical flair and ability to improvise. There was more than Obama's skill at work here: there was an entire establishment seeking to make Obama the capping figure of a radical political movement that began four decades ago.

In Senator Barack Obama's ode to himself, *The Audacity of Hope*, he speaks about his "transcendent" politics. Obama scorns, he says, "the psychodrama of the Baby Boom generation—a tale rooted in old grudges and revenge plots hatched on a handful of college campuses long ago—played out on the national stage." Obama praises the 1960s radicals: "The victories that the sixties generation brought about . . . the strengthening of individual liberties and the healthy willingness to question authority—have made America a far better place for all its citizens." He says, however, that "what has been lost in the process, and has yet to be replaced, are those shared assumptions—that quality of trust and fellow feeling—that bring us together as Americans."[2]

Let's analyze this 1960s psychobabble: Apparently, Obama believes that America is stuck in the past, refighting battles that should have ended long ago. And apparently, Obama believes those battles *did* end long ago, and that they ended in the overwhelming victory of the hard left. Now, supposedly, he wants to move *beyond* the 1960s.

And yet Obama's policies and rhetoric are precisely the same as the policy and rhetoric of his 1960s forebears. Scratch Obama, and you'll sniff Timothy Leary, Bill Ayers, Ward Churchill, Jeremiah Wright, Angela Davis, Christopher Hedges, and Tom Hayden. The radicals of the 1960s weren't concerned with women's rights or gay rights or racial equality—those were the appetizers served up before the Caligula-style entrees.

They were concerned with something far broader: transformational change.

Sound familiar? It should.

Obama has repeatedly stated that he wants to change America. Not just change our policies or our politics—he wants to change our souls. Michelle Obama, she of the never-proud-of-my-country-until-they-elect-my-husband crowd, openly claims that Barack will remove our hearts of stone and replace them with hearts of flesh: "We have lost the understanding that in a democracy, we have a mutual obligation to one another—that we cannot measure the greatness of our society by the strongest and richest of us, but we have to measure our greatness by the least of these. That we have to compromise and sacrifice for one another in order to get things done. That is why I am here, because Barack Obama is the only person in this who understands that. That before we can work on the problems, we *have to fix our souls. Our souls are broken in this nation.*" [3]

What, precisely, is wrong with our souls? Those tired old notions of personal responsibility. Capitalism. Individual liberty. The Constitution. Success and failure. Risk and reward. Mom and Dad. Family structure. Anything and everything traditional. Everything and anything that has made this country what it is. And all of that needs to change.

That's Obama's plan. It's a page torn right from the radical mantra of the 1960s. Obama isn't the man moving us beyond the conflicts of the 1960s—he's the culmination of the 1960s dream. And now he's going to implement its utopian visions.

TIMOTHY LEARY AND THE BIRTH
OF THE RADICAL MOVEMENT

It all started with Timothy Leary. Leary was an intellectual, a graduate of the University of California at Berkeley with a doctorate in psychology. His credentials were all in order: he was director of psychological research at the Kaiser Foundation Hospital from 1955 to 1958, and he joined the Harvard University faculty in 1959.

Leary was a brainiac, all right. There was only one problem: he was completely out of his mind. After his wife committed suicide in 1955, leaving him with two daughters, he began experimenting with drugs. In 1960, on a trip to Mexico, he started messing with 'shrooms. It was a transformative moment for him: aside from seeing early visions of the Goombas from *Super Mario Bros.*, Leary also came to the conclusion that psychedelic drugs could be useful in psychotherapy. Because what crazy people really need is to get high. (I happen to prefer a good bartender who knows how to pour and listen—but I digress . . .)

Leary brought this unique theory back to Cambridge, Massachusetts, where he promptly put it to work. He gave psilocybin, the active ingredient in 'shrooms, to various people including researchers, prison inmates, and divinity students. The divinity students, wrote Leary, found that "spiritual ecstasy, religious revelation and union with God were now directly accessible." Also, those lava lamps were way cool!

Harvard finally grew tired of his antics in 1963, after Leary began doping himself with LSD, tried to use it in experiments, and started getting high with his students. And to think, if only I had been born in 1946 instead of 1956, I wouldn't have wasted all that time and money with my flight instructors, Barry Allyson and Dick Erwin, learning to actually fly. I guess by today's standards, I would be considered a victim. Where's the ACLU when you need them?

Leary moved to a mansion in upstate New York and started a hippie drugged-up commune, his bills paid for by a rich and stupid admirer. Leary had a couple of run-ins with the law—he traveled to Texas, where they were less tolerant of his pot habit and arrested him; G. Gordon Liddy raided his house in New York and arrested him there, too. But that didn't stop this brilliant charlatan.

He moved to hippie paradise: Hollywood. Out in La-La Land, he held "deep" events like "love-ins" and "be-ins," presumably in order to get in touch with his "inner self." In reality, he was just trying to get laid. At his third wedding, according to the *New York Times*, all the guests were on acid trips. This explains the fact that his wife said "I do." Or "Till the DEA does do us part."

While Leary was busy telling kids to "turn on, tune in, drop out,"

Richard Nixon was labeling him the "most dangerous man in America."[4] Leary later tried to defend his slogan, explaining, "*Turn On* meant go within to activate your neural and genetic equipment. . . . Drugs were one way to accomplish this end. *Tune In* meant interact harmoniously with the world around you. *Drop Out* suggested an active, selective, graceful process of detachment . . . self reliance, a discovery of one's singularity, a commitment to mobility, choice and change." Leary acknowledged, however, that his words were "often misinterpreted to mean 'get stoned and abandon all constructive activity.' "[5] Perhaps they were misinterpreted that way because Leary's entire life was devoted to getting stoned and abandoning all constructive activity.

Leary's strange adventure was just getting started. He decided to run for governor of California in 1970, only to find himself arrested on pot charges and sentenced to ten years in prison (he had already been sentenced to ten years in Texas, but had somehow avoided serving time). He escaped, climbing onto a rooftop, up a telephone pole, on a cable strung across the prison yard, and over the barbed wire, where he fell into the waiting arms of the Weather Underground, who secreted him out of the country to Algeria, where he hooked up with the Black Panthers. From there, he headed to Switzerland and Afghanistan, was captured, and ended up back in the United States. In 1976, Governor Jerry "Moonbeam" Brown ordered his release from prison—one hippie moron helping another. He spent the next twenty years exploiting his dubious fame for cash while ripping capitalism.[6]

Throughout the course of his life, Leary preached hard-left, radical-hippie politics. A self-described pagan,[7] Leary hated the Bible[8] and challenged all authority.[9] Some of his more subtle sayings:

- "Each religion has got their own way of making you feel like a victim. The Christians say 'you are a sinner,' and you better just zip up your trousers and give the money to the pope and we'll give you a room up in the hotel in the sky."[10] Bill Maher, eat your heart out.
- "Drugs Are the Religion of the People—The Only Hope is Dope."[11] Al Sharpton, eat your heart out.

- "I've left specific instructions that I do not want to be brought back during a Republican administration."[12] Alec Baldwin, eat your heart out.
- "The key question to ask a candidate for office—or indeed, any person seeking to influence public opinion—has nothing to do with Vietnam or Marx or John Birch. The issue which determines who will be elected, who will be listened to, is: How much time did you spend making love last week?"[13] Dr. Ruth—oh, never mind.

Leary preached the virtue of youth. "Human beings born after the year 1943 belong to a different species from their progenitors," he wrote.[14] "Political experts puzzle over the results of recent elections. . . . But one single and simple clue will account, in almost every case, for the surprises and shifts in voting. Age. Can you think of an election return in the last two years which found a potent, seed-carrying candidate defeated by an oldster?"[15] Why were young people so special? Because they were catching on to the fact that they could *resist the system*: "The American youngster is beginning to catch on to the frightening fact (already known by the veterans of the underground, the Negroes, the free artists, the delinquent poor, and the kids of Cuba and Russia) that the affluence and bribery of things and the carnival of televised athletic and political spectacles are the come-on for grim monolithic mind-copping social machines, and for those rebels who spurn the seductive bribe there awaits, on either side of the Iron Curtain, the gun and steel to coerce those who will not conform."[16]

And Leary preached that politics was meaningless. "The political spectrum," he wrote, "which has colored social attitudes for the past 300 years has decreasing relevance today and by 1980 will have no political meaning. Left-Right. Liberal-Conservative. Radical-Reactionary. Communist-Capitalist. Democratic-Republican. Whig-Tory. Labor-Management. White-Colored. Brooklyn Dodgers. Twenty-three skidoo. . . . Mao and LBJ are blood-nerve brothers, twins of the same steel bosom; they think alike. Their world view is basically the same. Like intertwined quarreling lovers, they are both committed to the same marriage—capitalism—Communism. . . . Ho loves Reagan, (they share the same game consciousness, and they share the same game consciousness) and they both avoid the bright, far-seeing eyes of their turned-on teen-agers." [17]

This childish sense of the world became a rallying cry for an entire generation. "Moving beyond politics." "Change." "The wisdom of youth." And as the 1960s generation began to believe this crap, they began to explore their own power in heretofore unimagined ways.

STUDENTS FOR A DEMOCRATIC SOCIETY

Perhaps the most influential student group of the 1960s was the Students for a Democratic Society. Organized by Alan Haber, the organization was dedicated to encouraging "direct action"; such action, Haber believed, needed to provide "an integrating framework of values" to students "suspicious of ideology." He wanted to perfect the American public into "a body that shares a range of common values and commitments, an institutional pattern of interaction and an image of themselves as a functioning community. . . . It is now the major task before liberals, radicals, socialists and democrats." [18] Today, we call this the Department of Education.

Just what would be the unifying values, though? In 1962, sixty leaders of SDS congregated at Port Huron, Michigan, to declare their vision for the world. The resulting Port Huron Statement, written by Tom Hayden, would become the most famous expression of political thought in the 1960s. Major influences on the Port Huron Statement included socialist John Dewey, closet Marxist C. Wright Mills (Bob Dylan), and feminists Doris Lessing and Simone de Beauvoir. [19]

The document itself was a tremendously infantile piece of work. It embodied both ignorance and pretension. First, it embraced the Clintonian "third way" and Obama "beyond politics" language—"The decline of utopia and hope is in fact one of the defining features of social life today. . . . Perhaps matured by the past, we have no sure formulas, no closed theories—but that does not mean values are beyond discussion and tentative determination."[20] You really can't come up with this nonsense unless you're on drugs. Smoke a fattie, wait twenty minutes, read again—wow, that's deep!

These are empty words for empty minds. Immediately after SDS utters them, they embrace full-scale leftist utopianism: "We regard men as infinitely precious and possessed of unfulfilled capacities for reason, freedom, and love. . . . Men have unrealized potential for self-cultivation, self-direction, self-understanding, and creativity."[21] This is the kind of pie-in-the-sky liberalism that prompts coercion—after all, if men are not meeting their potential, they must be forced to do so.

It gets worse. In the economic sphere, says the statement, "work should involve incentives worthier than money or survival . . . that the *economy itself is of such social importance that its major resources and means of production should be open to democratic participation and subject to democratic social regulation.* Like the political and economic ones, major social institutions—cultural, education, rehabilitative, and others—should be generally organized with the well-being and dignity of man as the essential measure of success." Also, in pursuing world industrialization, "We should not depend significantly on private enterprise to do the job. Many important projects will not be profitable enough to entice the investment of private capital . . . the Federal government should have primary responsibility in this area."[22]

The statement is unabashedly critical of patriotism and business, which it derides with the blanket term "apathy." "There are no convincing apologies for the contemporary malaise," the statement continues. "[S]ubjective apathy is encouraged by the objective American situation—the actual structural separation of people from power, from relevant knowledge, from pinnacles of decision-making. . . . The American political system is not the democratic model of which its glorifiers speak. In actuality it frustrates democracy by confusing the individual citizen, paralyzing policy discussion, and consolidating the irresponsible power of military and business interests."[23]

Here's their bottom line on the economy: "In summary: a more reformed, more human capitalism, functioning at three-fourths capacity while one-third of America and two-thirds of the world goes needy, domination of political parties and the economy by fantastically rich elites, accommodation and limited effectiveness by the labor movement, hard-core poverty and unemployment, automation confirming the dark ascension of machine over man instead of shared abundance, technological change being introduced into the economy by the criteria of profitability—this has been our inheritance. . . . To change the Cold War status quo and other social evils, concern with the challenges to the American economic machine must expand. Now, as a truly better social state becomes visible, a new poverty impends: a poverty of vision and a poverty of social action to make that vision reality. Without new vision, the failure to achieve our potentialities will spell the inability of our society to endure in a world of obvious, crying needs and rapid change." [24] Fast-forward to 2009: Barack Obama basically says the same thing in his "poverty of ambition" speech at Wesleyan.

The statement drags on and on. It would be useless to quote further its arguments against nuclear deterrence and in favor of colonial revolution; its opposition to "unreasoning anti-communism," which demonstrates "paranoia"; its unfailing criticism of virtually every aspect of American life.

And it would be just as useless to cite its "solutions": solutions like "universal controlled disarmament," "creating a world where hunger, poverty, disease, ignorance, violence, and exploitation are replaced as central features by abundance, reason, love and international cooperation," "foreign aid . . . given through international agencies, primarily the United Nations," "[avoiding] the arbitrary projection of Anglo-Saxon democratic forms onto different cultures," "allocation of resources . . . based on social needs." [25]

Who says pot doesn't affect your brain?

Commercial moment: This is your brain. And this is your brain on drugs.

If all of this sounds tame now, that's because the folks who wrote it—and their disciples—are now in control of all levers of government, as well as much of the major media. The SDS counterculture, which at its height controlled thousands of students and young people across the country, became the mainstream culture. When it broke up in 1969 due to inner turmoil, the seeds had already been sown. If they hadn't already been planted and smoked.

WEATHER UNDERGROUND

One of the groups instrumental in the breakup of the SDS was led by Bernardine Dohrn. Dohrn, the SDS interorganizational secretary, sympathized with another SDS-allied group, the Black Panthers (more on them later), which she said "has posed the question of black/white revolutionary movements in clear, immediate and real form."[26] She also led a branch of SDS, the Revolutionary Youth Movement (RYM). That wing eventually split from SDS in 1969 in order to pursue a more violent policy. Dohrn, who considered herself a "revolutionary communist," idolized North Vietnam and felt that the glorious utopia she dreamed of would be brought about by conflict between the Third World and American blacks on one hand, and U.S. imperialism on the other. In the aftermath of the SDS breakup, Dohrn helped found the Weathermen, a terrorist organization that drew its inspiration from a lyric by Bob Dylan: "You don't need a weatherman to know which way the wind blows." Apparently, you did need a Weatherman if you wanted to blow things up. "Revolutionary violence," said Dohrn," is the only way."[27] I wonder what her profile would look like today on eHarmony.com.

Dohrn was, not to put too fine a point on it, stark raving nuts. On one flight, she bragged to the Weathermen, she and some friends had gone "up and down the aisle 'borrowing' food from people's plates. . . . They didn't know we were Weathermen, they just knew we were crazy. That's what we're about, being crazy motherfuckers and scaring the shit out of honky America." Dohrn, by the way, is white.[28] She routinely wore buttons proclaiming "Cunnilingus is Cool, Fellatio is Fun."[29] Scratch eHarmony. Check out her profile on ePsycho.com.

Among Dohrn's other charming views was the strange idea that serial killer Charles Manson was an agent of the revolution. In the aftermath of the brutal slaying of Sharon Tate and others, Dohrn celebrated: "Dig it, first they killed those pigs, then they ate dinner in the same room with them, then they even shoved a fork into a victim's stomach! Wild!" Weathermen began using their hands to form the shape of a fork as a gang symbol.[30]

Dohrn's allies were just as insane: two of them, Bill Ayers and Diana Oughton, were lovers. Ayers grew up rich; his father helped broker relations between Chicago mayor Richard Daley and Martin Luther King, Jr., and chaired both Northwestern University and the Chicago Symphony. That didn't stop him from embracing Dohrn's psychotic streak. Oughton, too, grew up listening to opera and playing both the piano and the flute. Her father was elected to the Illinois General Assembly. She, too, joined the clinically insane far-left revolutionaries.

Everyone in the Weathermen was sleeping with everyone else. Sleeping probably wasn't the operative word here. Ayers said they were attempting to "smash monogamy." The Weathermen, he claimed, were "an army of lovers." Ayers admits using his weathervane to show his male best friend which way the wind was blowing, so to speak. Ayers proved even more violent than Dohrn. An FBI agent who infiltrated the Weathermen during their heyday heard Ayers state that "after the revolution succeeded and the government was overthrown, they believed they would have to eliminate 25 million Americans who would not conform to the new order."[31] Ayers summed up the Weathermen's ideology succinctly: "Kill all the rich people. Break up their cars and apartments. Bring the revolution home, kill your parents, that's where it's really at."[32] He must have had a really small weathervane.

The Weathermen began planning armed revolt against the U.S. government. In February 1970, three Weathermen—including Oughton—blew themselves up accidentally while cooking up a bomb in a New York City townhouse.[33] In October 1970, the FBI issued a warning to field offices that the Weathermen were "going underground and forming commando-type units which will engage in terroristic acts, including bombings, arson, and assassinations."[34] Ayers and Dohrn eventually got married and settled down, finally turning themselves in in 1980. Despite their involvement in several bombings, including the bombing of the Capitol and the Pentagon, Dohrn received just three years of probation due largely to supposed prosecutorial misconduct.[35]

But the Weathermen weren't the most violent or dangerous of the 1960s–1970s sociopaths. That honor was reserved for the Black Panthers.

THE BLACK PANTHERS

The Black Panther Party was founded in 1966. Its platform substantially mirrored the SDS and Leary, although it added the component of radical racialism. "We want freedom," stated the platform. "We want full employment for our people. We believe that the federal government is responsible and obligated to give every man employment or a guaranteed income. We believe that if the white American businessmen will not give full employment, then the means of production should be taken from the businessmen and placed in the community so that the people of the community can organize and employ all of its people and give a high standard of living." As if creating millions of government employees just for fun wasn't enough, the Panthers also called for "decent housing, fit for shelter of human beings. We believe that if the white landlords will not give decent housing to our black community, then the housing and the land should be made into cooperatives so that our community, with government aid, can build and make decent housing for its people." Today, that's called Section 8 housing.

Worst of all, the platform called for the complete indoctrination of American schoolchildren into the evils of America: "We want education for our people that exposes the true nature of this decadent American society. We want education that teaches us our true history and our role in the present-day society." Other requests: total exemption of blacks from military service, the immediate release of all blacks from jails and prisons across the country, juries composed entirely of blacks for black defendants, and finally, "land, bread, housing, education, clothing, justice and peace."

The Black Panthers proposed to achieve these objectives by seceding from the United States. They quoted the Declaration of Independence in support of the proposition that the U.S. government create a "United Nations–supervised plebiscite to be held throughout the black colony in which only black colonial subjects will be allowed to participate for the purpose of determining the will of black people as to their national destiny." [36]

To be fair, the Panthers were reacting to decades of the evils of state Jim Crow and deliberate federal noninterference. But by the time of their founding, the Civil Rights Act had been passed and events were clearly moving in the direction of racial equality and justice. Such violent pretensions were not only unnecessary but counterproductive.

And violent they were. Aaron Dixon, a former Black Panther member from Seattle, describes their tactics. They would shoot at fire stations to "scare the firemen, to keep them inside so they couldn't fight the fires we were setting around the city." (Anyone remember the L.A. riots?) "We had a split personality," says Dixon. "You could see us patrolling here with rifles and shotguns. And then later you'd see us over there serving free breakfasts to schoolkids." [37]

They should have spent more time on the free breakfasts and less time on the shootings. They sponsored riots across the country. Prominent Black Panthers included prison inmates like Eldridge Cleaver and George Jackson. Jackson served time for armed robbery and the murder of a prison guard. Cleaver was arrested in 1957 for rape and assault with intent to murder.

Cleaver and Jackson both became causes célèbre for the radical left. Cleaver organized an ambush of Oakland police officers, in which one was shot thirteen times and killed. When the police tracked him down, he was with the young leader of the Oakland Black Panthers, Bobby Hutton; the police shot Hutton. Cleaver suggested that the police had targeted him because he was running on the little-known Peace and

Freedom Party presidential ticket. Hutton's death became a rallying cry for groups including the Weathermen.[38]

Jackson's story was even more spectacular. While George was imprisoned for life for his murder of the prison guard, Jackson's younger "revolutionary" brother Jonathan came up with a plan to free some of George's friends. During the trial of James McClain, a prisoner who stabbed a San Quentin guard, two witnesses were present: Ruchell Magee and William Christmas. Jonathan invaded the Marin County courtroom and threw McClain a pistol. While McClain taped a sawed-off shotgun to Judge Harold Haley's head, Jonathan held the crowd in check with an automatic weapon. The gunmen then tied together four hostages, including three female jurors, who they smuggled into a truck and began to drive away. The police opened fire, killing McClain, Christmas, and Jackson. The judge was dead, his head blown off by McClain's shotgun.[39] Just over a year later, three days before Jackson was scheduled for trial, he was shot and killed; his liberal lawyer Stephen Bingham was accused and later acquitted of smuggling him a pistol, which he had used to take over his cell block. The standoff ended with two dead prison guards, two dead white prisoners, and one dead Jackson.

Huey Newton, the founder of the Panthers, was just as violent. He murdered a cop, John Frey, and he allegedly murdered a seventeen-year-old prostitute named Kathleen Smith. He spent three years in exile in Cuba. He was eventually shot to death in 1989 by a black drug user; investigators suspected that Newton had stolen drugs from him.[40]

The Black Panthers weren't all men. Nice to see they didn't discriminate. Women were also invited to participate. How tolerant of them. Angela Davis was one of the most prominent of the Panthers. She was a communist, and she was so in love with George Jackson, she was charged with providing Jonathan Jackson with the shotgun used to kill Judge Haley. Ah, true love. She was soon a member of the FBI's Ten Most Wanted—which, among the hard-left crowd, was a badge of honor. She was eventually captured and imprisoned, but released when prosecutors were unable to use the gun ownership to prove her connection to the Jackson murders.[41] Soviet dissident Aleksandr Solzhenitsyn remembers the USSR stumping for Davis when she was in prison: "We had our ears stuffed with Angela Davis. Little children in school were told to sign petitions in defense of Angela Davis. Little boys and girls, eight and nine years old, were asked to do this."[42]

After Davis's release, she headed to Cuba to hang with Fidel. When she came back, she demonstrated the strength of her judgment by hooking up with the Reverend Jim Jones—you remember, the fellow who later had his followers commit mass suicide by drinking poison-laced Kool-Aid in Guyana.

These deeply violent men and women were beloved by the radical left. Journalist and author Tom Wolfe perfectly captured the worship for the Black Panthers in a 1970 essay describing a party at the home of composer Leonard Bernstein: "now, in the season of Radical chic, the Black Panthers. That huge Panther there, the one Felicia [Bernstein] is smiling her tango smile at, is Robert Bay, who just forty-one hours ago was arrested in an altercation with the police, supposedly over a .38-caliber revolver . . . And now he is out on bail and walking into Leonard and Felicia Bernstein's thirteen-room penthouse duplex on Park Avenue. Harassment & Hassles, Guns & Pigs, Jail & Bail—they're *real*, these Black Panthers. The very idea of them, these real revolutionaries, who actually put their lives on the line, runs through Lenny's duplex like a rogue hormone."[43] The white elites loved the black revolutionaries determined to kill them and redistribute their spoils; they felt they could buy them off with a few non-tax-deductible donations.

They couldn't. But it would take a better strategy for the revolutionaries to enter power and unleash their hatred for the wealthy. That strategy would begin to form with the Kent State massacre.

THE DEATH OF "INNOCENCE"

Everything seemed to be going relatively well for the hard left until May 4, 1970. It was then that the radicals realized that the government was not intimidated by their terroristic tactics. Because on May 4, 1970, at Kent State University in Ohio, the government proved that even an accidental response by the U.S. government was stronger than any concerted response by SDS, the Weathermen, and the Black Panthers combined.

It all began with the April 30, 1970, announcement by President Nixon that the United States had begun bombing Cambodia. The rationale for such an attack was clear: the Viet Cong had been using Cambodia as an easy way of skirting U.S. defenses and smuggling supplies to its troops. Nonetheless, the announcement provoked massive student protests across the country. On May 1, the Kent State students held a rally at which they burned the Constitution. That night, protesters started bonfires in the streets, stopped traffic, smashed bottles on police cars, and shattered surrounding store windows. The Kent State police force tried to deal with it but couldn't, eventually using tear gas to break up the crowd. The next day, the mayor asked the governor to send in the National Guard.

On May 2, the Kent State students set the ROTC barracks on fire. On May 3, rocks and tear gas were traded between police and protesters. Governor Jim Rhodes stated that he would petition the court for a declaration of a state of emergency.

On May 4, the students gathered to protest again. Kent State police and General Robert Canterbury of the Ohio National Guard ordered them to disperse. When they refused and began pelting a police jeep with stones, Canterbury ordered his troops to lock and load. They marched across campus and stopped on a practice football field. As the students threw stones, the Guard fired into the crowd. Four Kent State students were killed; another nine were wounded. The injuries ranged from paralysis of the legs to chest and forehead wounds.[44]

The Kent State shootings did not end the revolutionary movements—as we have seen, the Weathermen, Leary, and the Black Panthers all remained active throughout the decade. In fact, days later, 100,000 students and protesters descended on Washington to intimidate the Nixon administration. But Nixon's message was the one that resonated with most Americans, who were sick and tired of the bombings, the smelly hippies, the dope smoking, and the dumb slogans: "This should remind us all once again that when dissent turns to violence, it invites tragedy. It is my hope that this tragic and unfortunate incident will strengthen the determination of all the Nation's campuses—administrators, faculty, and students alike—to stand firmly for the right that exists in this country to dissent and just as firmly against the resort to violence as a means of such expression." [45]

Did the government overreact? Probably. Weapons are one tactic, but the easiest way to break up a group of hippie radicals is to toss them a bar of soap. Should you get shot for throwing a bottle at the National Guard? Probably not. But the best way to *not* get shot by the National Guard is to *not throw the bottle.*

And the hippies started to realize that. More and more, they recognized that they couldn't win by taking the establishment head-on; hippie protests and even bombings wouldn't convince Americans to approve their fringe point of view. They would have to do something different—they would have to infiltrate.

INFESTATION

In the aftermath of the turbulent 1970s, the radicals weren't going to simply surrender. They came up with a far more clever tactic: they turned in the Birkenstocks and put on Brooks Brothers suits. They were the same hippie, pie-in-the-sky utopians and sometimes violent idiots they had always been—only now they were less smelly and, in appearance, more mainstream.

They took over the pillars of the American establishment: They took over the education system. They took over the news media. They took over the government.

And gradually, they took over the nation.

Tom Hayden, the writer of SDS's Point Huron Statement, went on to a successful career in politics. In 1972, he traveled to North Vietnam with actress Jane Fonda, then married her. In 1976, Hayden challenged California Democratic senator John Tunney in the primaries and came close to beating him. He then allied with Governor Jerry "Moonbeam" Brown, using his quasi-socialist Campaign for Economic Democracy to implement his far-left ideas. From 1982 to 1992, he served in the California State Assembly; from 1992 to 2000, he served in the State Senate. He lost a run for governor in 1994 and a run for mayor of Los Angeles in 1997.

Not surprisingly, Hayden supported Barack Obama during the 2008 election cycle. He now teaches an aptly titled class at Pitzer College in Claremont, California: "From the 60's to the Obama Generation."

Bernardine Dohrn, after avoiding her prison sentence, used her husband's connections to get a law job at the prestigious white-shoe firm of Sidley Austin LLP. Howard Trienens, a partner at Sidley, hired Dohrn on the advice of Ayers's dad. "We often hire friends," said Trienens. Even friends with terrorist records and no license to practice— Dohrn couldn't be admitted to the bar due to past criminal activities, including failure to testify before a grand jury in 1981—an incident that brought her a seven-month prison sentence. If only she had apologized for her behavior, she could have practiced law—but, said Trienens, "she wouldn't say she's sorry."

Her continued allegiance to her radical past didn't stop her career ascent. In 1991, Dohrn was hired to teach law at Northwestern University. Not coincidentally, Ayers's dad was heavily involved with the university—in fact, he was chairman of the board of trustees. The university later explained, "While many would take issue with views Ms. Dohrn espoused during the 1960s, her career at the law school is an example of a person's ability to make a difference in the legal system." [46]

There's only one problem with that trite explanation: Dohrn continues to express those same views. She denounced terrorism in a 2005 letter to a right-wing Web site: "I fought the illegal, immoral war against Vietnam and the organized terrorism of my government—and I unequivocally oppose the terrorism of governments, individuals, and religious, political and irregular organizations." [47] But in an interview with PBS, she was far less forthcoming: "We were part of an authentic, aroused opposition to the U.S. empire and to racism at home. . . . Of course, I wish we had done better, and I wish we had stopped the war earlier, and I wish we had been more effective, and I wish we had been more unifying. . . . At the end of the day, I feel like we were lucky to be in that history."[48]

Dohrn's husband is even less apologetic. "Did we do something that was horrendous, awful? . . . I don't think so. I think what we did was to respond to a situation that was unconscionable. . . . We destroyed property in a fairly restrained level, given what we were up against."[49] In fact, says Ayers, "I don't regret setting bombs. I feel we didn't do enough." Would he do it again? "I don't want to discount the possibility."[50]

Like Dohrn, Ayers is now in academia, imprinting his extremism onto student minds. He teaches at the College of Education at the University of Illinois at Chicago, where he presumably talks about his own ideology—"radical, Leftist, small 'c' communist"—and teaches teachers to "teach against oppression."[51]

Angela Davis, formerly of the Black Panthers, became a political activist-educator, too. In 1980 and 1984, she ran for vice president of the Communist Party. Solzhenitsyn remembered Soviet and Czech dissidents sending an appeal to Davis: "Comrade Davis, you were in prison. You know how unpleasant it is to sit in prison, especially when you consider yourself innocent. You have such great authority now. Could you help our Czech prisoners?" Answered Davis: "They deserve what they get. Let them remain in prison." As Solzhenitsyn observed, "That is the face of Communism. That is the heart of Communism for you."[52]

She is now the presidential chair and professor with the History of Consciousness Department—yes, there is a History of Consciousness Department—at the University of California, Santa Cruz. She also directs the university's Feminist Studies Department.[53] In 1997, she started switch-hitting, coming out of the closet as a lesbian—which, she said, was a "political statement."[54] Says Davis, "The only path of liberation for black people is that which leads toward complete and radical overthrow of the capitalist class.[55]

What of Timothy Leary? Leary died in 1996, but not before lecturing on campuses all over the country. His legacy lives on in the halls of academia, the media, and governmental power.

TIMOTHY LEARY LIVES ON

The radicals of 1960 are now the mainstream of 2000.

With Ayers and Dohrn and Davis occupying the seats of ignorance at America's major universities, it's no surprise to see their disciples, such as Ward Churchill, following in their footsteps. Churchill, who taught ethnic studies at the University of Colorado at Boulder, was a former Weather Underground and SDS-involved Vietnam vet who began working at the university in 1978, lecturing on Indian issues. Despite claiming Native American ancestry, Churchill does not have a single Native American ancestor.[56]

That wasn't his biggest problem, though. His biggest problem was his hatred for America. On September 12, 2001, Churchill responded to the World Trade Center and Pentagon terrorist attacks as you would expect a former SDS-er and Weather Underground radical: he labeled the victims "little Eichmanns" and "Good Germans" and suggested that the chickens were "coming home to roost." Those who died in the World Trade Center, said Churchill, were not "innocent. . . . They formed a technocratic corps at the very heart of America's global financial empire—the 'mighty engine of profit' to which the military dimension of U.S. policy has always been enslaved—and they did so both willingly and knowingly." In fact, said Churchill, the attacks were carried out for purely Marxist reasons—the terrorists were victims of global capitalism and its militarist arm: "they were secular activists—soldiers, really— who, while undoubtedly enjoying cordial relations with the clerics of their countries, were motivated far more by the grisly realities of the U.S. war against them than by a set of religious beliefs."[57]

Churchill followed up that doozy with a clarion call for the utter destruction of the United States. In a 2004 interview, Churchill stated,

"[I want the] U.S. off the planet. Out of existence altogether." If I was allowed to say what I want to say about Churchill—well, I'll just have to leave that to your imagination.

The resulting furor was predictable and appropriate. In July 2007, the administration finally got wise and fired Churchill on plagiarism charges. His scholarship was horrendous—for example, he claimed that Captain John Smith had purposely infected Native American tribes by handing them disease-ridden blankets, and cited only "oral tradition" as a source.[58] Still, Bill Ayers, his fellow academic, said he was "persecuted because of his politics" in an academic "witch hunt."[59]

Churchill eventually filed suit for wrongful termination from the University of Colorado. Katherine Mangu-Ward was on hand from the *Wall Street Journal*, and she described the scene: "Old hippies with gray-streaked ponytails, sporting their best Indian radical-chic finery, arrived early and waited in a marble hallway of the District Court here, chowing down on breakfast burritos from the cafeteria." Churchill's case was predicated on the grounds that if not for his "little Eichmanns" comment, his plagiarism never would have come to light—a sort of "fruit of the poisonous tipi" argument. Nonetheless, he refuses to repudiate his ridiculous comments, stating, "When you bring your skills to bear for profit, you are the moral equivalent of Adolf Eichmann."[60] And you parents are paying *how much* for your kids to get educated at places like this?

Churchill isn't alone, of course. Ideological fellow travelers are common. Christopher Hedges represents the 1960s view well in the pages of the *New York Times*. A reporter, Hedges has routinely spouted his own views on current events; he considers himself a socialist. Writes Hedges, "We will either find our way out of this mess by embracing an uncompromising democratic socialism—one that will insist on massive government relief and work programs, the nationalization of electricity and gas companies, a universal, not-for-profit government health care program, the outlawing of hedge funds, a radical reduction of our military budget and an end to imperial war—or we will continue to be fleeced and impoverished by our bankrupt elite and shackled and chained by our surveillance state."[61] Hedges draws his worldview from the Vietnam era: "At the end of the Vietnam War, we became a better country in our defeat. We asked questions about ourselves that we had not asked before. We were humbled, maybe even humiliated. We were forced to step outside of ourselves and look at us as others saw us. And it wasn't a pretty sight . . . War is necrophilia."[62] Apparently, the 1960s chickens are coming home to roost.

It isn't just academia and the media. It's the federal government.

It's our president. A president who's present in the now, but percolating in the past.

Barack Obama is a disciple and practitioner of 1960s radicalism. During the 2008 campaign, Republicans left the political reservation with misguided attacks on Obama's patriotism based on lapel pins and failing to put his hand over his heart for the National Anthem and chasing down the smoking-gun birth certificate. It got so absurd that when Obama went to Hawaii to visit his dying grandmother, there were some suggestions that he was there to kill her because she had the goods on this anti-American Muslim sleeper agent.

But here's the reality. Barack Obama *is* very patriotic—patriotic to the radical ideology of the 1960s. Obama's not the beginning of something new; he's the culmination of something old and stale: the extremist collectivism and hippie naïveté of the 1960s. And now, he has the power to bring all of the 1960s dreams to fruition. He is an empty canvas that every special interest group, activist group, and socioeconomic group can project upon. He and his followers proclaim he is everything, but in reality, he is everyone else. As he himself puts it, "I serve as a blank screen on which people of vastly different political stripes project their own views."[63]

He says as a nation we have to move beyond the 1960s, but Obama remains an unrepentant child of the 1960s. Obama supporters say he is a window to the future; I say he's a mirror of the past.

Obama's love for and association with 1960s radicals is common knowledge. He has a close friendship with Bill Ayers, and his work with Ayers on the Chicago Annenberg Challenge is well known—Obama was recruited to join the board straight out of law school, possibly by Ayers but certainly with Ayers's knowledge and support. Also well known is Obama's endorsement of one of Ayers's books on education, a tome which suggested that America abolish the prison system, comparing the United States to South Africa, and saying that America is neither kind nor just.[64] Prominent sources like Jack Cashill have stated that Ayers ghostwrote portions of Obama's leap-to-prominence memoir, *Dreams from My Father*.[65]

Jeremiah Wright, Obama's spiritual advisor and pastor for twenty years, represents precisely the same vision from the pulpit that Angela Davis does from her perch at U.C. Santa Cruz. Wright, like Churchill, said that September 11 represented the chickens "coming home to roost." He has called America "AmeriKKKa"—a direct rip from the Weather Underground's "Amerika" language. His hatred for America and his belief that America is responsible for wrongs the world over are unquestioned.

But more than that, Obama's rhetoric and his politics are drawn straight from the 1960s. Compare his rhetoric of change and unity to the Port Huron Statement. The statement contains the word "change" forty-three times. It contains the word "hope" eleven times. Obama's TelePrompTer quotes almost word for word from the statement.

Think I'm wrong? Let's play a game. Here's a series of quotes. Which are from the Port Huron Statement, and which are from Obama?

1. "Doubt has replaced hopefulness—and men act out a defeatism that is labeled realistic."

2. "Do we participate in a politics of cynicism or a politics of hope?"

3. "Change will not come if we wait for some other person or some other time."

4. "We should not give up the attempt for fear of failure."

5. "Some will say this is a hope beyond all bounds; but it is far better to us to have positive vision than a 'hard headed' resignation."

6. "They know that we can take our politics to a higher level. But they're afraid. They've been taught to be cynical. They're doubtful that it can be done."

Here are the answers:

(1) Port Huron.
(2) Obama.
(3) Obama.
(4) Port Huron.
(5) Port Huron.
(6) Obama.

If you got 100 percent, you obviously went to an Ivy League university. That's the only place they still take this sort of nonsense seriously.

Even more than the trappings of rhetoric, Obama's internal belief system dictates that capitalism—and individualism more broadly—is soulless and cruel. In a commencement speech at Wesleyan, Obama proclaimed, "our individual salvation depends on collective salvation . . . thinking only about yourself, fulfilling your immediate wants and needs, betrays a poverty of ambition . . . it's only when you hitch your wagon to something larger than yourself that you realize your true potential and discover the role you'll play in writing the next great chapter in America's story." [66] This is the collectivism of the 1960s stripped of its tie-dye and garbed in a nice suit of clothes.

Obama reiterated this message at Arizona State University. "It may be tempting to fall back on the formulas for success that have dominated these recent years. Many of you have been taught to chase after the usual brass rings: being on this 'who's who' list or that top 100 list; how much money you make and how big your corner office is; whether you have a fancy enough title or a nice enough car . . . such an approach won't get you where you want to go; that in fact, the elevation of appearance over substance, celebrity over character, short-term gain over lasting achievement is precisely what your generation needs to help end." [67]

Obama doesn't just oppose profit—he opposes America on virtually all grounds. His blame-America-first policies were on display when he traveled to Europe and stated our nation was arrogant; catered to the Europeans' "leading role in the world" (they led us into World Wars I and II); kowtowed to the mullahcracy in Iran and apologized to them for the overthrow of Mossadegh in 1953; spoke in Arabic to the Muslim world; effectively apologized for the war in Iraq; threw Israel under the bus; appointed an attorney general who considers America a "nation of cowards" on race; purposely destroyed the U.S. economy with cap and trade; the list goes on and on. His politics is driven by the basic principles of the 1960s: America is fundamentally unjust. Capitalism is fundamentally unjust. The world community is far more beneficent and benign than the United States or its allies.

Obama's allegiance to the 1960s seems treasonous to the founding principles of this country: personal responsibility, free enterprise, the pursuit of liberty for us and our allies. These are in opposition to the communal aspirations of the 1960s radicals.

But, as Obama says, the "ground has shifted" beneath the feet of those who once opposed Ayers, Dohrn, Leary, & Co. They are now the radicals. *We*, the men and women who value traditionalism, constitutionalism, and classical liberalism, are the radicals.

If we are the radicals, we must fight for our freedoms. We must embrace the challenge. After all, they're not the only ones who can fight for hope and change. The only difference is that our change actually provides hope rather than despair, turning back the endless night of state-run lives and government-controlled destinies. Freedom over government oppression and a belief in the return of "we the people," not "we the government of the people."

I'll leave you with William Wallace's famous speech from the movie *Braveheart*: "Fight and you may die. Run, and you'll live . . . at least a while. And dying in your beds, many years from now, would you be willing to trade *all* the days, from this day to that, for one chance, just one chance, to come back here and tell our enemies that they may take our lives, but they'll never take . . . *our freedom*."

CHAPTER 7

WHERE'S MY PONY?

A government that robs Peter to pay Paul
can always depend on the support of Paul.
GEORGE BERNARD SHAW

What happens when there are more Pauls than Peters? The Pauls and the government keep growing and the Peters keep getting screwed.

That's exactly what's happening: the Pauls are growing and the Peters are shrinking. According to Adam Lerrick, a professor of economics at Carnegie Mellon University, "In 2006, the latest year for which we have Census data, 220 million Americans were eligible to vote and 89 million—40%—paid no income taxes. According to the Tax Policy Center (a joint venture of the Brookings Institution and the Urban Institute), this will jump to 49% when Mr. Obama's cash credits remove 18 million more voters from the tax rolls. What's more, there are an additional 24 million taxpayers (11% of the electorate) who will pay a minimal amount of income taxes—less than 5% of their income and less than $1,000 annually." The bottom line: under President Obama's taxation scheme, 60 percent of voters will pay virtually no income taxes.[1]

And that's leaving aside all of those Obama voters who will get *special* benefits: members of unions, who have been given shares in the nation's largest auto companies; government employees, who literally live on the government dole; and pensioners, who rely on the continued viability of Social Security to pay their rent. Obama has ensured that all of them vote for him by bulking up government programs, seizing American corporations, and raising taxes on those who will not benefit from government handouts.

The logical end point of this process of nonproducers voting is the end of capitalism: we vote ourselves directly into a government-controlled economy where all exercise of entrepreneurial vision is penalized. And politicians are okay with that. They aren't stupid. They want their pension, their salary, their perks, and their congressional pages. And so they take advantage of the situation. They get elected by promising endless benefits to constituents. They deliver those endless benefits by taxing the producers. They get the votes of the nonproducers next time around. And so the cycle continues. It's no wonder that in 2000, the same year the population split right down the middle on the presidential election, U.S. congressional incumbents won 98 percent of their races: local voters vote for candidates who will give them a pony.

Meanwhile, at our "education" centers, children learn that they *deserve* a pony—a pony paid for by someone else. Government-paid teachers tell our kids that, in the words of Barney, they are "special—everybody's special." They are graded with purple markers rather than red pens so that when they fail, it's not as harsh. This is a far cry from my grammar school experience in Brooklyn, New York, at Our Lady Help of Christians. When grades were compiled, the pastor of Our Lady Help of Christians church would go from classroom to classroom, and standing in front of our panting little faces, would proceed to read each student's grades out loud. In front of the entire class. I'm not sure how we survived the trauma of that experience without the benefit of the invention of Depends.

If you failed, you were left back a grade. Now students are "retained," which is so much more pleasant to the ears. But being "left back" was more accurate. When you're shaving in the eighth grade, there's a slight chance you're an idiot!

In most schools the kids who skipped class, failed to turn in assignments, or just generally were a pain in the ass ended up in detention. At my high school, Xavier, in lower Manhattan, they called detention something different: JUG—Justice Under God. JUG operated just as you would suppose it would. You would go to the prefect of discipline's office, and there your fate would be determined. A favorite punishment I suffered several times involved kneeling at attention on the edge of a hard wooden chair. This exercise typically lasted until you collapsed onto the floor in excruciating pain. Today, JUG in the public school system would likely result in a lawsuit.

It's no wonder kids think they deserve a spot in the Ivy League, a $200,000 salary from Goldman Sachs, a nice house in Chappaqua, and an eighty-foot yacht, all before they're thirty. And if it doesn't happen for them, they expect the government to *make it happen* for them. They expect the government to take care of them just as Mommy, Daddy, and their teachers have done.

Thankfully, there are enough sane, productive, pissed-off taxpayers that have finally started to say "enough is enough."

TEA TIME IN AMERICA

On March 15, 2009, the people of Cincinnati, Ohio, turned out into the streets by the thousands. They weren't there to celebrate the Ascension of the One; they weren't there to worship and praise He Who Must Not Be Questioned. They were there to protest his Economic Fascism. Cincinnati's rally was just one of dozens across the country called "tea parties," reminding Americans that there was a time when high taxes and redistribution of wealth were cause for revolution.

There were many clever signs and placards in the tumultuous Cincinnati crowd. Some people wore T-shirts emblazoned with the words "Got Tea?" Others carried signs reading, "Give Us Liberty, Not Debt." Eight-year-old Isabel Lynch held a sign stating, "Stop spending my allowance," and five-year-old Kate Lynch held one reading, "Stay out of my piggy bank."

But the best sign of all came from five-year-old Kaylee McChesney: "Where's my free pony?"[2] You have to love cynicism especially when it comes from a five-year-old. I know some people believe that her parents put her up to it or that they made the sign and forced her to carry it. Using children like that is akin to child abuse, right? Keep that in mind the next time you see a five-year-old carrying a sign that states "Stay Out of My Womb" or "It's My Right to Choose" at a pro-abortion rally.

"Where's My Pony" could be the slogan of the Economic Fascism movement. Why? Because when it comes to electing our leaders, a majority of Americans are now making their selections based on what the government will do for them personally. These people want the house, the car, the double Sub-Zero and the sixty-five-inch 1080p flat screen with 7.1 surround sound. They want free health care, subsidized health insurance, Social Security, and a four-year college education to give them a piece of paper that shows us just how smart they are for wanting all these freebies. And they don't want to pay for any of it—they want the government, the taxpayers, to pick up the tab.

Take, for example, Peggy Joseph. Joseph is a young woman who attended a Sarasota, Florida, rally for Barack Obama during the 2008 election campaign. A cameraman approached her to interview her, and she told him that Obama's campaign was "the most memorable time of my life." The cameraman asked why. Her answer was stunning: "Because I never thought this day would ever happen. I won't have to worry about putting gas in my car. I won't have to worry about paying my mortgage. You know. If I help [Obama], he's gonna help me."[3]

"If I help Obama, he's gonna help me." Could the payoff be any clearer? This is votes for cash. In any normal democratic society, that would be criminal bribery. In modern America, that's representative government at its finest.

Now, it's one thing to act like Peggy if you pay income tax. You're still a moron, but at least you're a moron who's putting your money where your mouth is. But here's the problem: Americans like Peggy generally *aren't* paying taxes. This means that most Americans are now putting your money where their mouth is. They're voting for the government to confiscate your cash and my cash on their behalf. And politicians are all too happy to comply.

Americans have become addicted to government-issued crack: money from your neighbor's pocket. It will take a dramatic shift in the voting requirements and a widespread realization that our very way of life is on the precipice in order to enter economic rehab.

HOW WE GOT HERE

It never used to be this way. Originally, property ownership was a voting requirement in most states. Virginia, Georgia, New Hampshire, New York, New Jersey, North Carolina, and Rhode Island required landownership to vote; other colonies required nonland property or tax payments. William Blackstone, the author of the single greatest treatise on the British legal system, explained property requirements this way: the "true reason of requiring any qualification with regard to property in voters is to exclude such persons as are in so mean a situation as to be esteemed to have no will of their own."[4] In other words, poor people could be pressured by richer people into voting in particular ways. It apparently had not yet occurred to Blackstone that those without property could simply vote themselves property.

The American founders were more practical. Gouverneur Morris of New York, his real name, not the governor of New York, stated, "The aristocracy will grow out of the House of Representatives. Give the votes to people who have no property, and they will sell them to the rich."[5] Morris worried about employees selling their votes to employers, but he did not anticipate the wild growth of government—if he had understood that government would become a source of cash and benefits, he surely would have worried about voters selling their votes to *politicians*. Then again, we should give Morris the benefit of the doubt—at that point in time, the income tax was unconstitutional, which put a severe crimp into the redistributionist plans of social levelers.

John Adams understood the threat even better than Morris. "Every man, who has not a farthing, will demand an equal voice with any other in all acts of state," Adams warned. "It tends to confound and destroy all distinctions, and prostrate all ranks, to one common level."[6]

Clearest-eyed of all was James Madison, who recognized that the absence of property qualifications would result in either socialism or oligarchy: "If *all* power be suffered to slide into hands not interested in the rights of property which must be the case whenever a majority fall under that description, one of two things cannot fail to happen; either they will unite against the other description and become the dupes and instruments of ambition, or their poverty and independence will render them the mercenary instruments of wealth. In either case liberty will be subverted; in the first by a despotism growing out of anarchy, in the second, by an oligarchy founded on corruption."[7]

The words of these men were overlooked more and more often as time went on. Soon, property qualifications were gone completely. And with good reason: America was far less susceptible to class warfare than other countries, since land was so easily available.

As America grew more crowded, however, the dangers of class warfare increased. The final straw came in 1913, when the Constitution was amended to allow the federal income tax. Now the politicians had the ultimate tool at their disposal: they could redistribute wealth openly. This made the politicians very happy. President Woodrow Wilson, for example, was an open advocate of "state socialism": "socialism is a proposition that every community, by means of whatever forms of organization may be most effective for the purpose, see to it for itself that each one of its members finds the employment for which he is best suited and is rewarded according to his diligence and merit, all proper surroundings of moral influence being secured to him by the public authority. 'State socialism' is willing to act through state authority as it is at present organized . . . it is very clear that in fundamental theory socialism and democracy are almost if not quite one and the same. They both rest at bottom upon the absolute right of the community to determine its own destiny and that of its members. Men as communities are supreme over men as individuals. Limits of wisdom and convenience to the public control there may be: limits of principle there are, upon strict analysis, none." [8] Kind of puts that Barack Obama "community organizer" in a whole new light.

Wilson did not have the power to effect the sort of change he sought. He tried, for example, to pass tax withholding through Congress in the aftermath of the Sixteenth Amendment; he wanted the government to be able to remove taxes from paychecks without the employees ever seeing that money, obfuscating the fact that government money *is* taxpayer money. The people turned him down flat, and in 1917, Congress passed a law banning tax withholding.[9]

Where Wilson failed, Franklin D. Roosevelt succeeded. Using the Great Depression as a club to wield against capitalism, FDR blatantly pandered to voters by using the power of the federal purse. His government-run make-work programs made millions dependent on the largesse of the federal government; meanwhile, FDR excoriated "speculators" and capitalist entrepreneurs. Another famous president frequently referred to senior bondholders and pension funds as "speculators." That would be Barack Obama in the shotgun wedding of Chrysler and Fiat. Are you starting to see a pattern of terminology here?

In his 1933 inaugural address, FDR used the most anti-economic-liberty lingo in the history of American politics: "Practices of the unscrupulous moneychangers stand indicted in the court of public opinion, rejected by the hearts and minds of men. . . . They know only the rules of a generation of self-seekers. They have no vision, and when there is no vision the people perish. The moneychangers have fled from their high seats in the temple of our civilization. . . . The measure of the restoration lies in the extent to which we apply social values more noble than mere monetary profit." [10]

What were those noble social values? Robbing the producers and growing the government.

He was pandering to those who were unemployed—he knew they would guarantee him office, and that his big government plans would gain him immortality in liberal history books. FDR raised non–income taxes repeatedly and invented new taxes, like the payroll tax. He debased the gold system and inflated the currency. His plans were a purposeful vote-buying scheme. When confronted with the argument that payroll taxes would increase the already gargantuan unemployment rates, for example, FDR merely stated, "I guess you're right on the economics, but those taxes were never a problem of economics. They were politics all the way through." [11]

FDR was able to ram through the program Wilson had abandoned: tax withholding. World War II was used as an excuse to confiscate people's taxes up front, without having to wait for people to file. The government put forward a propaganda effort incredible in scope—so big even Donald Duck was recruited to help Uncle Sam. A cartoon urged by the feds and produced by Disney appeared in theaters across the country, with Donald telling taxpayers, "it is your privilege to help your government by paying your tax and paying it promptly." What a privilege! According to Neal Boortz and John Linder, "Tens of millions of Americans saw this film, and Gallup reported that 37 percent of the people felt that Donald Duck actually had a positive effect on their willingness to pay taxes." [12] I don't have a problem with what they took the money for, it's how it was sold and done that bothers me. They had to find an emotional connection to get us to turn over our money to them. The war was the connection. Same for global warming. We were sold a big fat lie by selling us a polar bear. You don't want that cute little polar bear cub to die, do you Jerry? Only if it's the one that grows up and wants to rip me to shreds when I'm salmon fishing in Alaska. Then I don't have a problem with one fewer natural-born killer.

The combination of new taxes, tax withholding, and class warfare created a perfect nexus for the "Where's My Pony" crowd. Those who were paying taxes weren't aware just how much they were paying—the taxpayers didn't have to painfully sign away their cash, the government just grabbed it. And those who weren't paying taxes were reaping the benefits. The job wasn't finished, however. In order to increase the number of "Where's My Pony" voters, the government would make voters feel legitimate about stealing money from others. The government would have to conceal the theft by making people feel entitled to other people's money.

WE DESERVE A PONY

The government had the perfect tool to conceal its redistributionist theft: the public education system. By teaching children that they were entitled to other people's money, that they had no responsibility for earning or working, that by simply being fortunate enough to be born in America they were guaranteed certain magical benefits. The public schools could also accomplish another important goal; inoculate themselves against independent voters—the kind of voters who can't be bought.

The obsession with childhood self-esteem started in the 1960s with idiots like Carl Rogers, psychologist at the University of Chicago and the University of Wisconsin. Rogers suggested that all troubles could be traced to inferiority complexes, and that the best way to bring up kids was for parents and teachers to boost their egos. "The spontaneous feelings of a child," he wrote, "his real attitudes, have so often been disapproved of by parents and others that he has come to interject this same attitude himself, and to feel that his spontaneous reactions and the self he truly is constitute a person whom no one could love." In his 1969 treatise, *Freedom to Learn*, Rogers suggested that schools act as "personal-growth" centers, pushing students to feel that "At last someone understands how it feels and seems to be *me* without wanting to analyze me or judge me. Now I can blossom and grow and learn." [13]

Rogers was a complete nut job, by the way. He suggested that there be no moral judgments against misbehavior, since that misbehavior was clearly a product of childhood angst. In one group therapy session, he excoriated one teenager as close-minded after she condemned a fellow teenager who had raped his own sister. This kind of insanity was also reflected in his radically left-wing politics suggesting that right-wingers were plotting an imminent coup.[14] Clearly this guy was in left field, playing a bunt and facing the fence.

Rogers's ideas have now worked their way throughout our public school systems. Educational "experts" like Dr. Denise Clark Pope have embraced Rogers's ideas and have even carried them further. Competition, they say, must be entirely stamped out in order to make kids feel more special. Pope says, "In the American capitalist system, students learn to compete; the goal is to win, 'to beat the others' . . . even if this means acting in ways that are personally frustrating and dissatisfying. . . . One may ask, is it worth it?"[15]

With the anticompetition, "everybody's special" ethic in mind, it's no wonder so many kids are trained to feel entitled. They never lose at tag, because they never play tag. A school in Santa Monica, California, banned tag in 2002 because it creates self-esteem issues, since somebody has to be "it."[16]

They never lose in the classroom, because teachers don't grade them on objective measurements. Teachers have been told that self-esteem will magically raise scores by itself; when those scores don't magically rise, teachers themselves simply inflate the grades. In fact, the "everybody's special" idea has almost entirely destroyed honest grading systems in the classrooms. Grade-point averages at private colleges jumped from 3.09 in 1991 to 3.30 in 2006. The shift was almost as large at public universities, where the GPA moved from 2.85 to 3.01. At Brown University in 2008, the majority of undergraduate grades handed out were As.[17] Harvard University professor Harvey Mansfield puts it this way, "It has created a new atmosphere of consumerism among the students, who are demanding high grades, always negotiating for higher grades, and insisting on being able to produce a transcript that is near perfection. They are afraid of getting a 'B,' if you can imagine that."[18]

So we've got a generation of coddled narcissists who truly believe that the world begins and ends with them. Groups of praise craze junkies with Barney the Dinosaur squirting intellectual Cheez Whiz into their skulls with nonsense like this, "There isn't another in the whole wide world / Who can do the things you do / Because you are special—special / Everyone is special." Of course, if you're useless, the world isn't better if you're here. And if you're evil, the world is *worse* off if you're here. What's next? Pop-Tarts with morning affirmations?

But when everyone thinks he or she's the second coming of Albert Einstein or Abraham Lincoln, there's bound to be some inflated self-esteem. And we know that unrelenting narcissists have a higher shot at ending up as sociopaths who have no problem hurting or taking from other people.[19]

That's what the government seeks to promote: a class of voters who are unafraid to take from other people because they are "special." The rules of fair play don't apply to them, because the world owes them something. A group of voters who somehow feel that competition is indecent, because that would entail objective measurements of worth. A mass of voters who hate capitalism and all it stands for because it is "mean" and "unfair." That's what the government needs: future voters who believe they are incredible and different—and who will come to rely on the government to provide for them each and every day.

YOU DESERVE A PONY

It doesn't stop with the education system. Politicians are eager to tell voters—ethnic minorities in particular—that they deserve other people's hard-earned cash because of their victimhood status. Lyndon Johnson's Great Society program was designed to pander to specialized groups and to tear down achievers. In his speech announcing the commencement of the Great Society, LBJ explicitly announced his intent to hinder American economic growth in order to pay people off: "Your imagination and your initiative and your indignation will determine whether we build a society where progress is the servant of our needs, or a society where old values and new visions are buried under unbridled growth." Why should indignation play a part in building a society? Because in this vision, the squeaky wheel does just as much work as the most productive members of society—whining is equivalent to creating. Creating, in LBJ's view, would merely result in "soulless wealth";[20] only by redistributing that wealth could America regain its soul.

LBJ was less highfalutin in his first State of the Union Address. In that speech, he blamed American history and American society at large for the despair of minorities and the poor. By harping on victimhood, he contributed to the widespread sense of entitlement that would legitimize massive wealth redistribution. "Very often a lack of jobs and money is not the cause of poverty, but the symptom," he intoned. "The cause may lie deeper in *our failure to give our fellow citizens a fair chance to develop their own capacities*, in a lack of education and training, in a lack of medical care and housing, in a lack of decent communities in which to give and bring up our children." [Emphasis added] Poverty and racism were the fault of the taxpayer. And the taxpayer would pay dearly.

Johnson was only the beginning. The government has repeatedly and consistently told Americans that privileges like welfare and food stamps are "entitlements" that *must* be handed out. In *Goldberg v. Kelly* (1970), the Supreme Court decided that welfare benefits could not be classified as "privileges," and could not be removed from a person without a legal process to do so. Justice William Brennan famously wrote, "It may be realistic today to regard welfare entitlements as more like 'property' than a 'gratuity.' Much of the existing wealth in this country takes the form of rights that do not fall within traditional common law concepts of property. It has been aptly noted that '[s]ociety today is built around entitlement.' "[21] Similarly, in *Plyler v. Doe* (1982), the Supreme Court stated that illegal immigrants were entitled to public education paid for by taxpayers: "Public education is not a 'right' granted to individuals by the Constitution. . . . But neither is it merely some governmental 'benefit' indistinguishable from other forms of social welfare legislation. . . . Education provides the basic tools by which individuals might lead economically productive lives to the benefit of us all. In sum, education has a fundamental role in maintaining the fabric of our society." [22] And if illegal immigrants deserve a pony, naturally everyone else does, too—particularly "victimized" racial minorities.

Race baiters have consistently pushed the "You Deserve a Pony" idea to minorities in an effort to gain their political support. Rep. John Conyers (D-MI), for example, has long supported slavery reparations: "You deserve forty acres and a mule." His Web site currently endorses reparations, stating, "Over 4 million Africans and their descendants were enslaved in the United States and its colonies from 1619 to 1865, and as a result, the United States was able to become the most prosperous country in the free world. It is undisputed that African slaves were not compensated for their labor. . . . As a result, millions of African-Americans today continue to suffer great injustices. Our country can no longer afford to leave slavery in the past and the issue of reparations for African-Americans must be resolved." [23] Will Conyers ever get his slavery reparations through Congress? Time will tell. But by pushing the idea that African-Americans are *owed something* by taxpayers, he is able to continue getting reelected—Conyers's district is 61.4 percent African-American.

President Obama has been one of the main proponents of the "You Deserve a Pony" ideology. While speaking at UNITY '08, a journalists event catering to ethnic minorities, Obama decided to crank up the pandering machine. "I personally would want to see our tragic history, or the tragic elements of our history, acknowledged," Obama said. "I consistently believe that when it comes to whether it's Native Americans or African-American issues or reparations, the most important thing for the U.S. government to do is not just offer words, but offer deeds." [24] What kind of deeds? Obama did not specify. But the implication was clear: taxpayers would foot the bill.

GIVE ME CASH

Leaving aside race, politicians have repeatedly clothed redistributionist schemes in the guise of "tax cuts" because, after all, "You Deserve a Pony." Members of both parties are responsible for this pathetic ruse (which makes sense—every congressperson seeks reelection through payoffs). The longest-standing example of welfare masquerading as tax cuts is the Earned Income Tax Credit (EITC). The EITC was initiated by Congress in 1975, under President Gerald Ford. It was designed to reimburse poor people for paying Social Security taxes, but it has become an excuse to redistribute wealth, all the while lying that the beneficiaries have "earned" their "tax refund." You can receive an Earned Income Tax Credit simply by filing a tax return, even if you pay no taxes. It does not affect welfare benefits, meaning that your government payments won't be cut if you receive the "tax cut." The express purpose of the EITC: "to provide an incentive to work." [25] Because, apparently, you need a government handout in order to feel the incentive to work. In fact, you can only get an EITC if you make less than $33,995 for a taxpayer with one qualifying child and $38,646 for a taxpayer with more than one qualifying child,[26] which makes the EITC an incentive *not* to work.

The EITC has been expanded multiple times. Each time, it's been lauded as a perfect example of people getting what they deserve—except that if you pay taxes, you're likely ineligible.

Originally, the maximum benefit was $400. Jimmy Carter expanded EITC. Ronald Reagan raised the EITC not once, but twice. George H. W. Bush raised the EITC. Bill Clinton went wild with the EITC, raising the EITC maximum 235 percent.[27] The current maximum, as raised by George W. Bush, is now $4,824 for a family with two or more children.[28] We're now 4,000 percent above the original payout. And everybody receiving the EITC—and everybody paying for the EITC—has been informed by the government that recipients "deserve" that money.

The EITC is only one element of the "You Deserve a Pony" boondoggle. Food stamps have been reclassified in the public mind—instead of being recognized as a bureaucratic charity scheme, food stamps are now seen as an "entitlement." The government has worked long and hard at removing the stigma from taking food stamps. Renamed the Supplemental Nutrition Assistance Program (SNAP), food stamps can now be paid for by an "electronic card that is used like an ATM card and accepted at most grocery stores."[29] This, of course, makes everyone around the food stamp recipient unaware of that recipient's status, absolving the food stamp recipient of the social shame that might come with living off the taxpayer dole.

The most recent addition to the "You Deserve a Pony" phone book of taxpayer-provided benefits comes from Barack Obama. During the 2008 campaign, Obama told Americans that 95 percent of them would receive a tax cut. This is total Clintonspeak. Bill's famous line during the Monica Lewinsky fallout, "it depends on what the meaning of 'is' is," is being recycled by Obama. The new mantra—it depends on what the meaning of a "tax cut" is.

Over 50 percent of Americans do not pay taxes. As the *Wall Street Journal* explained, Obama's "tax cut includes tens of billions of dollars in government handouts that are disguised by the phrase 'tax credit.' " Among the handouts: a $500 "tax credit" to "make work pay" for anyone making under $75,000; a $4,000 "tax credit" to help with college tuition; a 10 percent mortgage interest "tax credit"; yet another expansion of the EITC allowing single workers to receive $555 even if they have no kids; a 50 percent child care "tax credit" that will pay up to $6,000 per year; a "clean car tax credit" of up to $7,000; a 50 percent "savings tax credit" of up to $1,000. None of these "tax credits" are available to taxpayers who make more than a given amount. And all of them apply to those who aren't actually paying taxes. Under Obama's plan, 63 million Americans who do not pay income taxes would get a check from the government.[30] Which makes the Obama "tax credit" phraseology about as honest as the George H. W. Bush's "no new taxes" pledge.

Worst of all, Obama's plan incentivizes people to make less money. As the *Wall Street Journal* points out, "Some families with an income of

$40,000 could lose up to 40 cents in vanishing credits for every additional dollar earned from working overtime or taking a new job."[31] This is precisely the point: Obama and his cronies want people to work less hard, make less money, and remain dependent on government officials for their bread. Politicians breed dependence like farmers breed prize stock—it's what keeps them in business.

GIVE ME A CAR

As if the plain cash weren't enough of a payoff, our elected officials are now trying to buy us off with cars. If any American citizen took a car in return for his vote, he'd be in violation of federal law. But when our legislators buy entire swaths of the country with promises of cars and jobs in the car industry, nobody says boo.

Take, for example, the government's latest payoff program: "cash for clunkers." On June 9, 2009, the House of Representatives approved a bill that would pay Americans $4,500 toward the purchase of a new car if they turn in an older, non-fuel-efficient vehicle. The bill had two purposes: give Americans with an old car some money toward a new car, and bribe the auto industry. "Stimulating sales is the only way to get the auto industry back on its feet," explained Rep. Donald Manzullo (R-IL). Rep. Betty Sutton (D-OH) agreed: the bill served "the multiple goals of helping consumers purchase more fuel efficient vehicles, improving our environment and boosting auto sales." The bill also allows the $4,500 to be used toward leasing a vehicle.[32]

There are several big problems with this idiotic piece of legislation. First, it assumes that $4,500 will be enough to incentivize someone to buy a new car—a ridiculous assumption considering that a new car runs about $30,000 these days. Second, it requires that you buy a *new car*, which means that poor folks who can't afford a new car are left out to dry. You can guess where this is going: soon the government, which now controls GM and Chrysler dealerships, is going to be deciding that those low-income folks deserve free and easy car loans. The poor folks will default on those loans, naturally, and the companies will lose money. But that doesn't bother the politicians—they already have the car company employees working for them. And we're paying their salaries.

Most of all, "cash for clunkers" means paying off the car companies yet again. Apparently it wasn't enough for Americans to foot the bill for GM's crappy management and Chrysler's pathetic policy; it wasn't enough for taxpayers to pay union benefits and screw shareholders. Now Americans can directly pay other Americans to buy fuel efficient cars. So taxpayers are subsidizing *both the buyers and the sellers* in these transactions. But at least Barack Obama and the representatives from towns reliant on car manufacturing can rest easy at night knowing their constituents have been well served.

GIVE ME A HOUSE

"Cash for clunkers" might as well be the slogan for the federal government's mortgage policies. Except that the clunkers would refer to the borrowers. Tying together racial pandering and economic bribery, the Democrats spent years pushing government-sponsored entities to give low-interest subprime loans to "racially diverse" bad credit risks, buying those voters. According to the *Los Angeles Times*, in 1992, the Democratic Congress "mandated that Fannie and Freddie increase their purchases of mortgages for low-income and medium-income borrowers. Operating under that requirement, Fannie Mae, in particular, has been aggressive and creative in stimulating minority gains." These policies required banks to look the other way, ignoring credit histories in favor of other criteria.[33] Under the Community Reinvestment Act, it's actually worse than that—as Professor Thomas DiLorenzo of Loyola College writes, if a bank wishes to change its operational structure in any way, it has to demonstrate that it has made " 'enough' loans to the government's preferred borrowers. The (partially) tax-funded 'community groups' like ACORN (Association of Community Organizations for Reform Now) can file petitions with regulators that stop the bank's activities in their tracks, perhaps defeating them altogether. The banks routinely buy off ACORN and other 'community groups' by giving *them* millions of dollars as well as promising to make even more dubious loans."[34] In fact, as of February 2009, loans were *still* available through the CRA with "100 percent financing . . . no credit scores . . . undocumented income . . . even if you don't report it on your tax returns." Countrywide spent $1 billion on low-income loans in 1992; by 2003, it was $600 billion.[35]

Liberal policy makers then took the "cash for clunker-borrowers" program and decided to kick it up another notch. They allowed minority applicants to claim entitlements as income for purposes of their applications. That's right—no joke—they allowed applicants to write down their *welfare payments and food stamps* as a proper source of income. One Freddie Mac program, aptly entitled "Affordable Gold," allowed borrowers to make down payments from entitlement programs and even from nonprofits; if you could sucker the Red Cross into putting up a few grand, you'd get the mortgage. These loans, by the way, defaulted four times more often than normal loans.[36]

The Democrats did this in the name of "diversity." As Steven Malanga of the Manhattan Institute reports, the Federal Reserve Bank of Boston told mortgagers that underwriting standards were "unintentionally biased" because they ignored "the economic culture of urban, lower-income and nontraditional customers." The Federal Reserve Bank explicitly noted that the "secondary market" for such mortgages— meaning Fannie Mae and Freddie Mac—would buy the bad loans. Unsurprisingly, Freddie Mac joined with Sears Mortgage Corporation to offer mortgages to clunker-borrowers who had an income-to-monthly-payment ratio of 50 percent. The typical rate is somewhere in the 28 to 33 percent range.[37] That means that they'd offer a $350,000, 6 percent, thirty-year fixed-rate mortgage to a borrower making $50,352 a year. The monthly income is $4,196.00 and the monthly mortgage payment is $2,098.43. That's not including property taxes, insurance, utilities, and maintenance, which typically add another 50 percent to the payment. Throw in a little food now and then and you just might be in over your head. All that under the assumptions that real estate never goes down in value and that people took out fixed rate loans. We know the pin punctured the balloon a long time ago. However, if that sounds like a winning financial program, chances are you might be reading this book in a homeless shelter.

The feds then threatened nonbank lenders, which were not subject to their dictates, with regulation if they did not water down their standards. According to Malanga, Clinton's Department of Housing and Urban Development threatened to apply the "racially diverse" Community Reinvestment Act to such lenders if they did not comply with the new, looser standards.[38]

All this was fine and dandy while real estate values, buoyed by inflationary fiscal policy and foreign investment, rose unabated. These horrible credit risks could simply sell the house for more than they bought it, pay back the banks, and walk away with the difference. But once supply of housing outstripped demand, the prices on real estate were bound to fall. And when they fell, these clunker-investors couldn't pay their mortgages. And so banks and lenders went under, and, were subsequently nationalized.

But that didn't stop liberal politicians from pursuing even *more* payoffs. Obama used the economic crisis to stump for low-interest student loans; according to the *Washington Post*, Obama wants to expand the Pell Grant Program, "making it an entitlement akin to Medicare and Social Security." Obama wants every American to go to college. The new program would be run by the Department of Education, and would "give priority to needier students." The program combines Obama's favorite practices: demagogue capitalism and pandering to poor voters. "In the end," Obama stated, "this is not about growing the size of government or relying on the free market—because it's not a free market when we have a student-loan system that's rigged to reward private lenders without any risk."[39]

And then there's Obama's mortgage revamping, which specifically helps only those who have lost money on their home purchases—serious money. In order to receive refinancing help under the Homeowner Affordability and Stability Plan, borrowers' loans must be worth 105 percent of the value of their house.[40] This means, for example, that if you owe $350,000 on a house now worth $320,000, you may be eligible for the program. If, however, you owe $350,000 on a house worth $360,000, no refinancing for you.

The same is true for people who spend far too much on their mortgage. If you're a homeowner spending 38 percent of your income on the monthly mortgage, you could get a subsidy. The government may allow you to reduce your payments to the 38 percent level; then the government (i.e., taxpayers) will actually pay your mortgage so that you are paying 31 percent of your income.[41] This means that I am paying your mortgage. You're welcome. When's dinner?

Of course, this defeats the purpose of the program, which is to keep people in houses they can afford—those who were smart enough not to pay gargantuan sums for overvalued properties are screwed by the program. If you're a smart homeowner, you're actually paying your mortgage and the guy's next door. This is dumb for any number of reasons, one of which is the fact that if I'm paying your mortgage, I can't buy a second home—which means that the housing market remains cool. And that's leaving aside the more basic problem: the program ends in five years, which means that Obama is simply kicking the can down the road—in five years, the housing market will collapse again.[42]

But the point of the housing bailout isn't actually to help people. It isn't to boost the economy. It's to give you the impression that Obama and other elected officials will pay your mortgage. That way, you'll vote for Obama again. It's the tax-paying minority that takes it in the shorts, as always.

THAT GUY'S GOING TO TAKE AWAY YOUR PONY

American politics has become simple bribery. So it's no surprise to see that politicians routinely accuse their opponents of maliciously taking away benefits from voters. It's the ultimate trump card: Candidate A is going to take away your Social Security! He's going to take away your Medicare! He's going to fire teachers! He's going to cut welfare payments . . . and he's probably a racist!

When Clinton ran against George H. W. Bush in 1992, he routinely accused him of targeting the poor, minorities, and the elderly. "If you are a millionaire," Clinton told seniors in one speech, "his budget promises a capital gains tax that would generate $500,000,000 over the next five years, but if you're one of the 30 million Americans who depend on Medicare, his budget makes you $2,000 poorer over the next five years. Four more years of George Bush means more millionaires with vacation homes and more older Americans struggling to come up with paying their gas and electric bills in their own homes." [43] (This, like most other things Clinton said, was a lie.)

When George W. Bush had the stones to discuss privatization of Social Security, for example, Democrats immediately accused him of cutting benefits for the elderly. Actually, they went a bit further: they produced an animated video showing Bush saying "Trust me" as he prods two wheelchair-bound elderly people over a cliff. "Bush and Republicans still want to push their privatization plan through Congress," says the narrator. "And they will, if you let them." [44]

During the last election cycle, Obama pulled the same sort of dirty tricks on McCain. In one of his TV spots, "It Gets Worse," the narrator announces, "The *Wall Street Journal* reports John McCain would pay for the rest of his health care plan 'with major reductions in Medicare and Medicaid.' Eight hundred and eighty-two billion from Medicare alone." This, of course, was complete bunk—the *Wall Street Journal* never claimed any such thing. [45]

What's even more pathetic is liberals' attack on true tax cuts as "tax cuts for the wealthy." Barack Obama incessantly cited "tax cuts for the wealthy" as a scurrilous legacy of George W. Bush. "[McCain] wants to continue the Bush tax cuts for the wealthy and he wants to put another $300 billion tax cut on the table for corporations," Obama blathered. "Why not small businesses? Because he thinks it is o.k. the way things are going right now. Let me tell you, we cannot afford to keep on doing more of the same, and that is why I am running for president of the United States of America!" [46] Obama conveniently ignored the fact that his own plan, designed to tax those who make above $250,000, would disproportionately affect small-business owners, who often file as individuals for tax purposes.

But the larger point is that the rich get more back when taxes are cut because *they pay more taxes.* You cannot expect people who do not pay taxes to receive lots of money from tax cuts. If they did, it would be called welfare—or, according to Obama, "tax credits."

As of 2004:

The top 1 percent of earners, who made 19 percent of the country's total income, paid 37 percent of the total income taxes.

The top 5 percent, who earned 33 percent of the country's total income, paid 57 percent of the total income taxes.

The top 10 percent, who made 44 percent of the country's total income, paid 57 percent of the total income taxes.

The bottom 50 percent, who earned 13 percent of the country's total income, paid a whopping 3 percent.

It makes sense, then, that cutting taxes would help the top earners, since they're paying, on average, almost twice what they bring in as a percentage of income.

The politicians know this. They lie about it in order to pander to those who want a pony. And the rich don't constitute enough of a voter bloc to do anything about it, even if they're hiring all of those who vote to confiscate their wealth.

THE END OF PROPERTY RIGHTS

If government payoffs are the best way to buy votes, it's only a matter of time until the government finds a way to openly confiscate property to help "the people."

Think I'm crazy?

It's already been done.

In *Kelo v. New London* (2005), the Supreme Court decided that the government could steal your house, pay you a small sum, bulldoze it, and hand it over to a giant corporation, so long as the corporation would be paying more taxes than you are. Here's the background. In 2000, the city of New London, Connecticut, approved a development plan that was supposed to create jobs and additional tax revenue. The city purchased certain plots of land for the development. Then they tried to confiscate others under the Fifth Amendment to the Constitution, which allows takings of private property for public use with just compensation. The key phrase there is "public use." You can't grab my house and hand it over to my neighbor—that's private use. You can, however, grab my property and turn it into a road if you pay me. Makes sense.

Or at least it *did* make sense. The Supreme Court, however, saw things differently. They decided that the government could confiscate your property and hand it over to another private party. Not for a road. Generally. They could literally rob Peter to pay Paul. Believe it or not, this was not a new doctrine. In a case called *Hawaii Housing Authority v. Midkiff* (1984), the Court decided that the state of Hawaii could confiscate big chunks of land held by single parties, then carve them up and hand them off to Hawaiian natives. The "public purpose" in that case? "Eliminating the 'social and economic evils of a land oligopoly.'" The public purpose in this case? "Economic rejuvenation." [47]

Even nutty Justice Sandra Day O'Connor recognized the importance of this decision: "Any property may now be taken for the benefit of another private party." The decision, she realized, destroys "any distinction between private and public use of property." [48]

But of course, this has been the case for decades with regard to cash. The government steals our cash and hands it out to the "less fortunate" in order to buy votes. Whether it's land or money, allowing the federal government to steal property and hand it over to others is a recipe for disaster. And it violates those basic principles of individual rights that underlie our Constitution and our political system.

THEY SHOOT HORSES, DON'T THEY?

The economy is not going to get back on track as long as Americans rely on the government to hand out ponies. It is our entrepreneurial spirit that makes our economy boom, and when the government force-feeds us into stupid reverie, our economy dies. Many Americans have gotten fat off the government dole—off the taxpayer dole—and now they're too feeble to move a muscle to protect their independence. Worse yet, many Americans don't want to protect their independence, so long as their needs are cared for by others. It's prolonged childhood, and it's crippling us.

There's an answer: make taxpaying a prerequisite for voting again. This isn't a radical idea. Think about it this way. If there were a teacher whose employment was based on student approval, the teacher would hand out As and gold stars to everyone. No one would be educated— everyone would have a 4.0 GPA and would simultaneously be a moron. But at least they'd feel good about themselves!

That's how our voting currently works. Our elected officials rely on our votes. And they buy our votes by paying us with cash, cars, houses, and loans. American republicanism is no longer based on honest and open debate about policy—it's now based on which official can guarantee more pork, more goodies for the voters.

It's time to rectify that by forcing Americans to "have some skin in the game." All Americans. No more Peter voting to tax Paul. No more poor voting to rip off the rich. No more legalized theft. And no more pretending that such theft is a legitimate outgrowth of group victimization. It's time for Americans to take responsibility for their own lives and *grow up*.

Thankfully, some Americans are waking up. The Cincinnati rally discussed at the beginning of this chapter wasn't an isolated incident. On April 15, 2009, hundreds of thousands of people showed up in cities across the country to challenge the destruction of American capitalism: the massive national deficit run up by the Bush and Obama administrations, the Big Bank Bailout Bonanza, the "stimulus" package that stimulated nothing but the United Auto Workers and assorted other Obama political buddies. This tremendous wave of public demonstration was called the tea parties in memory of the Boston Tea Party, when other Americans decided to strike back against a huge centralized government that ignored its constituents in favor of redistributionist policies.

The tea parties were a tremendous success, even if the mainstream media largely ignored them, or worse, made sophomoric jokes about "teabagging." Anderson Cooper of CNN was quoted as saying "it's hard to talk when you're teabagging." Thanks Anderson. We're a nation drowning in debt with Obama promises of more to come and you decide to make jokes at the expense of people who know that the course this nation is on is no laughing matter.

The tea parties were a beautiful illustration of the fact that American democracy is not dead—that there are people out there who still care about the value of personal responsibility, entrepreneurial freedom, private property ownership, and liberty of contract. People who believe in life, liberty, and the pursuit of happiness, not the guarantee of happiness by government.

Those are the only people who should be voting. If the government legalized armed robbery tomorrow, that wouldn't make it moral or right or decent. Forcing you to pay your taxes to others is armed robbery, pure and simple. It's time to make a citizen's arrest.

CHAPTER 8

GRAPEFRUIT, ANYONE?

I f the media pointed its billion-dollar technology-delivery system at a grapefruit, and if reporters from around the world asked the grapefruit their "compelling" questions, striving to deliver the "real" story about that grapefruit, within a reasonably short period of time we could parade that grapefruit across the country and people would come out of their homes and businesses, cheering, weeping, and screaming "Hey, that's the grapefruit I saw on TV!"

This is the "Grapefruit Mentality."

The "Great American Grapefruit" is served up daily to tens of millions of people around the world under the pretense of "news you can use," "news you absolutely need to know," and "news you can't live without." Whether it's thousands who trek to the Hard Rock Café in Las Vegas, Nevada, to see grilled cheese sandwiches emblazoned with the supposed image of the Virgin Mary, cinnamon buns that bear a striking image of Mother Teresa, the endless search for Natalee Holloway (a tragic regional story), the runaway bride Jennifer Wilbanks (Forrest Gump wouldn't be caught running with this one), or the latest musings from Paris Hilton, one of the deep thinkers of our time, the media is hell-bent on serving up "grapefruit segments" while real issues confront us on a daily basis.

Ted Koppel was accused of being an elitist when he thought reporting on the record 10 percent unemployment in this country was a bigger story than the death of John Belushi in 1982. One in ten Americans didn't have a job, yet his producers convinced him that the death of an extremely talented self-indulgent drug-and-alcohol-addicted actor who OD'd on cocaine and heroin in a Hollywood hotel was *the* story the nation couldn't live without. I guess they figured that 10 percent of Americans without a job was a TV market they could tap into. After all, without the hassle of going to work every day, there's more time to watch TV.

If John Belushi had been just another nobody named John, who would have cared? But care they did. They cared about the hotel, the room number, the last meal, the last drink, the last high. The story took over like a drug. How can I get through the day without my Belushi fix? And when the ratings died, we were weaned off that media drug and on to the next one.

The problem is this: the "Grapefruit Mentality" has an effect on how Americans view the world every day. The world we live in is far different from the one we're served up by the breathless anchors and helicopter reporters.

Take a little trip with me down memory lane.

It's 6:45 on a Monday morning in 1968. A five foot two, 102-pound twelve-year-old boy leaves home alone, in the dark, to head off to school. His first trek is a five-block walk to the bus stop. Then begins an eight-block bus ride to the junction in the Flatbush area of Brooklyn, New York. He then jumps on the No. 3 train to Franklin Avenue, where he gets off and waits for the uptown train to Manhattan. Upon arriving at the 14th Street station he has a three-block walk to Xavier High School, the all-boys Jesuit penal colony where a full military uniform is worn every day. At the end of the school day and some extracurricular activities, the process is repeated in reverse, arriving home in the dark. Total time round-trip was anywhere from two to three hours. This happened every day, day after day, week after week, year after year. All without a cell phone, a GPS, a credit card, an RFID chip in his head, and carrying about a $1.50 in his pocket just in case. Somehow he managed to live and tell the story. That story is my story.

If the media today found out that my mother allowed that same twelve-year-old to embark on that very same trek, there's a strong possibility she'd be on Child Protective Services' speed dial.

So why is it that what seemed so normal then seems so odd now? Grapefruit news and media sensationalism.

Airplane nondisasters. Reporters on the beach during hurricanes. Celebrity meltdowns. Freeway car chases. Lovelorn astronauts in diapers. Michael Jackson. Martha Stewart. O. J. Simpson. Scott Peterson. Missing blondes. Runaway brides. Overboard grooms and, of course, child abductions.

In 2008, New York–based syndicated columnist Lenore Skenazy allowed her nine-year-old son to shop by himself at Bloomingdale's, then take the subway and bus home by himself. "Was I worried?" she wrote. "Yes, a tinge. But it didn't strike me as that daring, either. Isn't New York as safe now as it was in 1963? It's not like we're living in downtown Baghdad." She didn't give her son a cell phone—she didn't want him to lose it. And she didn't watch him. "I trusted him to ask a stranger," Skenazy said. "And then I even trusted that stranger not to think, 'Gee, I was about to catch my train home, but now I think I'll abduct this adorable child instead.'"

The outcome? "Long story short: My son got home, ecstatic with independence. Long story longer, and analyzed, to boot: Half the people I've told this episode to now want to turn me in for child abuse."[1]

It wasn't just the people she knew. Half the country wanted to turn her in for child abuse. The day after Skenazy's column came out, she appeared on the *Today* show; she was grilled by Ann Curry, who asked, "Is she an enlightened mom or a really bad one?"[2] The title under Skenazy's picture: "America's Worst Mom?"[3]

And you'd probably agree with the media if you watched TV, read a newspaper, or explored the Internet. But here's the thing: Skenazy was right, and you'd be wrong. New York City is one of the safest big cities on earth. According to 2009 FBI stats, New York has the lowest crime rate of the twenty-five largest cities in the country. Of cities with more than 100,000 residents, New York ranked 246th in crime. It's actually safer in New York City now than it was when I was growing up. In 2007, there were fewer than five hundred murders in New York City; in 1963, there were just over five hundred, and by 1968, there were a thousand killings per year in New York City.[4] So if you were okay with letting your kid take the subway to school when Dick Van Dyke was on, you should feel comfortable now—but you don't.

So why aren't you okay with it? Because the media has scared the crap out of you. They've told us that if we let our kids play in the front yard without supervision, there is a 150 percent chance our kids will be kidnapped, raped, and dumped in a ditch somewhere. They've told us we're to blame if that does happen—and hey, we may even be involved in the kidnapping.

And the media has shown us that if the kid is blond and blue-eyed, the police will look harder for him or her and the press will give the kidnapping more coverage. Lesson here—if you're going to be an irresponsible parent, dye your kid's hair blond and ensure he or she's wearing steely blue contacts. You want your kid to look his best onscreen when Nancy Grace is grilling you for being a closet pedophile, kidnapper, murderer, or just the worst parent on the planet.

If you're black or Latino, skip it. You don't fit the demos. Apparently they think you're too black or too Hispanic for anyone to care.

The media-created paranoia about child safety is incredible. We can name the victims off the tops of our heads: fourteen-year-old Elizabeth Smart of Utah, kidnapped by a handyman (blond, with blue eyes); eighteen-year-old Natalee Holloway, kidnapped and presumably murdered in Aruba (blond, with blue eyes); twelve-year-old Polly Klaas, kidnapped from a slumber party and murdered; six-year-old JonBenet Ramsey, murdered, and her parents implicated (blond, with blue eyes); three-year-old Caylee Anthony, allegedly murdered by her mother;

eight-year-old Sandra Cantu, raped and murdered (blond); nine-year-old Amber Hagerman, abducted and murdered.

Each one of these cases in and of itself is a tragedy of massive proportions. But these are hardly run-of-the-mill affairs. Studies show that there are just 115 "stereotypical kidnappings"—defined as "a nonfamily abduction perpetrated by a slight acquaintance or stranger in which a child is detained overnight, transported at least fifty miles, held for ransom or abducted with the intent to keep the child permanently, or killed"—per year. That is in a country of over 300 million people. In fact, each person under age eighteen has approximately a 1:1,605,620 chance of being the victim of such a kidnapping. And that's just for kids under eighteen—the numbers go down for children under eleven.

But if you watch the media, there's no way to know that. According to the media, there are child rapists lurking around every corner, child murderers behind every bush, and "stranger dangers" everywhere.

There's a problem worse than overprotective parents, though: the problem of media malfeasance. While the talking heads were busy talking about Smart's abduction, America was at war in Afghanistan and preparing to go to war in Iraq. While the commentators were blustering about Holloway, the Supreme Court was stripping away Americans' property rights in *Kelo v. New London*.

While kidnapped kids are newsworthy on some level, what isn't newsworthy is the death of has-been celebrities. Such updates deserve thirty seconds of chitchat. Instead, they receive days-long odes. When alleged pedophile and singer Michael "It Doesn't Matter if I'm Black or White" Jackson dropped dead at age fifty on June 25, 2009, the media went crazy . . . for ten straight days. Every major media outlet mourned around-the-clock the so-called King of Pop—a man who hadn't released an album in eight years. He was heralded as an Elvis-type figure, a demigod with magical talent and mystical cultural properties.

Amidst all the hubbub, hardly anybody reported on Barack Obama's cap and trade bill, which passed through the House of Representatives. That version of the bill would have required that America lower its per capita carbon emissions to 1875 levels. You read that right: 1875. When horses were all the rage and black people were still being lynched.[5]

Here's a country that has 1875 carbon levels: Haiti. How's that working out for them? They've got 47 percent illiteracy and a life expectancy of forty-nine years. Sounds like a typical worker's paradise.[6]

And to achieve that tremendous benefit, just think of the low, low cost: only $1,600 per household, increases in gasoline prices of up to $2.53, and increases in electricity costs by up to 129 percent.[7] What a deal!

Pushing a 1,200-page Crap N' Tax bill through the House wasn't the only thing going on. As the media replayed *Thriller* for the ten thousandth time, things were exploding in Iran and Honduras. The Iranian government, which had been threatened by popular rioting, was declaring Mahmoud Ahmadinejad the president of Iran—and Obama was figuring his best "nonarrogant" U.S. response. In Honduras, a leftist would-be dictator named Manuel Zelaya was ousted from the country by the Honduran Supreme Court, Congress, and military—and Obama was condemning the country and asking for Zelaya's reinstallation.

But you didn't hear about any of that, did you? After all, it wasn't just Michael Jackson who died that weekend: we also lost Farrah Fawcett and Ed McMahon. So I understand if you were distracted from the federal government's $80 billion cash influx to non-TARP company General Electric—which, not coincidentally, owns NBC.

While Brian Williams was busy shedding distraction tears over the loss of Billy Mays, the OxiClean spokesman, and a personal friend, his bosses were quietly pocketing taxpayer cash handed over by the Obama administration.

The media doesn't just serve as a distraction from the real news, though: it makes politicians into stars and stars into politicians. Think Obama, a no-name default senator from Illinois, elected in 2004, now sitting in the White House. Think of *Saturday Night Live* alum Al Franken sitting in the Senate.

The media can turn a grapefruit into a star.

The media recognizes its own power—and it uses that power to manufacture grapefruit stars every single day. Then it uses those new stars to blind us to the real stories. It's a purposeful government-media alliance, and it's designed to keep you away from the truth.

TURNING GRAPEFRUITS INTO MEDIA STARS

Case in Point—Perez Hilton. Who is Perez Hilton and why do we even know he exists?

Hilton, aka Mario Armando Lavandeira, Jr., is a flamingly gay Cuban blogger (we can surmise that he enjoys a good Cuban cigar à la Bill Clinton only with a different type of wrapper). A graduate of New York University with a degree in drama, Lavandeira dubbed himself Perez Hilton, naming himself after another pseudo-celebrity, Paris Hilton, whose most famous celluloid exploit was a sex tape with her then-boyfriend entitled *One Night in Paris*. Classy.

He then worked as a media relations assistant to the Gay and Lesbian Alliance Against Defamation (GLAAD), which apparently did not realize that it was furthering gay stereotypes simply by employing him. He was also a receptionist at the New York gay club Urban Outings and the editor of *Instinct*, a gay men's rag.

His blog, PerezHilton.com, made him a semihousehold name. It features his "unique" commentary on celebrities, which includes childish scrawlings on tabloid pics, plus frequent use of curse words. There's nothing deep about Hilton's work—it's the equivalent of a three-year-old following around famous people with an Etch-a-Sketch. He's more freakish fan than journalist.

He uses paparazzi photos, which has earned him the everlasting enmity of the paparazzi—they've sued him for millions based on illegal use of their copyrighted work. At VH1's Big in '06 Awards in 2006, photographers refused to take his picture; Hilton responded by shouting, "Instead of wanting to have me as a friend or an ally you choose to be a c——! C——! And I don't wanna work with c——s."[8]

That hasn't stopped his ascent in the media. He's been profiled by the Associated Press, *GQ,* and the *New York Post.* He routinely "outs" supposedly gay Hollywoodites who would prefer to keep their sexuality private, including Lance Bass and Neil Patrick Harris. Says Hilton, "It upsets me that people think what I'm doing is a bad thing. . . . I know there is some controversy about outing people, but I believe the only way we're gonna have change is with visibility. And if I have to drag some people screaming out of the closet, I will." This is, to put it mildly, disgusting. Or, as *Us Weekly* editor-in-chief Janice Min put it, "I love Perez, but this is a guy who draws cocaine sprinkles falling out of celebrities' noses and writes things like 'sucks d——' on pictures of celebs he wants to out."[9]

Why is Hilton famous? Because in the media world, any Grapefruit can be a media phenomenon. And here's the thing about Grapefruit: their seeds become new Grapefruit. Just as Paris Hilton's idiotic celebrity created Perez Hilton, Perez Hilton's idiotic celebrity created Carrie Prejean.

Though Hilton should rightfully be relegated to Barney Frank's apartment whorehouse, his fame earned him a seat as a judge on Donald Trump's Miss USA panel. Now, Hilton had as much business judging Miss USA candidates as Congressman Charlie Rangel would in setting ethical standards for Congress.

That didn't stop Hilton from entering into political territory when he asked Miss California, Carrie Prejean, her final question. "Vermont recently became the fourth state to legalize same-sex marriage," Hilton asked. "Do you think every state should follow suit? Why or why not?"

Prejean's answer was simple and to the point. "Well, I think it's great that Americans are able to choose one way or the other. We live in a land where you can choose same-sex marriage or opposite marriage. You know what, in my country, in my family, I do believe that marriage should be between a man and a woman, no offense to anybody out there. But that's how I was raised and I believe that it should be between a man and a woman."

But Hilton ripped into Prejean as though she had asked him to wear purple and green together. "She gave the worst answer in pageant history," he said in a pathetically self-serving video blog on YouTube. "Miss California lost because she's a dumb bitch . . . I am so disappointed in Miss California representing my country . . . I could not believe when she became first runner-up. If that girl had won Miss USA, I would have gone up on stage, I s—— you not, I would have gone up on stage, snatched that tiara off her head and run out the door." [10]

Grapefruit Hilton's intolerance had created a new Grapefruit: Prejean. She appeared on all of the morning shows. She guest-hosted on Fox News. Turns out that association with crazy Grapefruits like Perez Hilton can be an excellent career path, at least for a few shining moments.

By the way, as the media focused incessantly on Prejean and Hilton, there were some other, minor items in the news: Obama was risking our national security by releasing CIA memos about our interrogation methods; Obama was considering converting bank bailouts into equity shares, which would give the government controlling stakes in the nation's major financial institutions; Janet Napolitano, homeland security secretary, was defending a report labeling anyone who didn't like big government a "right wing extremist" capable of terrorism; Obama was preparing to lash out at credit card companies and rewrite their rules.

But Prejean and Perez—the Grapefruit Sisters—were clearly more important than any of these little issues.

TURNING GRAPEFRUITS INTO POLITICAL COMMENTATORS

Katie Couric is charming and cute. But I believe I can say with some degree of authority that nobody really needed to see a camera up her butt . . . albeit a rather perky one!

That didn't stop her from airing her own live colonoscopy on NBC in March 2000. It was a procedure she would repeat in 2004.[11] "After I lost my husband, Jay, to colorectal cancer in 1998, I became determined to share my newfound knowledge about this deadly disease with the public," Couric said. "The whole reason I decided to air my colonoscopy publicly, is because I was hoping to demystify the procedure. A colonoscopy may not be on the top of your to-do list, but it is a lot more fun than being diagnosed with cancer," said Couric.[12]

Nonetheless, Katie's infomercial for colonoscopies had an effect—it helped boost rates of colonoscopies by 20 percent. Unfortunately, it was the wrong 20 percent—the populations most likely to contract colon cancer remained largely unaffected. "Perhaps next time a colon cancer screening campaign can be given during a show like *Touched by an Angel* so that the demographics are more in line with the people who are at increased risk," said Mark Fendrick, an associate professor of internal medicine at the University of Michigan.[13]

I'm not thoroughly concerned with Katie's colonoscopies—if it helped raise awareness, terrific. The bigger question is why Katie Couric moved from colonoscopies as coanchor on NBC's *Today* show to domestic policy and international affairs as anchor of the *CBS Evening News*. The answer is simple: CBS was desperate, and it needed a Star Grapefruit. Couric fit the bill. Most of Couric's career had been dedicated to soft news: dog stories, babies, barbecues, and makeovers. They needed someone with a household name, someone people would recognize and connect with. Heck, if they'd watch her in the morning, they'd tune her in at night to see her deliver the hard news. Or so they thought.

Despite the fact that she had never broken a major story, she became the highest-paid anchor on television ($15 million per year), replacing Dan Rather after Rather's inglorious exit from television in the aftermath of his botched hit job on George W. Bush.

CBS thought they had harvested a fresh-picked Grapefruit. But by the time she hit CBS, her charm had worn off. Her news broadcasts routinely finish at the bottom of the ratings each night. The criticism she received in the early months was written off by the suits at CBS as an indication of how sexist America is. Nice try but not even close. If that was the case then why did viewers reject Peter Jennings when he was first tapped to anchor ABC's *World News Tonight* in 1965? Because he was Canadian? Does that mean America is an isolationist nation?

Peter Jennings and the suits at ABC realized he needed to go out in the field and cover the hard news the right way, by being there. Seeing it, tasting it, and smelling it. Jennings became a foreign correspondent in 1968 and learned his craft covering the Middle East and I'm not talking Ohio.

Jennings covered the Arab-Israeli conflict and the Palestine Black September organization. He landed the first American interview with PLO chairman Yasser Arafat, reported live on the Munich Olympics massacre of Israeli athletes and followed that up with the Yom Kippur War. He sat down with the Ayatollah Khomeini of Iran, reported on the Iranian Revolution and the hostage crisis that lasted 444 days, the assassination of Egyptian president Anwar Sadat, the Falklands War, and Israel's 1982 invasion of Lebanon.

In 1983, ABC named Jennings as the sole anchor and senior editor for *World News Tonight*. After getting his legs under him, the ratings began to soar. From the 1986 Space Shuttle Challenger disaster to the 1991 Gulf War, Jennings knew how to cover a story: seriously.

In the mid-1990s, television critics praised him for not letting the O. J. Simpson circus dominate the newscast at ABC. But just a few short years later, Jennings and ABC decided to back off on international stories and hard news, instead serving up the softer, happy Grapefruit News. Viewers revolted. Ratings tanked and never recovered.

In early 2005, Peter Jennings stepped down from the anchor desk after being diagnosed with lung cancer. He passed away on August 7, 2005, at the age of sixty-seven. He left behind a wife and two children and the respect of those in the journalist community who rewarded his hard work and dedication with sixteen Emmys, two George Foster Peabody awards, Overseas Press Club and duPont Columbia awards, Best Anchor by the *Washington Journalism Review* in 1988, 1989, 1990, and 1992, and the Edward R. Murrow Award for Lifetime Achievement in Broadcasting.

Jennings was a pro and the audience knew it. Viewers of hard news served up around dinnertime and late night want someone they know has the chops to deliver. We want to believe them. We want to know that they know of which they speak. Katie Couric still has a chance to salvage her position and bring back the respect that Walter Cronkite earned as anchor of the *CBS Evening News*. She just needs to go learn her craft by *being* a journalist, not just acting like one.

B-LIST GRAPEFRUIT COMMENTATORS

Couric's story isn't rare. When it comes to the political commentariat, they're drawn far too often from the bottom of the barrel.

Take Frank Rich, for example. He was the chief drama critic for the *New York Times*, where he specialized in critiquing musicals. Then the paper elevated him to writing on politics. Clearly, watching Sondheim's *Follies* is wonderful preparation for writing an influential column on national and international politics.

Then there's Ana Marie Cox. She's currently the Washington editor of Time.com. And her background demonstrates her commitment to objective and important journalism. She wrote for suck.com—which, contrary to the site name, has nothing to do with pornography—and then moved on to Wonkette. Wonkette became a popular Web site only after she began pushing an anonymous blogger named Washingtonienne, who penned entries about her profligate sex life with politicians and their staff. Washingtonienne—a Senate staffer named Jessica Cutler, who had actually been a full-fledged prostitute—was another Grapefruit who became a media sensation. But while Cutler's exploits didn't gain her any lasting fame, Cox parlayed her slot at Wonkette into the Time.com job—which means that Perez Hilton will, in all likelihood, be the next editor of Time.com.

Keith Olbermann of MSNBC, a two-hundred-pound fish you could land on five-pound test, is another Grapefruit-turned-B-lister. Olbermann graduated from Cornell—well, actually, the non–Ivy League Cornell agricultural school—with a B.S. in communications arts (which ranks second to Art History on the list of useless majors). He then moved on to ESPN, where he became famous for spouting lines like "It's deep, and I don't think it's playable" and "Welcome to the Big Show."

That was before Olbermann went completely off his rocker. After burning bridges with ESPN, he moved on to MSNBC, where he hosted *The Big Show*, which specialized in Monica Lewinsky's oral abilities. In 2003, Olbermann's new show, *Countdown*, premiered. That show specialized in Olbermann saying the word "sir" with varying degrees of scorn. Because MSNBC lacks any show with ratings, Olbermann has remained on the air, where he names the Worst Person in the World and babbles mindlessly about his nonexistent intellectual credentials.

Maybe when Olbermann reads this book, I will be named his Worst Person in the World. Coming from Olbermann that's not saying much. If an idiot makes a noise in the forest does anyone really hear it?

CRIMINAL GRAPEFRUITS

The most popular type of Grapefruit is the Criminal Grapefruit. Usually, these are old-time Grapefruits who have withered away; they used to be popular, but now they're has-beens. When they commit a murder or a robbery or a rape, however, the media hyperventilates with joy: Martha Stewart or Robert Blake or Phil Spector or O. J. "Grapefruit Juice" Simpson or Michael Jackson can carry weeks' worth of newscasts. They can make careers—just ask Nancy Grace. And they can raise ratings.

There's been an interesting transition in America's love affair with Grapefruit Criminals. Originally, criminals used to be celebrities. Think of Al Capone, who gets profiled by Robert De Niro in *The Untouchables*, or John Dillinger, recently played by Johnny Depp in *Public Enemies*, or even Billy the Kid, profiled repeatedly in film. Think of all the criminal freaks: John Wojtowicz and Salvatore Naturile, the two men who robbed a bank so Wojtowicz could pay for his boyfriend's sex reassignment surgery (John and Salvatore got the big-screen treatment in *Dog Day Afternoon*); Eric Harris and Dylan Klebold shooting up Columbine High School (they, too, got the glitz makeover in Gus Van Sant's *Elephant*); Pauline Parker and Juliet Hulme, who murdered Pauline's mother (Kate Winslet launched her career in a remake of this crime, *Heavenly Creatures*); Leopold and Loeb (*Compulsion*); Bonnie (later, Faye Dunaway) and Clyde (later, Warren Beatty); Bugsy Siegal (Warren Beatty in *Bugsy*); Charles Manson; the list goes on and on.

Our fascination with crime has created copycat criminals who seek to get their faces and names on the TV screen. In 1982, after a spate of poisonings occurred around the country involving Extra-Strength Tylenol, copycat criminals began placing poisonous substances into both pharmaceutical drugs and food products.[14] The Columbine shootings themselves some suggest may have been inspired by *The Basketball Diaries* and/or *Natural Born Killers*. After the Columbine shootings, *Time* reported that "in recent weeks hundreds of schools have been hit with threats of Columbine-like violence." After the movie *Money Train* premiered in 1995, which included a scene in which a New York subway token booth was set on fire, street thugs tried to duplicate the feat. After *The Burning Bed* came out in 1984—a movie which included Farrah Fawcett pouring gasoline on her husband and setting him on fire—a man in Milwaukee repeated the experiment—with his wife as the victim.[15] Most recently, when Seung-Hui Cho committed mass murder at Virginia Tech in 2007, he was imitating the South Korean film *Oldboy*.

Culture has a clear impact on the Grapefruit Criminals—it both creates them and idolizes them. But more and more, the media has turned from idolizing outright criminals to featuring faded entertainment icons who commit crimes.

When celebrities commit crimes, it's always a story. Fatty Arbuckle, an early film star who lived up to his name with his massive girth, held a party in a hotel in 1921. One of his guests, Virginia Rappe, somehow suffered a ruptured bladder and died. Arbuckle was wrongly accused of raping her—varying accounts had him assaulting her with a champagne bottle or a piece of ice—and causing her death by crushing her with his bulk. The papers ate it up. Said newspaper magnate William Randolph Hearst of the scandal: "[it] sold more newspapers than any event since the sinking of the *Lusitania*."[16] Arbuckle's career was ruined, and the resulting scandal led to the voluntary imposition of the Hays Code on Hollywood, which was designed to keep moral values in film.

Sex symbol Errol Flynn, star of *The Adventures of Robin Hood* among other classics, was tried and acquitted for the statutory rape of two teenage girls. Roman Polanski ran from the United States after he was convicted of statutorily raping a thirteen-year-old girl. Chuck Berry spent time in prison for transporting a fourteen-year-old girl across state lines. Jerry Lee Lewis bigamously married his thirteen-year-old cousin. Rob Lowe videotaped himself servicing an underage girl. None of these men had their careers cut short[17]—and the media made a bundle by covering the scandals.

But the celebrity-as-criminal exploitation reached its height with the O. J. Simpson trial. Simpson's trial combined everything the media loves. It had sex—his wife was the smoking-hot Nicole Simpson, and O.J. murdered her while she was hanging out with another man, Ron Goldman. It had race—Nicole was white and O.J. was black. It had star power—O.J. was a former Heisman winner and NFL star. It had legal drama—the star-studded Simpson team included Alan Dershowitz, Johnny "If It Doesn't Fit, You Must Acquit" Cochrane, and Robert Shapiro. It had judicial weirdness—Judge Lance Ito became the subject of Jay Leno's "Dancing Itos" sketches, which featured Asian men in robes and beards gallivanting about to the *Perry Mason* theme song.

And Ito, like an idiot, allowed cameras into the courtroom. Even the *New York Times* was stunned. "To the relief of millions of voyeurs, court buffs and civic-minded students of the criminal justice system," wrote the *Times*, "Judge Lance A. Ito ruled today that a single television camera can remain in the courtroom for the trial of O. J. Simpson. . . . As Mr. Simpson sat nearby, intermittently attentive, Judge Ito spent much of the morning invoking the perils of television, including nervous witnesses, grandstanding lawyers and salacious sound bites." None of that stopped him from allowing the cameras. He laughably explained that "in a case crucial to public faith in courts, television was essential."[18]

The O.J. trial turned into a total and complete debacle, splitting the nation down racial lines. With Mark Fuhrman's racist comments broadcast throughout the country, the trial became less about O.J.'s brutal slaughter of two innocents and more about whether we like police officers who use the n-word. But the media reveled in every moment of it. When O. J. "Still Looking for the Real Killer" Simpson went free, the media had a field day. After all, now he could dedicate his time to tracking down the one-armed man who had murdered his wife. This was Grade A Grapefruit Juice.

If the O.J. trial is Exhibit A in the Celebrity Criminal Grapefruit Hall of Fame, Martha Stewart's trial for insider trading is Exhibit B.

Stewart was jailed for five months and given a charming electronic anklet for home confinement after her release from the women's prison in Alderson, West Virginia. The media thought this was the greatest story since the birth of Christ. When she was released from Alderson, two female media members breathlessly reported on national television: "Martha Stewart has been released. Stewart has been released from Alderson Women's Correctional Facility. I assume she's on her way to the airport right now and what will take place there? Well, first of all, it's about a thirty-minute drive and it's a very dark road that she has to travel on. It's about ten miles before she actually goes onto the highway and, um, there are deer out there, there are pheasants there and a lot of animals along that road so she's going to have to go carefully." Deer and pheasants? Really? I left out your names to protect your careers but you know who you are. Well done! And the Emmy goes to . . . Drumroll, please!

Now, I'm not condoning insider trading, but this is way over the top. While the helicopters were buzzing her 153-acre New York estate,[19] Bernie Madoff was making off with tens of billions of dollars in a Ponzi scheme that made Stewart's crime seem like stealing pennies from a gumball machine; Sir Allen Stanford was allegedly engaging in an $8 billion CD Ponzi scheme; and Senator Dick Durbin was selling $115,000 worth of stock the day after Treasury Secretary Henry Paulson and Federal Reserve chairman Ben Bernanke informed him that if

Congress did not act quickly, the economy would be gone by the following Monday morning.[20] Priorities, anyone?

Michael Jackson's trial for child molestation is Exhibit C. Jackson had been a star since childhood, of course; his songs and music videos had made him a household name. But when he wasn't filming *Thriller,* he was busy serving up "Jesus juice" to underage kids. In 1993, thirteen-year-old Jordan Chandler and his father were befriended by Jackson, who began inviting Jordan over for sleepovers. Jordan accused Jackson of performing sex acts on him. In early 1994, Jackson paid Jordan $20 million to go away.[21] Despite the settlement, many believed that Jackson was innocent of the charges.

That all changed in 2005. With documentary cameras rolling, Jackson was shown holding hands with a thirteen-year-old boy, Gavin Arvizo, a child suffering from cancer, and for whose chemo treatments Jackson was paying. Jackson and Arvizo also discussed where they were going to sleep. In the documentary, Jackson stated, "Why can't you share your bed? The most loving thing to do is to share your bed with someone." Maybe so, Jacko, but not when it's a thirteen-year-old boy.

Arvizo's parents were questionable characters in their own right—his mother sued J.C. Penney after using the children to shoplift from the store; his father pled no contest to child cruelty. In any case, the Santa Barbara County district attorney filed charges against Jackson. Soon the world would watch as Jackson danced atop an SUV amongst a throng of his supporters while exiting the courtroom. The media deemed the case "the trial of the century." After several months, Jackson was acquitted on June 13, 2005.

While the country was mesmerized by the Jackson case, there were a few events of vital significance taking place. One was the World Economic Forum in Davos, where international financiers and economic experts were busy skiing while ignoring all the warning signs of an imploding economy. Another was President Bush's attempt to regulate Fannie Mae and Freddie Mae—efforts stifled by Barney Frank and company. Still another story was the Bush administration's decision, along with the SEC's, not to prosecute AIG for cooking the books.

The media was too busy covering Grapefruit Jackson and his disgusting escapades with young boys to worry about the impending tsunami on the financial front. AIG, Fannie, and Freddie don't sell advertising—Michael Jackson's no-no's at Neverland apparently did.

TURNING A GRAPEFRUIT
INTO A PRESIDENT

On January 30, 2003, Barack Obama was a forty-two-year-old unknown member of the Illinois State Senate and an unsuccessful challenger for Bobby Rush's seat in the House of Representatives. On January 20, 2009, Barack Obama was sworn in as the forty-fourth president of the United States.

There's one very powerful component that can solidify true star power, and Obama's meteoric rise is proof of the power of the media. That and the fact that Obama is one hell of a Grapefruit. And the media was ready to demonstrate the power of its Grapefruit Machine by turning him into president of the United States.

It truly began long before Obama's ascent to the Senate. When he was in law school in 1990, Obama became president of the *Harvard Law Review*—an elected position, not an academic one. And for some reason, this brought him tremendous notice. As the *Boston Globe* wrote in a glowing 2007 profile, "Obama gained instant fame, was profiled glowingly in newspapers across the country, and landed a contract for a book that would become *Dreams from My Father*, his best-selling memoir. . . . Blair Underwood, the actor who played a black lawyer on L.A. Law, one of the campus's favorite shows, came to visit Obama at the Law Review and took him out for a Chinese food banquet." [22] Let's be honest—this wasn't exactly Rosa Parks material. Obama was already attending Harvard Law, and he was being selected by a bunch of friends, many of whom were eager (like Americans eighteen years later) to select a black man. So why the attention? The media was clearly picking Obama out for future stardom.

And they didn't leave him hanging when *Dreams from My Father* came out in 1995. The *New York Times* inexplicably gave Obama an 855-word review. Reviews that length are unheard of for no-name first-time authors, let alone no-name first-time authors writing self-serving auto-biographies. And it wasn't just a review—it was a drooling, sycophantic review. "All men live in the shadow of their fathers—the more distant the father, the deeper the shadow," gushed Paul Watkins. "Barack Obama describes his confrontation with this shadow in his provocative autobiography . . . and he also persuasively describes the phenomenon of belonging to two different worlds, and thus belonging to neither. . . . Mr. Obama was born into a cultural milieu that on the surface made for perfect social and racial diversity, but living such a life proved extraordinarily difficult."

Yes, Obama had such a tough childhood that he could afford cocaine, live the high life in Hawaii, pay the bills at the wholly private Occidental College, and then go on to Columbia University and Harvard Law School. But Watkins never challenged Obama's credibility. Instead, he wholeheartedly endorsed Obama's book: "At a young age and without much experience as a writer, Barack Obama has bravely tackled the complexities of his remarkable upbringing." [23] The *Washington Post* quickly followed suit with an even less critical review: "Barack Obama is never flip or hip. Fluidly, calmly, insightfully, he guides us straight to the intersection of the most serious questions of identity, family, class and race." [24]

Obama's story wasn't that remarkable, nor was it that important. But it earned him national media attention nonetheless.

By the time of the Democratic National Convention in 2004, Obama was a Senate candidate. Because he was young, black, and extremely articulate, he was given the honor of delivering the keynote address. It was, reportedly, the first time he had used a teleprompter; a lifelong love affair began. Despite the fact that Obama's speech was not very different from those delivered by VP candidate John Edwards and presidential candidate John Kerry—in fact, one line in Obama's original draft was so similar to Kerry's that Kerry insisted the line be cut—Obama was feted by every newspaper and media outlet in existence.

The *New York Times* predictably started his campaign for president before he was even elected to the Senate. "On Tuesday, at about 9 P.M., Barack Obama was an Illinois state legislator running for the Senate," wrote Scott Malcomson in the *Times*. "A half-hour later, after he had given the keynote address at the Democratic National Convention, he was the party's hot ticket. Pundits even predicted he would be the first black president. . . . Most people can find something to identify with in Barack Obama, and he can find something to identify with in them. We have never had a politician quite like this. It may be a paradox, but only someone this rare could be so universal." [25]

The Great Grapefruit Campaign of 2008 had begun.

Soon the media was clamoring for him to run for president. And despite previous promises that he would not run in 2008, Obama obliged. With the help of some of his star-making friends, of course. Obama raised tens of millions from his Hollywood buddies. As early as February 2007 he was getting checks from George Clooney, Eddie Murphy, and Barbra Streisand; at one fund-raiser that month, he told Hollywoodites that they were "the storytellers of our age." [26] He also used their image-making talents to craft his entire Democratic National Convention presentation— with contributors including Steven Spielberg, Tom Hanks, and *An Inconvenient Truth* director Davis Guggenheim.[27] Obama also reportedly received image-crafting advice and foreign policy advice from Clooney.[28] Ben Affleck explained how Hollywood loves Obama: "In Hollywood, what I've noticed . . . the vast majority of people I know out here support Obama. He's really sort of taken over Los Angeles in dramatic fashion. And he's swept up a lot of money from Hillary." [29]

Obama became a celebrity in his own right, garnering cover shoots in *Rolling Stone, GQ, Ebony, Vibe, Us Weekly, Vanity Fair, Men's Vogue, Tiger Beat*, and multiple features in *Time* and *Newsweek*. The cover of *Rolling Stone* was particularly egregious, labeling him "A New Hope" and backlighting an animation of him that made him seem a cross between Superman and Jesus Christ. He danced on *Ellen*. He got Oprah's endorsement. *Saturday Night Live*'s most cutting critique of Obama was that he was too "cool." Chris Matthews experienced a "thrill going up his leg" on national television while talking about Obama.

The Grapefruit was growing in fame and exalted stature.

Meanwhile, the media busied itself tearing down Hillary Clinton, treating her like an aging mistress. Hillary supporter and ultrawealthy founder of the Shorenstein Center on the Press and Politics at Harvard University, Walter Shorenstein, wrote a memo to Democratic superdelegates complaining about the media bias against Hillary. "Is it in the country's best interest that voters received far more information about Hillary's laugh than Obama's legislative record?" Shorenstein asked. "Our democracy depends upon the fourth estate to fulfill the uniquely critical role of informing voters about the important issues facing our nation—yet far too often, the campaign coverage has been biased, blasé, or baseless."[30] According to the Center for Media and Public Affairs, 84 percent of press coverage of Obama was favorable through the primaries, with just 51 percent favorable to Clinton.[31]

While the media focused on Hillary's mental lapse about her trip to Bosnia (she claimed she was shot at on the tarmac—photos and video proved she was lying, which she later explained away by saying she was suffering from jet lag), they utterly ignored Obama's deep and abiding relationships with radical racialist Jeremiah Wright, unrepentant terrorist Bill Ayers, unrepentant terrorist spokesman Rashid Khalidi, the voter fraud group ACORN, and anti-Israel Merrill McPeak, Samantha Powers, and Robert Malley, among others. They overlooked his gaffes—fifty-seven states, anyone?—and his outright fabrications on his policy positions. They did not press him on who he was or why he was running; instead, they focused on Hillary's pantsuits.

Once Hillary was out of the picture, the media turned its fire on John "My Friends" McCain, another former beloved of the mainstream press. Now McCain was an extremist who had no business attacking Obama over his racist pastor and radical wife. He was a right-wing loon who couldn't be trusted with national security, since he had been tortured in Vietnam. He was even an adulterer, carrying on an implied affair with a former staffer. All of it was baseless, and all of it was designed to turn Grapefruit Obama into president of the United States.

The media actually celebrated the fact that Obama was a Grapefruit without any discernible positions. They loved the fact that he was a blank canvas. He had no record and no policies—at least none he was willing to share. The media reveled in it—and it worked.

Obsessed with his self-image, enamored of hearing his voice on TV, Obama has actually usurped the power of the press. Now members of the press including super-liberal Helen Thomas are upset about Obama's habit of rigging his press conferences. "What the hell do they think we are, puppets?" she complained on July 1, 2009.[32] Well, yes. Mainly because you *are* puppets, dancing for the master. Next time Obama lies, catch him on it rather than laughing at one of his stupid jokes. Then perhaps Obama will start treating you like reporters rather than housebroken pooches.

ONE BIG HAPPY BOWL OF GRAPEFRUIT

The media's support for Obama—its demonstration of the Grapefruit Mentality once and for all—was a bargain with the devil. They sold their journalistic souls in order to make their man president—and in the process, they became wholly owned and operated subsidiaries of the Obama White House. Obama knows it; during the Radio and TV Correspondents Dinner in 2009 he openly joked about it. "Why bother hanging out with celebrities when I can spend time with the people who made me one?" he quipped.[33]

On June 16, 2009, Matt Drudge reported that ABC News would be running a series of specials focusing on Obama's attempts to nationalize the health care industry. From inside the White House. With no opposition. In other words, a bunch of campaign commercials. The network broadcast *Good Morning America* from the South Lawn, *World News* from the Blue Room, and *Questions for the President: Prescription for America*, with a fully screened audience chosen to ask "questions." The

Republican National Committee protested ABC News's blatant sellout: "Today, the Republican National Committee requested an opportunity to add our Party's views to those of the President's to ensure that all sides of the health care reform are presented. Our request was rejected. . . . In the absence of opposition, I am concerned this event will become a glorified infomercial to promote the Democrat agenda. If that is the case, this primetime infomercial should be paid for out of the DNC coffers." ABC News refused the RNC's request, stating instead, "ABC News alone will select those who will be in the audience asking questions of the president."[34] This was hilarious. Obama's White House would only grant access to ABC News knowing they would ask softball questions—there's a reason Obama didn't choose Fox News to do this series of specials. To be fair, the same could be said of George Bush and his mutual love fest with Fox News.

NBC, too, has become a wing of the Obama Press Office. Obama actually joked about Brian Williams sleeping with him: "A few nights ago, I was up tossing and turning, trying to figure out exactly what to say. Finally, when I couldn't get back to sleep, I rolled over and asked Brian Williams what he thought."[35] MSNBC, meanwhile, is home to the three amigos of the Obama love fest: Rachel Maddow, Chris Matthews, and Keith Olbermann.

NBC and MSNBC are owned by General Electric. General Electric is one of the biggest beneficiaries of the government's Temporary Liquidity Guarantee Program (TLGP), even though it is not a bank. GE Capital, the company's financing wing, has issued over $80 billion in debt backed by the TLGP. Meanwhile, they are not subject to banking restrictions. How convenient for both Obama and for GE.[36]

Those are only some of the most obvious sycophants. Others include the *New York Times*, which has yet to issue an editorial overtly condemning Obama on anything, and for the most part every other major newspaper in the country is lined up nuts to butts. For their hard work on behalf of the president, these newspapers have been rewarded with rumors of government bailouts dancing in their heads.

Hollywood has received rich reward from the Obama administration, which has pushed for tax breaks in the hundreds of millions. Meanwhile, comedians continue their hands-off policy with regard to Obama. Even the Obama-supporting *Los Angeles Times* has taken notice: "On his HBO show, *Real Time with Bill Maher*, the comedian routinely makes vicious fun of celebrities, politicians, presidents and even God. But he's learned that, for much of his audience, Barack Obama is off-limits. . . . 'Obama is the new God,' quipped Maher. . . . TV's leading political humorists have largely backed away from their ritual comic hazing of the president, a colorful tradition in the medium, especially in its late-night time slots, since at least the Nixon administration."[37] In fact, when Obama appeared on Jay Leno as president and cracked a not-so-funny joke at the expense of the Special Olympics, no comedian dared respond.

Our fourth estate has made its living turning Grapefruit into stars and their greatest feat was turning a political Grapefruit into the president. Unfortunately for them, that Grapefruit is now turning the media into his plaything. Call it *Revenge of the Grapefruit*.

The mass media is all about massive ratings. I get it. But don't we have a responsibility to look at the bigger issues that confront us as a nation? The bigger issues, remember? Winning the war against Islamists who use terrorism as their main tactic, reducing the number of people who live below the poverty line in America (41 million), raising educational results across America, congressional accountability, reducing out-of-control federal spending, securing our nation's borders—all of these issues, and many more, affect every one of us. We're all in the same "situation room." What "news alert" we choose to get swooshed by is up to us.

A GRAPEFRUIT-FREE CHILDHOOD

How we choose to be affected by the Grapefruits we're served is up to us. We can cower in fear, focus on matters that don't matter, waste time with time wasters or just waste away watching a synthetic life on a fifty-two-inch flat screen too frightened to go outside and confront the evil world that's just on the other side of our fortress walls. Not me.

A listener to my radio show e-mailed me back in 2005 something I reread often to remind me of the way it used be—and in a lot of ways still is today. I don't know if Charlie B is the author, but whoever wrote it nailed it. I hope you enjoy it as much as I do.

TO THE KIDS WHO SURVIVED
the 30s, 40s, 50s, and 60s

First, we survived being born to mothers who smoked and/or drank while they carried us. They took aspirin, ate blue cheese dressing, and didn't get tested for diabetes. Then after that trauma, our baby cribs were covered with bright-colored lead-based paints.

We had no childproof lids on medicine bottles, doors, or cabinets and when we rode our bikes, we had no helmets, not to mention the risks we took hitchhiking. As children, we would ride in cars with no seat belts or air bags. Riding in the back of a pickup on a warm day was always a special treat. We drank water from the garden hose and NOT from a bottle. We shared one soft drink with four friends, from one bottle, and NO ONE actually died from this.

We ate cupcakes, bread and butter, and drank soda pop with sugar in it, but we weren't overweight because WE WERE ALWAYS OUTSIDE PLAYING! We would leave home in the morning and play all day, as long as we were back when the streetlights came on. No one was able to reach us all day. And we were okay.

We would spend hours building our go-carts out of scraps and then ride down the hill, only to find out we forgot the brakes. After running into the bushes a few times, we learned to solve the problem. We did not have PlayStations, Nintendos, Xboxes, no video games at all, no ninety-nine channels on cable, no videotape movies, no surround sound, no cell phones, no personal computers, no Internet or Internet chat rooms . . . WE HAD FRIENDS and we went outside and found them!

We fell out of trees, got cut, broke bones and teeth and there were no lawsuits from these accidents. We made up games with sticks and tennis balls and ate worms and although we were told it would happen, we did not put out very many eyes, nor did the worms live in us forever. We rode bikes or walked to a friend's house and knocked on the door or rang the bell, or just walked in and talked to them!

Little League had tryouts and not everyone made the team. Those who didn't had to learn to deal with disappointment. Imagine that! The idea of a parent bailing us out if we broke the law was unheard of. They actually sided with the law!

This generation has produced some of the best risk takers, problem solvers, and inventors ever! The past fifty years have been an explosion of innovation and new ideas. We had freedom, failure, success, and responsibility, and we learned HOW TO DEAL WITH IT ALL!

And YOU are one of them! CONGRATULATIONS! Send this on to others who have had the luck to grow up as kids, before the lawyers and the government regulated our lives for our own good.

Kind of makes you want to run through the house with scissors, doesn't it?

DISCLAIMER BY JERRY DOYLE: In the highly litigious atmosphere in which we live, I have to add this disclaimer: Do not run through the house with scissors at my behest. I'm not condoning this activity. Run with scissors at your own risk!

I don't want to wake up one day with half a dozen helicopters over my house and Nancy Grace at my front door, asking, "Why did that poor, blond-haired, blue-eyed four-year-old girl have to die because of your irresponsible behavior? Isn't this going to set a trend of copycat scissor runners?" Nuff said.

CHAPTER 9

DRAIN THE POLITICAL SWAMP

*Not since the beginning of time
has the world beheld terror like this!*

That's the tagline from the 1954 horror classic *Creature from the Black Lagoon*. Fast-forward half a century, and the creatures, our esteemed members of Congress, have firmly entrenched themselves in the political swamp known as Washington, D.C. This is only fitting, since the nation's capital is built on a swamp. Literally!

In 1790, the Residence Act declared that the federal government would establish a permanent seat by 1800. The act allowed President George Washington to select the location for the capital of the newly formed United States; in the meantime, Philadelphia would serve as the capital until the new structures were in place.

There was a healthy debate over where the capital would be located. Southern states refused to be governed by a capital located in the North, and Northern states wanted the capital located away from the South.

177

There was another concurrent problem. Certain states, mainly concentrated in the North, were loaded with financial liability; the Revolutionary War had left many of them facing huge debts. Treasury Secretary Alexander Hamilton was pushing a financial plan in which the federal government would assume all state debt. (You might call it the first federal bailout package in American history.) And the Southern states didn't want any part of it—large Southern states like Virginia had already paid off their debts and didn't want to foot the bill for Massachusetts's spendthrift ways.

This led to a compromise: representatives from the North agreed to a capital site to their south. In exchange, Southern delegates agreed to the federal government assuming debts from the states. You might call it the first pork-barrel roll in American history.

The site chosen for the new capital was far from ideal. It was located along the Potomac River, and was designed to comprise an area of one hundred square miles. George Washington was granted the power to decide where the actual buildings would be placed, and so hired a surveyor. The land chosen for the Capitol was known as "Jenkins Hill." The hill was surrounded by a muddy swamp and untamed wilderness along the bank of the river. Oliver Wolcott, Jr., secretary of the treasury under Washington and John Adams, the first president to reside in D.C., said the place was "cold and damp in winter . . . built to be looked at by visitors and strangers, and will render its occupants an object of ridicule with some and pity with others." [1] Abigail Adams, the first First Lady to occupy the White House, described Georgetown as "the very dirtiest hole I ever saw." The country was "romantic but wild." And the city of Washington, D.C., was "only so in name." [2]

Since then, Washington has been built up. The first stone was laid for the Capitol in 1793 and it has been consistently restructured, restored, and updated since then. The highest point on the Capitol is capped with a statue depicting Freedom in female form; the idea is that nothing stands above Freedom. The statute faces east, symbolizing that the sun never sets on Freedom.

Underneath, though, D.C. is still a swamp. Below the statue of

Freedom dwell the Swamp Creatures of the U.S. Congress. And despite Speaker of the House Nancy Pelosi's commitment to "drain the swamp,"[3] some of the most despicable swamp dwellers are the highest-ranking members of Congress. She should know—she's one of them. And with each misstep, scandal, and lie, they gain more and more power, continually failing upward.

Let's take a look at the swamp dwellers. Only by examining them directly in the light of day will Americans come up with the guts to drain the political swamp.

SWAMP CREATURES

Just take a walk around the halls of the U.S. Congress, and you're likely to see the who's who of the Swamp Creatures. These are the folks who claim ignorance when it's convenient and brilliant foresight when it's politically expedient. These are the folks who claim they can predict trends decades down the line, but somehow never figure out when there's dirty business afoot in their own offices. These are the Swamp Creatures who undermine American security for their own personal benefit, who cover up financial scandals to rake in campaign cash, who pretend foreknowledge of disaster but somehow never speak up when they can prevent it. While the case can be made for many of the 535 Swamp Members, let's take a look at some of the more high-profile, ethically challenged, and just downright pathetic.

Senate Majority Leader "Whorehouse" Harry Reid (D-NV)

SWAMP STATUS: *Senate Swamp Leader, Possible Drainage in 2010*

First and foremost among the Swamp Creatures is Senator "Whorehouse" Harry Reid. Reid's nickname is no empty swipe—my esteemed senator has been very public about his connection to a brothel in his hometown of Searchlight, Nevada. It's not as bad as it sounds. As a boy growing up in the small mining town, little Harry Reid learned to swim at a whorehouse. Senator Reid recalls those fond childhood memories: "As a boy, I learned to swim at a whorehouse. Nobody in town had ever seen such a fancy in-ground tiled pool in their lives as the pool at the El Rey. Or any pool at all, for that matter. At least nobody that we knew. The El Rey was the main bordello when I was growing up in Searchlight. Every Thursday afternoon, the whoremonger in town, a kindly bear of a man by the name of Willie Martello, would ask the girls who worked the El Rey to clear out, and he'd invite the children in town, usually no more than a dozen or so at a time, to swim in his pool. And we would live the life of Riley for a couple of hours, splashing in the azure blue of that whorehouse pool."[4] The problem is that in the five decades since Harry's whorehouse swimming, he's moved from the pool to the cathouse—he's perfectly used to whoring himself out for the cash at this point.

You may remember one Jack Abramoff. Abramoff was a well-connected lobbyist in Washington. He spent his time wining and dining our elected representatives to ensure that his clients received favorable treatment. In 2006, Black Jack pled guilty to fraud, tax evasion, and conspiracy to bribe public officials. He originally aroused suspicion because of payments totaling $82 million that he and a partner received from Native American casino owners. Tribes who ran gaming operations spent a boatload of money on lobbyists to help them gain political backing for their casinos, and to help block rival casinos from opening. Abramoff admitted to defrauding several of these tribes out of millions, and also copped to conspiring to persuade former Capitol Hill staffers—i.e., low-level Swamp Creatures—to violate the ban on lobbying their former bosses.[5]

Prior to his indictment, Abramoff headed the Government Affairs Department of Greenberg Traurig, a Washington, D.C., law firm. His silent partner in the tribe scam was Michael Scanlon, who owned Capitol Campaign Strategies. Scanlon's firm provided grassroots political campaign support, organized letter-writing and telephone campaigns, and handled coalition building for its clients. Scanlon and Abramoff worked out a sweet deal for themselves: Abramoff would steer clients to

Scanlon's firm, and in turn, Scanlon would charge inflated fees, kicking back money to Abramoff. Abramoff called these clients "Troglodytes . . . lower form[s] of existence . . . plain stupid . . . morons." And he swindled them wholeheartedly. The Chippewa Tribe in Michigan paid over $14 million to Scanlon for various services.[6] They were charged $4.5 million for a database of Michigan voters they hoped to contact on behalf of a new casino, but they were never given the names. They could have simply bought the database from the state for $75,000.[7] Between 2001 and 2004, six different Native American tribes paid Scanlon's firm a total of $66 million; during those same years, Scanlon paid Abramoff's firms $21 million.[8] Sweet deal.

It wasn't such a sweet deal for Republicans, many of whom had taken lobbying cash from Abramoff. Abramoff bragged that he had funneled $10 million in tribal cash to Republican-minded groups. Speaker of the House Tom DeLay, Grover Norquist's Americans for Tax Reform, Ralph Reed's political consulting firm, and Rep. Bob Ney (OH) were all implicated.[9] The media jumped on Republicans with alacrity, painting the Abramoff scandal as solely a Republican one.

And it wasn't just the media capitalizing on the Abramoff scam—it was one Whorehouse Harry. On January 18, 2006, Whorehouse Harry sent out a letter to the Democratic Senatorial Campaign Committee mailing list. "I have been in public service for over 40 years and never been as disillusioned as I am today," Reid fumed. "In 1977, I was appointed chairman of the Nevada Gaming Commission. It was a difficult time for the gaming industry and Las Vegas, which were being overrun by organized crime. During the next few years, there would be threats on my life, FBI stings, and even a car bomb placed in my family's station wagon. What is happening today in Washington is every bit as corrupt as when Las Vegas was run by the mob, but the consequences for our country are worse. These Republicans have created the most corrupt government in our history. Their 'K Street Project' is a shakedown machine that would make the mafia blush. We cleaned up Las Vegas, and we will clean up Washington, D.C.

"Today, Democrats from Howard Dean . . . to Nancy Pelosi and me in Washington are declaring our commitment to a government as good and honest as the people it serves," Reid continued. "To achieve that vision, this morning we introduced the Honest Leadership and Open Government Act. Our tough, real reforms go beyond the public relations fixes Republicans suggest. For example, a key proposal in the Act, known as 'The Jack Abramoff Rule,' will ban staff and members from receiving gifts, meals and travel from lobbyists. This is not just about talking the talk; we are going to walk the walk." [10]

In actuality, Whorehouse Harry was walking the street walk. In 2005, the Associated Press revealed that Reid had accepted tens of thousands of dollars from Native American tribes who were Abramoff clients. In one case, he received $5,000 from the Coushatta Tribe after sending a letter to Secretary of the Interior Gale Norton on their behalf.

Here's the story: After seven years of running their casino, the Coushattas were having trouble getting Louisiana governor Mike Foster to renew their gambling compact. They hired Abramoff to help them get the compact renewed. After flooding the governor's office with thirty thousand letters, the Coushattas were allowed to continue with their casino. Governor Foster, however, didn't shut down the competition—he awarded a new compact to a rival tribe, the Jena Band of Choctaw Indians. Abramoff called in the big guns to fight his client's rivals, mounting a letter-writing campaign and getting numerous congressmen and state and federal officials to petition on his client's behalf. Reid and the junior senator from Nevada, John Ensign, both signed the letter to Norton urging her to reject the Jena Band Compact, claiming it was invalid. The day after the letter was sent to Norton, the Coushatta Tribe sent a check for $5,000 to Reid's PAC, the Searchlight Leadership Fund. That's some high-falutin morality for you.

Reid wasn't the only one. Many other members of Congress intervened on behalf of Abramoff and the Coushattas, and they all received "donations" within days of their letters. Most of these legislators have no constituents in Louisiana and no clear interest in the matter. They claimed at the time that they petitioned the secretary of the interior to block the new casino because they opposed the expansion of tribal casinos. None of the legislators, however, felt strongly enough about the expansion of tribal gambling to reject tribal dollars. The Associated Press uncovered thirty-three lawmakers who wrote letters to block the rival tribe from opening a casino near Abramoff's client—and those lawmakers raked in over $830,000 in donations.

Whorehouse Harry's Indian Adventure didn't end with the Coushattas. He intervened on behalf of Abramoff's clients in multiple states . . . none of which were in Nevada! While he was Senate majority whip from 1999 to 2000, he sponsored a bill that would have blocked a Native American tribe in Northern California from opening a casino near Oakland. He claimed that the casino would have posed substantial competition to casinos in Nevada. A more likely explanation: one of Jack Abramoff's clients was the California Agua Caliente Band of Cahuilla Indians. In return for the attempt to block the new casino, the Agua Caliente Tribe made a $7,500 "donation" to the Searchlight Leadership Fund, followed by another of $2,000.

In 2002, Reid did it again, blocking a proposal for a casino in Michigan that would have directly competed with Abramoff's client, the Saginaw, Michigan, Chippewa Tribe. Federal Election Commission records show that Whorehouse Harry received $14,000 in "donations" from the Saginaw Chippewas.

In total, Reid received nearly $68,000 in donations from Abramoff's firm, lobbying partners, and clients. His staffers had regular contact with Abramoff's team about legislation. Reid's office admitted having "routine contacts" with Abramoff's lobbying partners and intervening in government matters.[11] Reid's office denied, however, that there was any connection between Reid's letters and the political payoffs from Abramoff's clients. "There is absolutely no connection," blustered Reid spokesman Jim Manley. "The only connection was Senator Reid has consistently opposed any effort to undermine the Indian Gaming Regulatory Act."[12] Reid claims he "never met the man." It was later uncovered in Abramoff's firm's billing records that his lobbying partners had face-to-face or phone contact with Reid's office over two dozen times in 2001 alone.[13]

On April 17, 2006, with the assistance of Judicial Watch, I sent a formal complaint regarding Harry Reid's Abramoff corruption. My letter to the Senate Ethics Committee detailed Reid's numerous efforts to support Abramoff-related tribes or thwart their competition. Even though Whorehouse Harry was obviously paid to use his influence to benefit Abramoff's clients, he was never accused of violating Senate ethics rules. He also happened to be the chairman of the Senate Ethics Committee from 2001 to 2003. What a coincidence.

The only response I got to my letter was the signature on the FedEx tracking receipt.

Senator Chris "Countrywide" Dodd (D-CT)

SWAMP STATUS: *Possible Swamp Refinancing in 2010*

Perhaps the worst Swamp Creature of all is Senator Chris "Countrywide" Dodd. If medals were handed out for causing the current economic crisis, Dodd would bring home the gold. Not coincidentally, he *does* bring home gold from various financial institutions seeking to pay him off. Also not coincidentally, Dodd chairs the Senate Banking Committee.

Let's start with Countrywide. Countrywide, which has now become a subsidiary of Bank of America, made its fortune on risky subprime loans and political payoffs. When Bank of America announced its intention to buy Countrywide in January 2008, Countrywide had just reported a shocking $1.2 billion third-quarter 2007 loss.[14] In June 2009, the Securities and Exchange Commission announced that it would accuse Countrywide CEO Angelo Mozilo of fraud for withholding information from investors about the mortgage lender's financial situation and selling shares based on inside information.[15]

Countrywide was shielded from investigation for years by one Christopher Dodd. Countrywide's ethics code bars anyone at the company from "improperly influencing the decisions of government employees or contractors by offering or promising to give money, gifts, loans, rewards, favors, or anything else of value." That didn't stop Countrywide from enrolling Dodd in its so-called V.I.P. Program, in which Dodd received an insanely preferential mortgage. In 2003, Dodd borrowed $506,000 to refinance his Washington, D.C., townhome; he received another $275,042 to refinance his home in Connecticut. The interest rates were reduced from 4.875 percent on the Washington house to 4.25 percent; the interest rates on the Connecticut property were reduced to 4.5 percent. The lower rates saved Dodd $58,000 on his Washington home and $17,000 on the Connecticut home. Dodd paid nothing for the refinancing. Countrywide also has contributed $21,000 to Dodd since 1997.

Other legislators and regulators were also part of the Countrywide V.I.P. Program, including James Johnson, former Obama advisor; former Secretary of Housing and Urban Development Alphonso Jackson; former Secretary of Health and Human Services Donna Shalala; and former U.N. ambassador and Assistant Secretary of State Richard Holbrooke. These lucky few were known at Countrywide as F.O.A.: Friends of Angelo. "These loans are incredibly important to Angelo," wrote one Countrywide manager regarding a Holbrooke-related loan, "and as such they are incredibly important to us." [16]

Dodd stepped up on behalf of Countrywide in a major way. Countrywide was the single biggest customer of Fannie Mae; Countrywide sold its risky loans to Fannie, even as Mozilo pushed riskier and riskier loans. According to the *Wall Street Journal*, "Mr. Dodd in turn supported this goal by pressing Fannie to do more for 'affordable' housing." [17]

This brings us to Dodd's relationship with Fannie Mae and Freddie Mac. While the Bush administration was attempting to tighten regulations on Fannie Mae and Freddie Mac, Dodd and his cronies were out to weaken regulations. In February 2004, the Bush administration's 2005 budget was published. It stated that Fannie and Freddie were "highly leveraged, holding much less capital in relation to their assets than similarly sized financial institutions. . . . A misjudgment or unexpected economic event could quickly deplete this capital, potentially making it difficult for a [government-sponsored enterprise] to meet its debt obligations. Given the very large size of each enterprise, even a small mistake by a GSE could have consequences throughout the economy." [18] Dodd's response: do nothing. As late as July 13, 2008, Dodd was claiming, "To suggest somehow that [Fannie and Freddie] are in trouble is simply not accurate. . . . The facts are that Fannie and Freddie are in sound situations. They have more than adequate capital, in fact more than the law requires." [19] Since Dodd was in charge of the Senate Banking Committee, he presumably could have helped rewrite those laws.

Over the course of his political career, Dodd has taken $165,000 from Fannie Mae and Freddie Mac. [20] And yet Dodd questions the *Bush administration* for its failures on Fannie Mae and Freddie Mac: "I have a lot of questions about where was the administration over the last eight years." [21] He absolves the CEOs and blames everybody but himself: "The problems of Fannie and Freddie weren't created by these two CEOs, they go back a long time. . . . Where were the regulators? Why weren't people stepping up? How did this housing problem expand into the broader economic problems we're seeing today?" [22] Well, Chris, why don't you give us some answers?

Dodd's biggest concern in the aftermath of Fannie's and Freddie's nationalization? Perpetuating the same bad loans that got us into this mess. "We need to know whether or not this plan is going to maintain the role of the GSEs in providing affordable mortgages to Americans," he said. [23] And so the cycle continues.

Neither Dodd's involvement with Countrywide nor his corrupt relationship with Fannie and Freddie compares to his unbelievably reptilian record with regard to American International Group, AIG. In March 2009, the press realized that employees and executives of the bailed-out AIG were slated to receive bonuses—$165 million, to be precise. Those bonuses came on the heels of a $170 billion taxpayer bailout. The press went bananas. And so the Obama administration and Congress decided that employees of the bailed-out AIG could not, under any circumstances, receive bonuses. "How do they justify this outrage to the taxpayers who are keeping the company afloat?" asked President Obama incredulously. "I warned them this would be met with an unprecedented level of outrage," said Dodd.[24]

The Swamp Creatures did protest too much. As it turned out, Dodd had written the amendment to the original stimulus bill allowing AIG to pay bonuses to employees with retention contracts. This did not stop Dodd from protesting his innocence: "if I knew [the purpose of the changes] was to protect bonuses . . . I would have flatly rejected it."[25] This begs the question: did Dodd read the Dodd amendment? How could he let a $787 billion spending bill with his name on it pass through the House and Senate without fully understanding what was in it?

Dodd later admitted that he did in fact know about and understand the language permitting the AIG bonuses. In fact, he admitted far more: that the Obama administration—the same administration so outraged at excessive bonuses at AIG—had asked Dodd to put the language in the bill to protect the contractual agreements AIG made with its employees. Officials in the administration realized they could face numerous lawsuits if they tried to break the existing contracts.[26]

Dodd, it should be mentioned, is the leading recipient of AIG employee cash since 1989—he's raked in over $281,000.[27] Most of the bonus money was paid out to the AIG Financial Products Division, which happens to be based in Dodd's home state of Connecticut. Perhaps Dodd thought he could slip the amendment through without anyone but his constituents noticing. When somebody did notice, he tried to hide it, lie about it, and cover it up. In addition, he vilified the AIG employees who were begging to stay at the company to try and salvage or sell off what little was left, and who were promised retention bonuses if they stayed. Several executives were asked to take a salary of $1 per year, with the understanding that their retention bonuses would be honored.

In the end, Dodd's fellow Democrats tried to push through a bill that would tax any bonus over $100,000 to any AIG executive at a 100 percent rate; they also passed a bill that would tax any bonus to a person making $250,000 per year at a 90 percent rate if their company received more than $5 billion in TARP funds. Senator Chuck Schumer railed against AIG: "If [AIG CEO Edward] Liddy does nothing, we will act and will take this money back and return it to its rightful owners, the American taxpayers. We will take this money back by taxing virtually all of it." [28]

The bill was killed in the Senate, which saved the courts the trouble of striking it down—the bill would have violated the "Bill of Attainder" and "ex post facto" clauses of the Constitution, which protect people from being punished without trial and stop Congress from retroactively changing the legal consequences of a law. [29]

It was a pathetic situation. But then again, Dodd and his fellow Swamp Creatures are pathetic excuses for legislators. They vote for bills, and then react with outrage when those bills are implemented. They take kickbacks from companies, and then feign shock when those companies cheat, lie, and steal.

Speaker of the House Nancy "For the Children" Pelosi (D-CA)
SWAMP STATUS: *Swamp Den Mother, Entrenched Creature*

Reid's House counterpart, Swamp Creature Speaker of the House Nancy "For the Children" Pelosi, is just as dirty. She lies more than a Persian rug—and, come to think of it, she's about as thick as a Persian rug, too.

In May 2009, Pelosi made her most egregious claim: she falsely claimed she had been lied to by the Central Intelligence Agency.

It all began with a bit of political opportunism. On April 22, 2009, looking for a chance to rip President Bush's authorization of enhanced interrogation techniques for terrorist detainees, Pelosi called for a "truth commission." That "truth commission" would determine who had authorized and who had carried out the dastardly deeds (i.e., waterboarding) that kept Americans safe for eight long years. "It might be further useful to have such a commission so that it removes all doubt that how we protect the American people is in a values-based way," Pelosi preached. Immunity for witnesses, she noted, would not be granted "in a blanket way." Which meant that prosecutions for everyone involved would be on the table.[30]

There was only one problem with this: Pelosi herself had been briefed repeatedly about the CIA's use of enhanced interrogation techniques. On September 4, 2002, Porter Goss, at the time chairman of the House Permanent Select Committee on Intelligence, and Pelosi were briefed by the CIA on enhanced interrogation techniques. The CIA's briefing included specific information on the use of such techniques with regard to Abu Zubaydah, an al Qaeda operative captured in Pakistan.

Pelosi's answer: she was lied to by the CIA. "We were not—I repeat—were not told that waterboarding or any of these other enhanced interrogation methods were used," she said. "What they did tell us is that they had . . . the Office of Legal Counsel opinions [and] that they could be used, but not that they would." Goss disagreed with Pelosi, explaining, "we were briefed, and we certainly understood what the CIA was doing . . . not only was there no objection, there was actually concern about whether the agency was doing enough." Pelosi's explanation doesn't square with the CIA's notes regarding the briefing: "Briefing on EITs including use of EITs on Abu Zubaydah, background on authorities, and a description of the particular EITs that *had been employed.*" The CIA briefing wasn't focused on legal opinions about the future use of techniques. The briefing concerned techniques that had *already* been used.[31]

That wasn't the only briefing. In fact, the CIA compiled no fewer than *forty* CIA briefings to Congress on enhanced interrogation techniques.[32] A Justice Department memo from 2005 stated that "The CIA used the waterboard 'at least 83 times during August 2002' in the interrogation of Zubaydah"—one month before the Pelosi-Goss hearing on Zubaydah and waterboarding.[33] Even Leon Panetta, Democratic hack and new head of the CIA, denied Pelosi's allegations, stating that she had been told nothing but the truth.[34]

But Pelosi still wouldn't admit her lie. She stuck to it like a terrier gnawing on a raw steak. "The only mention of waterboarding at that briefing was that it was not being employed," she maintained. "Those briefings gave me inaccurate and incomplete information. . . . At the same time, the Bush administration was misleading the American people about the threat of weapons of mass destruction in Iraq." The briefers, she repeated, had lied to her.[35] "They mislead us all the time," she blurted.[36] Pelosi apparently had no such qualms about the CIA's intelligence when she stated on December 16, 1998, "As a member of the House Intelligence Committee, I am keenly aware that the proliferation of chemical and biological weapons is an issue of grave importance to all nations. Saddam Hussein has been engaged in the development of weapons of mass destruction technology which is a threat to countries in the region and he has made a mockery of the weapons inspection process."[37]

Of course, Pelosi had no evidence of these purported lies by the CIA; when asked to provide proof of her allegations, she ran from the press. "I have made the statement that I'm going to make on this," Pelosi told reporters. "What we are doing is staying on our course and not getting distracted from it."[38] To avoid becoming distracted by the burgeoning CIA scandal, Pelosi promptly ran off to China, where she kowtowed to the Chinese communist dictators by calling for unity on global warming—and, more specifically, calling on Americans to restrict their lives: "Every aspect of our lives must be subjected to an inventory . . . of how we are taking responsibility."[39] She did not mention her own responsibility not to slander members of the CIA.

Former Senator Hillary "I Lied, People Died" Clinton

SWAMP STATUS: *Cabinet Swamp Consolation Prize Winner*

The lies told by Senator Hillary Clinton fill books. Reams of them. Clinton is almost wholly responsible for the dearth of trees in the Amazon rainforest—they've all been pulped to print the books refuting her lies. So we'll just focus on her biggest, boldest lie: the blatant falsehood that President Bush purposely lied about weapons of mass destruction in order to sucker Congress into approving military action in Iraq.

On October 10, 2002, Senator Hillary Clinton made the case for the invasion of Iraq. "In the four years since the inspectors left," she said, "intelligence reports show that Saddam Hussein has worked to rebuild his chemical and biological weapons stock, his missile delivery capability, and his nuclear program. He has also given aid, comfort, and sanctuary to terrorists, including Al Qaeda members, though there is apparently no evidence of his involvement in the terrible events of September 11, 2001. It is clear, however, that if left unchecked, Saddam Hussein will continue to increase his capacity to wage biological and chemical warfare, and will keep trying to develop nuclear weapons. Should he succeed in that endeavor, he could alter the political and security landscape of the Middle East, which as we know all too well affects American security."

Clinton wasn't the only one acknowledging Hussein's pursuit of WMDs. President Clinton, too, felt that Hussein had WMDs: "One way or the other," he said on February 4, 1998, "we are determined to deny Iraq the capacity to develop weapons of mass destruction and the missiles to deliver them. That is our bottom line." [40] President Clinton's secretary of defense, William Cohen, stated in April 2003, "I am absolutely convinced that there are weapons. . . . I saw evidence back in 1998 when we would see the inspectors being barred from gaining entry into a warehouse for three hours with trucks rolling up and then moving those trucks out." [41] President Clinton's National Security Advisor Sandy "Documents Down My Pants" Berger agreed: "He will rebuild his arsenal of weapons of mass destruction and some day, some way, I am certain he will use that arsenal again, as he has ten times since 1983." [42] And President Clinton's secretary of state stated: "He has chosen to spend his money on building weapons of mass destruction, and palaces for his cronies." [43]

Now Hillary has changed her tune. Now, Bush and Cheney "lied" to her. Not her husband. Not her husband's national security advisor. Not her husband's secretary of state. And she *certainly* didn't lie. It was the Bush administration.

And so on April 22, 2009, Clinton ripped into former Vice President

Dick Cheney: "It won't surprise you that I don't consider him a particularly reliable source of information," she told the House Foreign Affairs Committee.[44] During her presidential campaign, she retracted her vote for the Iraq war resolution: "Obviously, if we knew then what we know now, there wouldn't have been a vote," she said, "and I certainly wouldn't have voted that way."[45]

It's easy to make decisions based on hindsight. Swamp Creatures are long on hindsight and short on courage of conviction. And Hillary is a Charter Swamp Creature.

Rep. Barney "Pimp My Apartment" Frank (D-MA)

SWAMP STATUS: *Slithers on Both Sides of the Swamp*

Rep. Barney "Pimp My Apartment" Frank is one of the most repulsive members of Congress. In 1989, he admitted that his gay lover, Stephen L. Gobie, was running a gay prostitution ring out of Frank's Capitol Hill apartment. Said Gobie, "He knew exactly what I was doing. It was pretty obvious. . . . He was living vicariously through me. He said it was kind of a thrill, and if he had been 20 years younger he might be doing the same thing." Frank admitted that he had paid Gobie $80 for sex—a cheap date. He admitted that he had met Gobie through an ad in the *Washington Blade*, the local gay weekly; the ad read, "Exceptionally good-looking, personable, muscular athlete is available. Hot bottom plus large endowment equals a good time." And Frank portrayed himself as *Pygmalion*'s Henry Higgins to Gobie's Eliza Doolittle.[46]

Frank's gay old time in D.C. was just beginning. In July 1998, a column in the *Washington Post* indicated that Frank had a new lover: Herb Moses, an executive for Fannie Mae. Frank was apparently referring to Moses as his "spouse." Another report stated that Frank referred to Moses as his "lover." The relationship lasted approximately ten years. For all ten years, Frank served on the House Banking Committee. Moses headed up Fannie Mae's affordable housing and home improvement lending programs—the same subprime programs that brought down the GSE. Frank's bias was clearly in evidence: he repeatedly defended Fannie Mae and Freddie Mac. In 2003, he told the *Washington Post* that he wouldn't stand for any restrictions on Fannie Mae that "would sacrifice activities that are good for consumers in the name of lowering the companies' market risks." "These two entities—Fannie Mae and Freddie Mac—are not facing any kind of financial crisis," he said. "The more people exaggerate these problems, the more pressure there is on these companies, the less we will see in terms of affordable housing." Frank has received over $40,000 from Fannie Mae and Freddie Mac over the past twenty years.[47]

Now, Frank gleefully blames the Republicans for the financial meltdown: "The Republicans—their own philosophy blew up in their face. They were so extreme in their insistence that there be no government intervention that they have wound up provoking far more government intervention than the Democrats ever would have. . . . I don't think anybody really thought that this subprime thing would reverberate as much as it did."[48]

And here's the funniest part: Frank is still trying to loosen restrictions on Fannie Mae and Freddie Mac to allow them to make *more* bad loans, even in the aftermath of the subprime meltdown. Although Frank tried to "roll the dice"—his phrase—on bad loans once, he wants to do it again, this time by allowing Fannie and Freddie to give low-interest loans on condos, properties with an extreme likelihood of falling into default. Frank is unconcerned with the ramifications—after all, he says, Fannie and Freddie are only going to sell the loans to the Federal Housing Administration (FHA), which already gives away cheap condo loans: "While the underlying goal may be to reduce taxpayer exposure relating to the current conservatorship of the GSEs, such a goal would not have an effect if it merely results in a shifting of loans from the GSEs to the FHA."[49] Hey, if we're going to screw the taxpayer, why not do it with alacrity?

There are lots of snakes in the Swamp. Frank is a feather-boa constrictor.

Former Senator Ted "Bridge to Nowhere" Stevens (R-AK)

SWAMP STATUS: *Drained!*

It isn't all Democrats. Republican Senator Ted Stevens is another Swamp Creature. He gobbled up government cash like it was going out of style, siphoning it to his buddies—and then he invested with his buddies, increasing his income. In 2003, the *Los Angeles Times* reported that "in 1997, he got serious about making money . . . in almost no time; he too was a millionaire—thanks to investments with businessmen who received government contracts or other benefits with his help." [50]

One of those schemes involved preserving a $450 million military housing contract for a friend. That friend turned around and made Stevens a partner in several real estate investments that netted him $750,000 from an initial investment of $50,000. Another scheme involved an Alaskan company to which Stevens directed defense contracts. The company repaid Stevens by leasing an office building for $6 million per year. Stevens owned the office building. "I am a passive investor," Stevens claimed. "I am not now nor have I ever been involved in buying or selling properties, negotiating leases, or making other management decisions." [51] Right. And Michael Corleone was registered with the Better Business Bureau.

The excrement truly hit the fan for Stevens when he was indicted in July 2008 on charges that he took illegal gifts. The indictment stated that Stevens "schemed to conceal" over $250,000 in gifts from Veco, an Alaska-based energy company he helped in Congress. Veco's CEO Bill Allen, for example, swapped a new 1999 Land Rover worth $44,000 for Stevens's 1964 Ford Mustang plus $5,000—a total loss for Allen of about $20,000. In exchange, said the indictment, Stevens used "his official position and his office on behalf of Veco." [52] Veco also did $250,000 worth of work on his house, turning Stevens's mountain cabin into a "modern, two-story home with wraparound porches, a sauna and a wine cellar." On October 27, 2008, Stevens was convicted on all counts. [53] In April 2009, Stevens's conviction was overturned on appeal—the prosecutors made several crucial errors in his trial. [54] At least that was the cover story. Protect one corrupt former senator to protect the status quo of current corruption might be the real story.

Stevens lost his seat in the Senate over the trial. But in all likelihood, he'll be back. After all, it's tough to keep a Swamp Creature out of his natural habitat in Washington, D.C.

Rep. Shelley "The Neck" Berkley (D-NV)

SWAMP STATUS: *Swamp Narcissist*

I'm not proud to say that this little-known congresswoman from Las Vegas, Nevada, my hometown, is my Swamp Creature. While there are many reasons to drain her from the swamp, the most glaring one is how she got her nickname "The Neck."

On September 8, 2005, Shelley Berkley skipped the vote to authorize $51.8 billion in emergency funding for Hurricane Katrina relief and recovery. For those of you who may have forgotten the details of the Hurricane and its aftermath, here's a brief look back.

Hurricane Katrina made landfall on Monday, August 29, 2005, as a Category 3 storm with sustained winds of 125 mph. The wind and rain overwhelmed the levee systems in and around New Orleans and for the most part the entire city and surrounding regions flooded. The estimated economic damage was $89.5 billion. Within days the human toll was obvious. The final numbers were a tragedy.

There were 1,836 deaths mostly in Louisiana and Mississippi, 1,577 in Louisiana, 238 in Mississippi. Twenty-six thousand people struggled to survive in the New Orleans Superdome. Twenty-three hundred people missing, mostly from New Orleans, mostly black. Three million people without electricity. Seven hundred thousand families and individuals without housing. To this day the aftereffects of Hurricane Katrina and follow-on Rita can still be seen.

So what was so important, so pressing in nature that Shelley Berkley missed this important House vote? She was having cosmetic surgery on her neck!

Despite Congress's five-week summer recess, recess being a fitting term for a class of kindergartners, this narcissist decided to have a neck lift at the end of the five weeks, not the beginning. She must have had other pressing matters to attend to before she got around to her neck. According to her, she didn't like the way her neck looked whenever she saw it in photographs. She said it was distracting. After the surgery there was some discoloration and swelling. Berkley said that those weren't her true colors. Her true colors, she said, were red, white, and blue. She went on to say the surgery was worth it and she loves her new neck and they didn't need her vote anyway since the bill passed in the House 410–11.

On September 2, 2005, there was a benefit concert on NBC called "A Concert for Hurricane Relief." There was the usual blame hurled at President Bush, Michael Brown, Michael Chertoff, Homeland Security, the National Guard, and of course those cold and heartless Republicans. While I don't hold any of them blameless, there was plenty of blame to go around.

At one point in the concert actor Mike Myers and rapper Kanye West went onstage. After their preplanned verbal exchange took place Kanye West went off script and said the following: "George Bush doesn't care about black people." If that's true, then the same can be said about Democrat Shelley "The Neck" Berkley.

Drain her![55]

HOW DEEP IS THE SWAMP?

It isn't just a few isolated Congressional Creatures who currently inhabit the swamp. It's hundreds of members from across the country. Just look at the elected officials who got nailed by ABSCAM, a sting operation set up by the FBI from 1978 to 1980.

The operation was designed in coordination with a con man named Mel Weinberg, who made his career by bilking idiots seeking to get rich quick. Weinberg and the FBI set up "Abdul Enterprises, Ltd." in 1978. That's just way too funny. Abdul Enterprises. How about Scam, Inc.?

FBI employees staffed the fake company, and Weinberg led it. The company told marks that the company's fictitious backer, Kambir Abdul Rahman, wanted to (a) buy asylum in the United States; (b) get a return on his invested cash, which was forbidden under Islamic laws barring usury; or (c) get his money out of Saudi Arabia. All of these activities involved bribes.[56]

Weinberg eventually got in touch with or was connected to dozens of federal and state officials; names that came up in the investigation included House Majority Leader Jimmy Wright (D-TX), Majority Whip John Brademas (D-IN), House Speaker Tip O'Neill (D-MA), Senator Ted Kennedy (D-MA), Congressman Jim Howard (D-NJ), Rep. William Hughes (D-NJ), Rep. Frank Guarini (D-NJ), Rep. James Mattox (D-TX), Rep. John Murphy (D-NY), Rep. John Murtha (D-PA), Rep. Frank Thompson, Jr. (D-NJ), Senator Strom Thurmond (R-SC), Rep. John Jenrette, Jr. (D-SC), Senator Harrison Williams (D-NJ), Rep. Richard Kelly (R-FL), Rep. Raymond Lederer (D-PA), Rep. Michael Myers (D-PA), Rep. Edwin Patten (D-NJ), Senator Larry Pressler (R-SD), and Rep. James Florio (D-NJ).[57]

When ABSCAM was revealed, those in Congress reacted predictably—they excoriated the FBI rather than the corrupt representatives. "It was a setup, a goddamn setup," said Speaker O'Neill. "I deplore the fact that the rights of those being investigated have not been protected; and I deplore the rush to condemn, to joke and be cynical," averred Senator Bill Bradley (D-NJ). Congressman John Seiberling of Ohio objected to "the idea of giving some people of dubious moral standards free rein to entice anyone they can entice to commit a crime." The *Washington Post*, that ethical standard-bearer, editorialized against ABSCAM, stating, "No citizen, member of Congress or not, should be required to prove his integrity by resisting temptation."[58]

This was a pathetic response to a well-designed sting operation. No elected official was forced to get in a room with the scam artists, nor was anyone forced to take cash. All they had to do was stay away. And they couldn't.

Murtha testified against Thompson and Murphy and was not prosecuted.[59] He's still sitting in the House of Representatives, and it's been said he's just as corrupt now as he was then. When he's not busy accusing U.S. Marines of cold-blooded murder in Iraq,[60] he's busy grabbing federal cash for his district. According to the *Pittsburgh Post-Gazette*, Murtha has directed billions of dollars to his constituents. "If I'm corrupt," says Murtha, "it's because I take care of my district. My job as a member of Congress is to make sure that we take care of what we see is necessary. Not the bureaucrats who are unelected over there in whatever White House, whether it's Republican or Democrat. Those bureaucrats would like to control everything. Every president would like to have all the power and not have Congress change anything. But we're closest to the people." Federal agents have repeatedly raided beneficiaries of Murtha's generosity, suspecting out-and-out corruption. And those beneficiaries have repeatedly given to Murtha's reelection coffers.[61]

Murtha is the model congressman: the self-serving bureaucrat who directs others' money to his buddies in return for political benefit. Whether it's open bribery, as in ABSCAM, or whether it's the implicit pay-for-play promise of donations for influence, our elected officials are far too comfortable in the moral swamp.

Just look at the numbers. Lawyers and law firms, for example, spent $236 million in donations during the 2008 election cycle. Barack Obama received over $44.4 million; Hillary Clinton clocked in second with $16.5 million. Among nonpresidential candidates, the chief recipients were Senator Mark Warner (D-VA), who picked up $1.3 million; Senator Dick Durbin (D-IL), who grabbed $1.3 million; Senator Chris "It Wasn't Me" Dodd (D-CT), $1.3 million; Senator Mary Landrieu (D-LA), $1.0 million; Georgia senatorial candidate James Martin (D), $1.0 million; Rep. Mark Udall (D-CO), $1.0 million; Senator Al Franken (D-MN), $1.0 million.[62] Notice anything? All the cash goes to Democrats. That's because Democrats are most likely to push back against rules regulating class actions and barring medical malpractice suits.

The same holds true for educators, where the only Republican in the top ten recipients of cash is Rep. Ron Paul (Kook-TX). Teachers and teachers unions are interested only in who will give them their federal payoff.[63]

Here's something truly egregious: hedge fund donors' top three recipients were Barack Obama ($1.3 million), Hillary Clinton ($723,350), and Senator Chris "It Wasn't Me" Dodd ($707,750). Dodd clocked in above presidential candidate John McCain.[64] No surprise, since Dodd was going to control the bailout system. The top nonpresidential recipients outside of Dodd: Senator Mark Warner (D-VA) and Rep. Rahm Emanuel (D-IL). Why Emanuel? Everyone recognized that he was going to join the Obama administration and influence bailout policy.

Payoffs are the only way to survive in the swamp. And both donors and candidates know it.

STUPID SWAMP TRICKS

So Congress is corrupt, you say. Fine. At least they get things done. That's true. They do get important things done. Let's review some of Congress's heavy lifting.

Like declaring National Watermelon Month. On April 29, 2008, the House considered whether to establish a "National Watermelon Month." The same day, the House decided whether to declare a "National Funeral Director and Mortician Recognition Day."[65]

Here are some other useful congressional acts this term:

- On March 23, 2009, the House considered whether to express support for designating March as "National Nutrition Month." The purpose: to encourage "local communities to raise awareness surrounding nutritional health."[66] Thank God for Congress. Without them, we'd surely try to eat the drywall in our homes. Hopefully, it's not the Great Drywall of China, another toxic product courtesy of our friends, the communist Chinese.
- On March 17, 2009, the House introduced, but did not support, a resolution designating September as "National Atrial Fibrillation

Awareness Month."[67] Good thing Congress rejected that one. We wouldn't want to mislabel a month.

- On March 18, 2009, the House introduced a resolution designating September as "National Brain Aneurysm Awareness Month."[68] September is going to be a real upper.

- Reminding us all that we should not stab ourselves in the eye with a fork, Congress considered on May 19, 2009, whether to create a "National Safety Month."[69]

- Congress decided whether to declare May "National Link Awareness Month." Congress sent it to committee to die.[70] Fans of *The Legend of Zelda* are still crying.

- In case you don't wear a facemask while playing football, Congress is considering whether there should be a "National Facial Protection Month." Seriously. Congress is particularly concerned that "5,000,000 teeth are knocked out each year during sports activities."[71] Where do they get these statistics? How many of these teeth are baby teeth? The voting public suffers sleepless nights waiting for the answers.

- On March 26, 2009, the Senate considered whether April 18, 2009, should be "National Auctioneers Day."[72] Shockingly, the bill passed, despite the fact that no one understands what the hell auctioneers are saying, which makes their arguments unconvincing.

- In case you missed it, April 23, 2009, was "National Adopt a Library Day."[73] Unfortunately, this declaration did not solve the problem of library orphanage.

- Congress declared on May 12, 2009, that it liked mothers: "Resolved, That the House of Representatives celebrates the role of mothers in the United States and supports the goals and ideals of Mother's Day."[74] A bold position taken by our esteemed members of Congress.

- Congress is also worried that we'll forget about our children. So they've decided to make us aware of them through "National Child Awareness Month."[75] Now try to ignore little Billy.

I could literally list dozens of these. As of June 7, 2009, there were fifty-six bills containing the words "national" and "month" in close proximity. There were another fifty-two bills containing the words "national" and "day" in close proximity. Dozens of other bills concern similar topics. And *that's just this session*. These are our tax dollars at work. Can we declare "National Disband Congress Month" yet?

PROTECTING THE GUILTY

Congress is filled with sleazeballs and scumbags.

(I know. Not your sleazeball. How is it that Congress has a single-digit approval rate but a 90-percent-plus reelection rate?)

Unfortunately, Congress is also tasked with policing itself. This is somewhat like allowing Lindsay Lohan to act as her own Alcoholics Anonymous sponsor.

The House's chief agency for punishing the corrupt is the vaunted Committee on Standards of Official Conduct, more colloquially known as the Ethics Committee. The job of the Ethics Committee: to recommend administrative actions to establish or enforce standards of official conduct; investigate alleged violations of the Code of Official Conduct or any other rules or regulations; report evidence of violations to federal or state authorities; render advisory opinions regarding conduct; and consider requests for waivers of the gift rule.[76] The Ethics Committee is always split 50/50 between Republicans and Democrats to prevent partisan hit jobs. That also means that the Ethics Committee is the home of the "you scratch my back, I'll scratch yours" mentality that pervades Congress.

In the past, the Ethics Committee has demonstrated its utter uselessness time and again:

- On Monday, May 22, 2006, FBI agents raided the Capitol Hill offices of Rep. William Jefferson (D-LA). Jefferson was being investigated for bribery charges; the FBI searched Jefferson's home in August 2005 and found $90,000 in cash in his freezer.[77] The House Ethics Committee did not recommend impeachment; instead, it was left to the voters to throw Jefferson out during the 2008 election.

- Rep. Charles Rangel has faced several House Ethics investigations. In June 2009, the Ethics Committee began investigating Rangel, along with Reps. Donald Payne (D-NJ) and Carolyn Kilpatrick (D-MI) for attending a conference sponsored by groups including Pfizer, Citigroup, and Macy's. Payne and Kilpatrick actually thanked the corporate sponsors. Others who attended included Rep. Sheila Jackson-Lee (D-TX), and Rep. Bennie Thompson (D-MS). The panel was already investigating charges that Rangel used congressional stationery to solicit donations from companies he had power to regulate, as well as tax evasion charges.[78] Said Rangel: "What I did or did not do is being investigated by a committee, by me."[79] That's some serious oversight there. So far, nothing has actually happened to Rangel.

- Rep. Mark Foley (R-FL) sent sexually explicit e-mails and pictures of himself for a decade to underage congressional pages—building a farm team for when they came of age, in all likelihood. The House Ethics Committee did virtually nothing. Foley resigned. Only then did the House Ethics Committee begin investigating just why nothing had been done to stop Foley for ten years.[80]

- Rep. John Murtha has never been investigated by the Ethics Committee. After the ABSCAM sting, Tip O'Neill quietly arranged for the House Ethics Committee to drop all investigations related to Murtha.[81]

- Rep. Gerry Studds (D-MA) had sex with a congressional page. The House Ethics Committee investigated him, and he was censured. He went on to be reelected six more times. All of which demonstrates the weight of a House Ethics Committee investigation and the stupidity of the voters.

- Rep. Nancy Pelosi (D-CA) lied about the CIA, as described above. No investigation has been initiated.

Here's how much of a sham the Ethics Committee is: when Rep. Tom DeLay (R-TX) was investigated by the House Ethics Committee regarding certain political donations, DeLay simply deposed the Republican head of the Ethics Committee, Rep. Joel Hefley (R-CO). In his place, the Republican leadership implanted Rep. Doc Hastings (R-WA), a favorite of then-Speaker Denny Hastert (R-IL). The Republicans also added Rep. Lamar Smith (R-TX) and Rep. Tom Cole (R-OK), both of whom had contributed money to DeLay's legal defense fund. Said Hefley, "[there is] a bad perception out there that there was a purge in the committee and that people were put in that would protect our side of the aisle better than I did. Nobody should be there to protect anybody. They should be there to protect the integrity of the institution." [82] That's a laugh. Democrats routinely do the same thing.

The Ethics Committee isn't the only way Congress Creatures protect themselves and each other. They also do it by delegating lawmaking power to the executive branch, then creating immunity for executive officials.

Here's how it works. Members of Congress decide they don't want to be held responsible for legislative acts. Instead, they allow executive officials to exercise enormous amounts of power unchecked by Congress. And they create prosecutorial immunity, so that those officials can't be charged for their malfeasance.

The best example: Bush's Treasury Secretary Henry "Shifty" Paulson. When it came to the economic crisis, Congress didn't want to be held responsible for either bailing out companies or refusing to bail them out. So they simply granted the authority to handle bailouts to Good Ol' Shifty. Under the originally proposed Section 8 of the Emergency Economic Stabilization Act of 2008, Paulson was granted unlimited authority: "Decisions by the Secretary pursuant to the authority of this Act are non-reviewable and committed to agency discretion, and may not be reviewed by any court of law or any administrative agency." [83] Talk about sweeping powers! Paulson didn't get quite that much. But he still got to spend TARP money at his total discretion, barred only by court actions for injunctive relief.

Congressmen love these tricks. They pass bills they didn't write. They pass bills they haven't read. They pass bills that abdicate all authority.

In February 2009, Democrats were so eager to ram through President Obama's $787 billion "stimulus" package that they didn't bother to allow members the luxury of actually reading the bill before voting on it. The Democrats released the text of the 1,000-plus-page bill at 10 P.M. the night before a 9 A.M. vote.[84] The bill passed 246–183.[85] For all the congressmen knew, they had just legislated an elongated version of *The Cat in the Hat*. But that didn't matter. There's no accountability. The only people the Swamp Creatures are accountable to are the voters. And the voters are doing nothing to stop them.

HOW TO DRAIN THE SWAMP

Congress is in the business of vote buying. They spend our tax money on their constituents, bribing them for their support. They help particular groups in order to cash those groups' checks. They constitute a Country Club La Cosa Nostra—no disrespect meant to La Cosa Nostra.

Congress has existed on political payoffs for so long that they've forgotten what truly makes our economy run: entrepreneurial freedom. They're more interested in taking money from Peter to pay Paul, in order to get Paul's vote. In order to pursue that "fairer system," they pretend to be friends of free enterprise while covertly undermining it.

And they're getting away with it. We've entered an age of Congressional Stagnation: most Americans hate Congress, but love their congressperson. Incumbents almost always win—since 2000, the House incumbency rate has *averaged* 96 percent. The Senate isn't much better: since 2000, the Senate incumbency rate has averaged 85.2 percent.[86] That's because we have a basic collective action problem: voters want their congressmen to keep bringing home the bacon, but object when other congressmen take voters' tax dollars home to *their* districts.

This is how Economic Fascism gets started: congressional cockroaches seeking to maintain their seats, inflating the currency, stealing taxpayer dollars, and going to bat for lobbyists. It's not long before those lobbyists are controlling Congress, and using that power to restrict market competition. It's not long before Congress is buying off more and more voters with glorious neon promises like "free" health care and "free" Social Security and "free" wages.

So how do we drain the swamp and do away with the Swamp Creatures? By taking responsibility. We have to run candidates who can win and vote for candidates who will do the right thing. We have to stop tolerating Swamp Creatures just because they're *our* Swamp Creatures. We have to recognize that when Washington, D.C., remains a swamp, we all pay for it. Alexander Hamilton relied on the people to check the encroachment of elected officials: "Let me now ask what circumstance there is in the constitution of the House of Representatives that violates the principles of republican government, or favors the elevation of the few on the ruins of the many? . . . Who are to be the electors of the federal representatives? Not the rich, more than the poor; not the learned, more than the ignorant; not the haughty heirs of distinguished names, more than the humble sons of obscurity and unpropitious fortune. The electors are to be the great body of the people of the United States." [87] The people of the United States were to guard their own liberty. We have failed to do so over the past few decades. Let us begin now.

CHAPTER 10

THE RIGHT STUFF

When I was eighteen years old, I was dating a girl I knew from high school and things were starting to get pretty serious. One night after dinner we were sitting around her parents' kitchen table and the "What are your plans for my daughter" question was tossed my way. I told them that I really cared for her but first I needed to figure out what I wanted to do with my life. Her mom then asked me if I had any kind of career in mind. I responded that I was thinking about becoming a cop. She replied, "Anybody can be a dumb Irish cop."

I was stunned by her remark, seeing as how she knew my dad had been a New York City cop. I tried to reason away her words as being one of two things. Either it was the booze talking or she was just an uppity bitch. Turns out it was both.

The reason I thought about becoming a cop was because that was the family I grew up in: Irish Catholic, cops and firemen, a true blue-collar clan. When my dad got out of the Navy after serving in the Korean War, he was hell-bent on becoming a police officer. His dream was to wear the uniform and walk the beat. There was only one problem: he was an unimposing guy. He wasn't a six foot four, 230-pound Irishman with hands the size of catchers' mitts. He was barely five foot eight, the minimum height requirement. So for months he slept on the floor in order to straighten out his spine before taking his exam. He wanted to make sure he hit that minimum height requirement. That's how much he wanted to be a cop. I'm not so sure my newly married mom was thrilled with the sleeping arrangements, but she "slept by her man."

It wasn't frightening to me in those days to have a cop for a dad. It never entered my mind that every day when he left home, he might not come back. I didn't have the run-ins with the scumbags and bottom-feeders that the cops had to deal with every day, because for the most part, the cops kept that element of society from reaching out and touching us. They saw criminals for what they were: losers who thought the laws didn't apply to them.

Just as my dad saw it as his duty to serve his country by enlisting in the Navy at seventeen (yes he lied about his age), he felt the same obligation to serve his community in the NYPD. The same goes for firefighters—when everyone else is running out of a burning building, they're running in. When the World Trade Center terrorist attacks took place on September 11, 2001, tens of thousands of New Yorkers were running uptown, while New York cops and firemen ran downtown.

If there is anything that can be viewed as a positive resulting from the horrors of 9/11, it's that Americans, by and large, grew to appreciate the sacrifices made by the men and women of the police and fire departments.

It's not athletes, rock stars, or Hollywood actors who deserve our respect: it's the police, the firefighters, the first responders, the military and all their families. It's the folks who grind it out every day to make our lives safer and better.

So why do so many people in our society give a crap about Brangelina (i.e., the combination of Brad Pitt and Angelina Jolie) and other Grapefruit while the real superstars are too often taken for granted? It's because too many Americans have lost their bearings. We now treat the Hollywood Grapefruit as though they're the cream of the crop, while some of us treat our military, police, and adventurers as though they're relics of an imperialist past.

It's ignorance that springs from the left's unceasing attack on America and her values. A recent poll revealed that 11 percent of Americans view the military unfavorably, and 14 percent are undecided. That means one in four Americans is unsure whether to back the men and women who fight to protect their right to be idiots. And, you guessed it, there's a significant statistical difference between Democrats and Republicans on this score. While 85 percent of Republicans have a favorable view of the U.S. military, just 68 percent of Democrats do. It's no wonder that on Memorial Day 2009, a scant 23 percent of adults said they would attend a service to honor fallen soldiers.[1]

The same ignorance applies to police officers. Only 59 percent of Americans express a great deal or quite a lot of confidence in the police.[2] Among ethnic minorities, blacks in particular, trust for the police lags far behind even that statistic. While 67 percent of white Americans say that police in their communities treat all races fairly, just 30 percent of blacks agree.[3]

Why do so many people not trust the police, firefighters, and military anymore? Why do these people see them as alternatively incompetent, stupid, and brutal? Why is it that our illustrious president once opined on national television that, although he did not know the facts of the case, the Cambridge, Massachusetts, police "acted stupidly" when responding to a 911 caller who reported a suspected house break-in?

Here's why: our society confuses heroes and victims with perpetrators.

Those who gamed the financial system—the myriad bankers and financial institutions who profited handsomely from the inflationary monetary policies of the 1990s and 2000s—are portrayed as victims. They're perpetrators, not victims.

The fools who bought mortgages with 0 percent down, lied about their income, and then abandoned those homes when real estate values dropped are seen as victims. They're not victims—they're perpetrators.

Soldiers who engage in hard-nosed acts in order to keep us safe at night are seen as perpetrators. They're not perpetrators—they're heroes. Soldiers who are killed on the battlefields protecting our rights are seen as victims. Nuts! They're not victims—they're heroes.

We need to remember what turns ordinary people into heroes. It's not by magic, yet it is something that's awe-inspiring. It's the willingness of others to put themselves in our place—not just with their money or with their intelligence, but with their lives. It's the sense of risk taking and daring that allows mankind to scale the heights. It's a meritocracy of skill and guts. As Tom Wolfe wrote about the test pilots of the Air Force:

> A career in flying was like climbing one of those ancient Babylonian pyramids made up of a dizzy progression of steps and ledges, a ziggurat, a pyramid extraordinarily high and steep; and the idea was to prove at every foot of the way up that pyramid that you were one of the elected and anointed ones who had *the right stuff* and could move higher and higher and even—ultimately, God willing, one day—that you might be able to join that special few at the very top, that elite who had the capacity to bring tears to men's eyes, the very Brotherhood of the Right Stuff itself.[4]

There is no affirmative action when it comes to the Brotherhood of the Right Stuff. Bribery won't help; victimology won't help. It's one of the last pure bastions of the American competitive spirit. And no movement, no matter how powerful or ideologically driven, should be allowed to destroy that competitive spirit, for when that competitive spirit dies, so does America's future.

MILITARY "VICTIMS"

When not slandering military members as beasts, bigots, and boors, antiwar activists and "bring them home" Democrats enjoy labeling them "victims" of a cruel, heartless society and military command structure.

They say that our soldiers are all poor and undereducated, and therefore targeted to fight and die on the front lines as cannon fodder. They say that they're all bamboozled into joining up, that recruiters deceive teenagers into signing their papers. And they cite the seemingly endless stream of stories about military members who become unstable, commit suicide, are plotting to become a home-grown terrorist or suffer from post-traumatic stress disorder.

Take, for example, our president. On Memorial Day 2008, when Obama was just a candidate, he spoke about his supposed uncle:

> I had an uncle who was one of the, who was part of the first American troops to go into Auschwitz and liberate the concentration camps. . . . And the story in my family is that when he came home, he just went into the attic, and he didn't leave the house for six months. All right? Now, obviously something had affected him deeply, but at the time, there just weren't the kinds of facilities to help somebody work through that kind of pain.

The media picked up on the obvious fact that Obama's great-uncle (not his uncle) could not have liberated Auschwitz. The Russians liberated Auschwitz.[5] What they didn't pick up on was the obvious tone of the comments: Obama wasn't paying homage to a World War II hero, he was portraying him as a victim. Why, on Memorial Day of all days, would the future president of the United States choose to focus on the psychological damage suffered by his warrior great-uncle?

Obama isn't the only one who loves repeating the troops-as-victims theme. Hollywood uses this cliché as the basis for most of its war movies. Famous Vietnam war movies include *Platoon*, in which Charlie Sheen joins up, only to learn about the evils of war; *Rambo*, in which a Vietnam vet comes home and goes psychotic; *Coming Home*, in which one Vietnam vet, the "stupid" careerist, commits suicide when his wife has an affair with another "heroic" paralyzed and disillusioned former military vet; and *Jacob's Ladder*, in which we are treated to conspiracy theories about military higher-ups using soldiers for guinea pigs. The television show *M*A*S*H*, which was purportedly about the Korean War, was an obvious slap at the Vietnam War; as creator Larry Gelbart acknowledged, an attempt to speak more broadly "about the futility of war."[6]

Modern Hollywood has done its part to undermine our military men and women. *Stop-Loss* featured Ryan Phillippe as a soldier gone AWOL to avoid being arbitrarily reupped and shipped back to Iran. *In the Valley of Elah* starred Tommy Lee Jones as a father seeking to uncover the circumstances surrounding his son's death; his son, as it turns out, was a victim of his brutal colleagues, who cut him to pieces over an insignificant quarrel because they had been so damaged by war. John Cusack's *Grace Is Gone* was designed to portray families of soldiers as victims as well. "[There is no way] I would support an ultra-authoritarian administration that wants to open up new markets using the U.S. military and Blackwater," Cusack said while publicizing the film. "I mean, that ain't gonna happen, ever. But you can be pro-military and anti-war and anti-war profiteering."[7] This makes no sense to me. It's the "I support the troops but not the war" mentality. If you support the soldiers who are fighting the wars, then you have to support their efforts. What's the point of having soldiers if we never send them into battle?

The "soldiers as victims" lie has gained traction in recent years, with the left consistently insisting that a disproportionate number of the military are poor minority suckers. Rep. Charles Rangel, a black former Bronze Star of Valor recipient for his service in the Army during the Korean War, has called for reinstitution of the military draft on the grounds that "A disproportionate number of the poor and members of minority groups make up the enlisted ranks of the military, while most privileged Americans are underrepresented or absent."[8]

Brilliant military expert and girly leading man Matt Damon echoes Rangel's comments:

> I don't think that it's fair as I said before, that it seems like we have a fighting class in our country. That's comprised of people who have to go for either financial reasons or, I don't think

that that is fair. And if you're gonna send people to war . . . if we all *get together* and decide we need to go to war then that needs to be shared by everybody. You know and if the President has daughters who are of age then maybe they should go too.[9]

New York Times columnist Bob Herbert, a black Korea War veteran, was even more explicit:

There was a time, long ago, when war required sacrifices that were shared by most of the population. That's over. . . . For the most part, the only people sacrificing for this war are the troops and their families, and very few of them are coming from the privileged economic classes. . . . This is a war fought mostly by other people's children. The loudest of the hawks are the least likely to send their sons or daughters off to Iraq. . . . College kids in the U.S. are playing video games and looking forward to frat parties while their less fortunate peers are rattling around like moving targets in Baghdad and Mosul, trying to dodge improvised explosive devices and rocket-propelled grenades. . . . If Mr. Bush's war in Iraq is worth dying for, then the children of the privileged should be doing some of the dying.[10]

A few points: first, these fine folks somehow didn't think to protest the percentages of minority soldiers during the U.S.'s military involvement in Bosnia, Somalia, and Haiti under Clinton.

Second, we now have an all-volunteer military—which means that all of those "poor minorities" have signed up because they want to, not because they have been forced to fight by evil white men.

Third, and most important, is the fact that poor, undereducated members of the military are not substantially overrepresented. In fact, they are underrepresented. According to a 2005 Heritage Foundation study of 1999 recruits, recruits were generally more highly educated than the general population, more rural and less urban, and on a par as far as income: "We did not find evidence of minority racial exploitation (by race or by race-weighted ZIP code areas). We did find evidence of a 'Southern military tradition' in that some states, notably in the South and West, provide a much higher proportion of enlisted troops by population." [11] It seems that Herbert's point—that members of the military are drawn from minority populations—is largely false.

A 2008 Heritage Foundation study reiterated the point:

> U.S. military service disproportionately attracts enlisted personnel and officers who do not come from disadvantaged backgrounds. . . . Members of the all-volunteer military are significantly more likely to come from high-income neighborhoods than from low-income neighborhoods. Only 11 percent of enlisted recruits in 2007 came from the poorest one-fifth (quintile) of neighborhoods, while 25 percent came from the wealthiest quintile. These trends are even more pronounced in the Army Reserve Officer Training Corps (ROTC) program, in which 40 percent of enrollees came from the wealthiest neighborhoods. [12]

Despite the ROTC's overwhelming recruitment of high-income youths, many leftists hate the ROTC, stating that it "targets minorities." In 2005, for example, the *Los Angeles Times* ran a story claiming that ROTC was going out of its way to target poor minority kids from downtrodden high schools. "This year," reported the *Times*, "the Army and Marines plan not only to increase the number of recruiters, but also to penetrate high schools more deeply, especially those least likely to send graduates to college." Such criticism caused certain high schools to restrict military recruiting. [13] Apparently, it is better for kids to become high school graduates working in menial professions than to graduate, join the Army, get training, and go to college.

CRAZY VETS AND OTHER
LEFTIST NONSENSE

When the antimilitary left isn't too busy complaining about recruitment of minorities into the armed services, they're busy portraying America's soldiers as unstable men and women on the verge of psychological melt-downs. Leaving aside the movies, which see every military member as a potential psycho murderer, the news media has consistently pushed the image of the violent PTSD veteran. On January 13, 2009, the *New York Times* ran a piece entitled "Across America, Deadly Echoes of Foreign Battles." The article trumpeted ex-military violence. "Town by town across the country headlines have been telling similar stories," the *Times* breathlessly reported. "Lakewood, Wash.: 'Family Blames Iraq After Son Kills Wife.' Pierre, S.D.: 'Soldier Charged with Murder Testifies About Postwar Stress.' Colorado Springs: 'Iraq War Vets Suspected in Two Slayings, Crime Ring.' . . . The *New York Times* found 121 cases in which veterans of Iraq and Afghanistan committed a killing in this country, or were charged with one, after their return from war. In many of those cases, combat trauma and the stress of deployment—along with alcohol abuse, family discord and other attendant problems—appear to have set the stage for a tragedy that was part destruction, part self-destruction."[14]

Do men and women who serve often suffer from PTSD? Unfortunately the answer is yes. But the vast majority do not, and the vast majority also don't kill people when they get back home. As Ann Coulter has pointed out, when we compare murders by veterans to murders by eighteen to thirty-five-year-old males, it turns out that "the homicide rate among veterans of [Afghanistan and Iraq is] 7.6 per 100,000—or about one-third the homicide rate for their age group (18 to 35) in the general population of both sexes." When women are removed from the calculations, "we see that Iraq and Afghanistan veterans are about 10 times *less* likely to commit a murder than non-veterans of those wars."[15] So much for the nutty vet myth.

But the Obama administration buys into the "violent vet" nonsense.

A report by the Homeland Security Office of Intelligence and Analysis released in April 2009 specifically mentioned homecoming veterans as a security threat—among other threats posed by "right wing extremists." "The return of military veterans facing significant challenges reintegrating into their communities could lead to the potential emergence of terrorist groups or lone-wolf extremists capable of carrying violent attacks," the report said. It then referenced Timothy McVeigh, the military vet responsible for the Oklahoma City bombings. After the report was uncovered, Homeland Security Secretary Janet Napolitano apologized for its reference to veterans.[16]

Meanwhile, the Obama administration said nothing about the continuing threat of Islamic terrorism, even as American-born Muslim convert Abdulhakim Mujahid Muhammad aka Carlos Bledsoe shot two American soldiers in Little Rock, Arkansas. His motivation: retaliation for the War on Terror, the murders committed for "the sake of Allah, the lord of all the world." [17]

American vets apparently have their hands full planning the murder of American citizens. But when they have extra time, according to the left, they plan their own suicides due to the psychic wounds received in battle. And the media says it happens to dozens of vets every year. On May 29, 2008, the *Chicago Tribune* ran a story revealing that Army suicide rates had increased again; 115 troops committed suicide in 2007, a 13 percent increase over 2006's 102. According to the *Tribune*, the Department of Veterans Affairs also reported 144 suicides among the 500,000 members of the military who retired from 2002 to 2005.[18]

Egregious, to be sure. But the military suicide rate is still lower than the rate for people of similar age and education level in the rest of American society. And 26 percent of the troops who committed suicide never served in either Iraq or Afghanistan.[19] The military isn't the psycho ward in *One Flew Over the Cuckoo's Nest*. Not every soldier is Private Leonard Lawrence from *Full Metal Jacket*. In fact, the vast majority of soldiers are not. They are well-adjusted, heroic men and women who willingly put their lives on the line every day. Portraying them as mentally unstable kooks who are all one moment away from turning into Charles Joseph Whitman and shooting people from the University of Texas at Austin bell tower is disgusting.

PAINTING THE POLICE AS RACISTS

The left's scorn for the military pales in comparison to their disdain for the men and women in blue. Prominent minority faux leaders like Al "Ain't Nothin' Strange About Your Daddy" Sharpton and Rep. Maxine "Too Black to Fail" Waters (D-CA) have built careers from tearing down the police.

Sharpton in particular has a pattern: he finds a police shooting, pretends the shooting is unjustified no matter what the circumstances, and calls for a crackdown on police officers. On April 7, 2001, for example, black nineteen-year-old Timothy Thomas fled from Cincinnati police after they recognized that there were fourteen warrants on him. Thomas was a repeat criminal—he had been pulled over eleven times by six white officers and four black officers, and ticketed twenty-one times for driving without a seat belt and without a license. Thomas led police on a short chase through the Over-the-Rhine Cincinnati area and into an alley. A police officer later testified that he thought Thomas was reaching for a gun and the officer shot Thomas dead.[20] The Cincinnati black population rioted in response.

Sharpton immediately swung into action. He flew to Cincinnati to condemn the police. "It's Cincinnati today, it could be anywhere else tomorrow," Sharpton ranted, calling on President Bush to meet with him. "Anytime you mess with God's children anywhere," he said, "God's children everywhere need to stand up and demand what is right. You don't need to act in a way to destroy your community. You do need to fight—until those that wear blue uniforms are subjected to the same laws as those who wear blue jeans."[21]

Sharpton should have spoken to the rioting Cincinnati black community. Since 1995, fifteen black men had been killed by police. That made Sharpton fighting mad. But the men killed by police were all criminals, and twelve of them were armed. The so-called victims included:

> Harvey Price, who axed his girlfriend's fifteen-year-old daughter and then attacked police with a knife.

> Daniel Williams, who hailed a police cruiser, then punched the female cop in the face and shot her point-blank four times. She somehow managed to shoot him dead.

> Jeffrey Irons, who stole a cop's gun, shot the cop in the hand, and then was shot himself.[22]

Upstanding citizens all. But according to Sharpton and Co., the police were the villains.

That theme—police as brutalizers, criminals as victims—has become a hallmark of the left. And it has deep roots. Back in December 1990, a twenty-five-year-old unemployed construction worker named Rodney King was released from prison after serving a sentence for robbing a grocery store with a tire iron. Three months later, Rodney decided to go for a drive with two friends. At the time he had a blood alcohol level of .19—almost three times the legal limit, and elected to drive 115 mph on the freeway. In addition, he failed to stop when followed by police patrol cars with flashing red lights.

When King was finally stopped, he hopped out of the car and taunted a female police officer (his two friends heeded the commands of the police and emerged totally unscathed). When two male police officers attempted to pin him, he fought them off. Officer Stacey Koon then took action, Tasering King twice. King *still* didn't quit, even though the Taser could take down a large farm animal. Koon thus concluded that King was high on PCP, a drug that makes users impervious to pain. Koon tried to subdue King, and failed. At that point, three other officers began

hitting King with their batons, finally putting him down. The King beating made waves across the nation when a nearby resident videotaped the
incident.[23]

The four officers were acquitted of all charges after their trial in
Simi Valley. But that didn't stop the African-American mayor of Los
Angeles, Tom Bradley, from condemning the officers. "Today, the system failed us," he said. "The jury's verdict will not blind us to what we
saw on that videotape. The men who beat Rodney King do not deserve
to wear the uniform of the LAPD."

Governor Bill Clinton, the not-yet-first "black" president, issued a
statement agreeing with Bradley: "Like most of America I saw the tape
of the beatings several times, and it certainly looks excessive to me so I
don't understand the verdict."[24]

Even as Bradley and his liberal cohorts condemned the officers,
blacks in South Central Los Angeles were using the Rodney King verdict as an excuse to riot. The Los Angeles riots caused the death of fifty-
three people,[25] the injury of over four thousand, and over $1 billion in
property damage. The most famous tape from the riots showed African-
American high school football standout Damian Williams bashing in
white truck driver Reginald Denny's head with a cinder block, cracking
it in ninety-one places and causing severe brain damage.[26]

There is some "happy" news to the story. Rodney King went on to
lead a full and productive life, blessed with a lifetime get-out-of-jail-free
card. In May 1991, King hired a transvestite prostitute and was caught
by police but no charges were filed. In June 1992, King's second wife
told police that he had hit her (he also hit his first wife in 1987). In
July 1992, King was arrested for DUI; again no charges were filed. In
August 1993, King crashed into a wall in Los Angeles; his blood alcohol level was again .19. In May 1995, King was picked up yet again for
DUI in Pennsylvania. In July 1995, King began fighting with his second
wife again and threw her out of his car; he was tried for assault with
a deadly weapon, reckless driving, spousal abuse, and hit-and-run. In
March 1999, King allegedly assaulted his out-of-wedlock sixteen-year-

old daughter and her mother. In September 2001, King was charged with indecent exposure and was arrested for using PCP.[27]

Yep, it sure must have been the cops who were the bad guys.

HOUSTON, WE DON'T HAVE A PROBLEM

While we're on the subject of a false impression heaped upon genuine heroes of our era, the men and women of NASA come to mind.

NASA has fallen in the public mind in the last few years. For me, however, the people of NASA represent everything that makes America great: they're risk takers, adventurers, dreamers, and modern-day explorers.

I've had a lifelong fascination with space and space travel and the NASA program. My uncle, Bob McCarthy, was a producer on the Apollo missions for NBC News. I remember going down to the Space Center in the days when the NASA enthusiasts lined the causeways to watch a launch wearing goofy shirts and straw hats drinking Busch beer out of a can. How many would show up? A million people lined up to watch the launch of Apollo 11, the first time man walked on the lunar surface.

So for me, when the call came from the producers of *Babylon 5* that anybody who wanted to come down to the Kennedy Space Center (KSC) to witness a Shuttle launch from the VIP viewing area, I said, "Hell yes!"

My escort at KSC was Louise Kleba, who worked in the Vehicle Integration Test Team (VITT) office, a NASA lifer. "NASA could probably live without me," she said, "but I couldn't live without NASA." That's how the twelve thousand men and women at NASA think. That's true from the suit techs to the close-out crew to the security team to the astronauts—they are all mission-focused. I was amazed at how they could take all the thousands of pieces and parts from all over the world, assemble a vehicle, stack it, load it, and launch it, and make it look easy.

But the real challenges of NASA arise when something goes wrong:

Apollo 13, Challenger, and Columbia. When most of the pundits after the Challenger disaster were saying "Shut it down, it's too dangerous," they launched another mission within a few years.

When astronauts get into shuttles, they realize there's a statistical probability that there's going to be a major malfunction, which some estimates put at greater than 1 in 100. In spite of that, they suit up, strap into a five-million-pound bomb built by the lowest bidder, and hurl themselves into orbit on an eight-and-a-half-minute 3G burn. They're either chasing the international space station at 17,500 mph, or trying to catch up to the Hubble telescope. And they do.

Here's a visual one of the guys gave me down at NASA's Kennedy Space Center: extend your arms out to your side as far as they can go with your hands in a pistol grip position. As fast as you can, bring your arms together trying to have only your index fingertips touch—with your eyes closed. That's not even close to how difficult their task is. I'll admit we were in a bar *near* KSC but you get the idea.

And think about the feat they pulled off on Apollo 13 using slide rules. The computer onboard Apollo 11 was 64K technology, which is what some calculators have today.

After Challenger, the press agonized over whether it's worth it. But every astronaut I've ever met—and I've met at least seventy-five—says he or she would go the next day.

These guys have double degrees, triple languages—classic over-achievers. There were twins, Scott and Mark Kelly, who both became F-16 fighter pilots. They both applied to NASA. They both got accepted. And they have both commanded shuttle missions. I played basketball with them when I was down at Johnson Space Center and I got to fly the Shuttle Motion Simulator. They're both about five foot ten, I'm six three and my astronaut buddy Rick Linnehan is about the same height as me. They destroyed us and I had played college ball! They're relentless. They decide that this is what they're going to do. This is their mission. And they do it.

Once you've been accepted to the NASA program—and that's a challenge in and of itself—you're still not guaranteed a slot in the corps much less heading off into the wild blue yonder. If you're claustrophobic, you learn early on that you're not in the right line of work. They test you in a rescue ball—a three-foot-in-circumference rubberized bladder. They track your vitals, and then zip you up. It's not for the faint of heart. It ain't the pleasurable comfort of the womb.

I had the opportunity to try the claustrophobia test. I was stuffed into a Soyuz mockup—the Russian capsule—with two other guys, even though this was configured for a two-man team. When they closed the hatch, my infatuation with space travel was limited to perhaps six seconds. I was attempting to let them know I was done without sounding panicked and alarmed; they laughed.

Here's the kind of mind-set these NASA people have. I met one astronaut who had just returned from a mission. I asked him how he planned to decompress.

"I'm going right into training," he said.

"You got reassigned already?" I asked, "How cool."

"No," he said, "I'm training to climb Mount Everest."

He promptly put on a sixty-pound training pack and ran on a treadmill for three hours. Then he went to Thailand at a base camp, and then climbed Everest. I'm officially a slacker.

Watching a launch is fantastic but knowing the people on the inside is a connection that's difficult to explain—you attend the launch, follow the missions, watch the NASA channel, get the e-mails, and you know that your friends are spiraling over the earth at thousands of miles per hour. The human drama is enormous.

On February 2, 2003, right after Columbia broke up; I got an e-mail from my NASA friend Rick Linnehan, who had been called back to headquarters to assist with the recovery efforts. This is the message he sent to his friends and NASA supporters:

> Just returned early this AM from northern Quebec. We were extracted by snow cat half way through a winter survival skills course with the Canadian military following the word yesterday morning about Columbia. I wanted to thank all of you for

your thoughts, words and friendship over the past 24 hours and through the years. You've all been involved with NASA and the US space program. The good will and imagination of people like you form the marrow of what is best about this country and humankind. The seven people we lost yesterday were people like you. They had families like you and many friends that cared about and supported them in their desire to explore science and space just as you have done for me. They were my friends. And they did what they did because they knew that it was important and they wanted to explore and contribute to the advancement of our species. There isn't anything more important than that.

No, there isn't.

SCI-FI FANS

All this was made available to me because I was the chief of security on a plywood space station on a Warner Brothers soundstage.

Even in Hollywood, science fiction has always been the stepchild of the industry. And the fans of science fiction have been unfairly criticized or ridiculed or mocked, when in fact they tend to be members of the military, cops, firemen, minority communities, scientists, doctors, engineers. They like the science, and they are that forward-thinking group that looks at what the future holds.

Now there are some who truly embrace the fiction part of science fiction. And if you want to have an understanding of what a science fiction convention can be like for some, watch the movie *Galaxy Quest*. It is spot-on.

I remember at one convention, as I looked up to greet the next attendee and sign the photos and memorabilia he had for me, he said, "Guess who I am?"

He had fashioned a homemade replica of what I had worn on *Babylon 5*. At a biscuit short of 350, it wasn't clear who he was supposed to be. He said, "I'm you! I'm Garibaldi!"

"I wonder how I missed that?" I asked.

Sometimes you meet a fan and that experience will stay with you for a lifetime for much different reasons than a funny costume. I was at a convention in Hunt Valley, Maryland, back in 1995. I was in the bar holding court, and a guy came up to me and asked if he could talk to me privately. "Sure," I said. "What's up?" He told me there was someone who wanted to meet me but she was too shy to come over and say hello. "Where is she," I asked. He pointed across the room to a gal who was in a wheelchair sitting by herself. We walked over and I got down on one knee to be at her eye level. I spent at most maybe ten minutes with her. We laughed, had a nice conversation, and as she was leaving I gave her a kiss on the cheek and told her how much of a pleasure it was to meet her and that I hoped our paths crossed again in the future. Later on after her friend had put her to bed for the night he approached me again at the bar and thanked me profusely for spending a few minutes with her. I told him it was nothing. He said it was not nothing. He said that all her life people made fun of her severe physical challenges. They would point at her. Stare at her. Mock her. He told me that as he tucked her in she said that no matter what people do or say to her in the future, it won't matter because Jerry Doyle liked her. I don't remember her name but I will always remember the smile on her face and the one she puts on mine whenever I think of her.

I really appreciate all the fans I had the chance to meet and who supported the show. In reality: without the fans, there's no show. When fans dress up in costume and show up at conventions, it's just Halloween or the Super Bowl or Mardi Gras for them. Those fans are the dreamers in this world, the ones who can visualize making science fiction into reality.

And you never know when you're really going to need them. Watch *Galaxy Quest* and you'll see what I mean.

HEROES AMONG US

Think of the pioneers about whom you studied in school. I refer to the men and women who crossed the plains in order to spread American civilization. Crossing rivers. Fighting for survival. Surviving. And building.

Heroes are not relegated to remaining characters in history books. Yet the true modern-day pioneers are taken for granted: the adventurers, the explorers, the risk takers, the defenders. They give us the opportunities and the technology, the right of self-determination, and the freedom that make our lives not only rich, but possible.

I salute all of you. The men and women of the armed services. The cops. The firemen. The NASA family. And all of you who appreciate all of them.

Stephen Wilbanks, a Marine vet who, at thirty-five, thought he was too old to reenlist, rejoined the Marines in the aftermath of September 11. Here's what he had to say about "Going Green Again," as quoted by Matthew Currier Burden in *The Blog of War*, an essential read for all Americans:

> As I watch the kickoff of Operations Enduring Freedom and Iraqi Freedom from the sidelines, I couldn't stand the fact that Marines were out there doing what Marines do and here I was, a man of eligible age, riding the bench. . . . Serving my country is not a four-year contract. It is a lifelong membership fee. It is a deeply personal obligation and it is certainly not time "to be done" like some felony prison sentence. It is nothing short of an honor that I hold in the highest regard, an honor I must prove worthy of, an honor that must be earned every single day.

Bloggers questioned why Wilbanks would reenlist despite having a family, a wife, and kids. This was his response:

> Without question, my family is the single most important part of my life on earth. But just what kind of husband and fa-

ther do I want for my family? What kind of man do I want my wife to devote her life to? When my children are grown, what is the picture of their father going to look like in their minds? I will tell you: I want my beloved wife to go through her days without a shadow of a doubt that the man she married is a man of honor and commitment, a man that knows there are things in life worth giving one's own life for, if necessary. I want her, as she looks out upon all of the world's deceptions, falseness, infidelity and evil, to know that her husband is on the right side of things.

I want my children to have a father that they can unwaveringly look up to as an example. I want them to grow up not with an attitude of entitlement, but with a sense of duty, honor, obligation and reward. I want to teach them that we don't always say, "Let the other guy do it." Instead, I want them to learn that there are times when we must ask, "If not me, then who?" I want to be the best father I can be, and I can think of no better lessons to teach them than the value of honor, integrity, dedication, perseverance and selflessness. I can offer no better example for my family than to strive to live those values every day in my own personal life.

These are my heroes.
These are your heroes.
These are America's heroes.
If we don't appreciate them, they'll become a relic of the past.
Let's honor them not only for what they are now but also for what we can become because we are blessed to stand upon their shoulders, look into the future, and see America for what it can become once again.

CHAPTER 11

A CALL TO ARMS

Were we to label today's America, we may well be justified in calling this the "Age of Indifference." Much of our country seems to be content with living a life of passive existence.

But life is full of choices. There are choices in life that define us, crucial choices we make that may mean life or death, liberty or oppression, prosperity or poverty. Sometimes those choices are as simple as what movie you want to see this weekend. Sometimes those choices are more complex—choices like "What should I do with my life?"

Then there are those choices that happen in the blink of an eye.

Back in 2002, I was in a movie called *Devious Beings*. This one definitely wasn't made for the children—it was a little dark, a little creepy. It also starred Patrick "Patty" Van Horn from the movie *Swingers*, Kevin Connolly of HBO's *Entourage*, and Andre Blake, a series and film actor who played the lead role. The producers did what producers usually do with an independent film: they planned a multicity tour to generate buzz for the movie. So the principal cast, producer, and director hit the road.

One of the first places we stopped was Las Vegas, where I now make my home. After we did the screenings and the signings, we decided that when in Rome, it was time to roam. Patty and I headed out to the casinos, where we spent the entire night gambling at blackjack, exercising our freedoms, and taking advantage of the most expensive free drinks in the world. Shockingly, I actually made out pretty well. I wound up with $1,400 in my pocket, and, I must admit, I was feeling pretty good about my newfound fortune.

At 8:15 in the morning, Patty and I decided to call it a night or should I say a morning and headed out through the parking lot to our hotel. The sun was already blazing, strip joints were offering their breakfast specials, and the hookers were saying good night to their last clients. All seemed right with the world.

I was walking slightly ahead of Patty, totally oblivious to the real world, when I heard him call to me.

"Ah . . . J.D. you might want to stop right there."

"Why, am I walking too fast for you?" I asked.

"Dude, just stop," said Patty. This time he spoke as firmly as would a drill sergeant. "There's a guy behind you and he's got a gun," Patty said."

"That's funny," I said.

And it was funny, until I spun around and saw that, yes indeed, there was a gun pointed right at my head.

The guy with the piece was a traditional gangbanger thug type: he was a black guy, and yes, he wore a silver gray do-rag, and yes, he slung his pants low. He was right out of Central Casting. In typical highbrow street vernacular he told me to give him my money or he'd blow my head off. Something came over me and I knew I had to change this up real quick because I firmly believed that even if I gave him the money, he was going to unload on me and maybe Patty, too. Dead witnesses make lousy witnesses.

I stared him square in the eyes for a few seconds and then said, "Not today." Maybe my reaction was prompted by some liquid courage but there was something else. A weird sense of calm overcame me. I decided if I was going to get capped at least I wouldn't be a compliant corpse.

This took the little street entrepreneur by surprise. He took a step back and cocked his head to the side, his eyes open wide with amazement at what I had just said.

"What chu mean, motha f-----? I'll blow your f----- head off," the gangbanger sputtered intelligently. Still staring him down I said, "No . . . Not today you won't."

Patty yelled, "Just give him your money."

"F--- that," I said. I'd spent the entire night winning that money, and I wasn't going to part with it just because some bottom-feeder felt an overblown sense of entitlement. It was my money not his.

The gangbanger turned and pointed the gun in Patty's direction.

"I don't want any trouble, man," said Patty, dropping to his knees. He spilled all the money from his pockets. The gangbanger scooped it up.

Then he turned back around to me, leveled the gun at me, put his finger on the trigger, and mouthed the word, "Bang."

"F--- you," I responded in a tone indicating that I was getting bored with this whole scenario. The slightly richer scumbag turned and ran off.

Patty got up off the ground and looked at me as though I were wearing a pink bunny suit. "What the f---?" he yelled. "*Not today? Not today!* You think you're Wyatt ----ing Earp? He had a *gun to your head.* And you said, 'No thanks, I don't feel like being robbed today.' What's wrong with you?"

I looked at Patty and said, "What's wrong with me? I still have my money."

I'm not telling this story so that I look like Dirty Harry. I'm not interested in being a tough guy—I'm not going to start fighting mixed martial arts and drinking deer blood. In fact, the police told me later that it was the dumbest thing I could have done. But as I pointed out to the cop, "You know how hard it is to win in a casino in Vegas? That degenerate wasn't going to get *my* cash."

That was a moment when I made a choice. From some perspectives, it was a dumb choice; from other perspectives a smart one.

But the underlying idea—saying "Not today!" to anyone who wants to take what's not theirs—is the right thing to do. And it's time for Americans to stand up and say "Not today!" to our government.

The government has a gun to each and every one of our heads. It's the coercive force of the state. And they're bringing it to bear every day through higher taxation, more regulation, massive inflation, and nationalization of private industry.

We're watching the tyranny of the minority overpower the will of the majority: a minority composed of corrupt oligarchs, making laws for the few at the expense of the many. The bad bankers get bailed out by the taxpayers; the bad borrowers get bailed out by the taxpayers; the criminals get bailed out by the honest people. And we think we can't do anything about it.

But we can.

We can start by standing up and saying "Not today!" en masse. We've already started to do it. That's what the tea party movement is all about: hundreds of thousands of Americans across the country, joining hands and linking minds, recognizing that freedom and liberty require constant vigilance, and that resistance to arbitrary exercise of government power is mandatory. The media may ignore us now, but soon they won't have any choice but to recognize the burgeoning resurgence of true American idealism.

We can start by seizing the day.

DOING NOTHING

It's as if we're standing motionless on a sidewalk, watching a passing parade of strutting politicians carrying signs scribbled with illogical promises such as: "Free medical care for everyone with no tax increases." Bureaucrats are the next in the parade, playing a tune that at first sounds like upbeat Dixieland jazz only to dissolve into a New Orleans dirge normally reserved for funerals. Bringing up the rear, pushing wheelbarrows heaped to overflowing with dollar bills, are lobbyists.

Their eyes dart from side to side as they look for ways to weave through the bureaucrats in order to get close enough to whisper into the ears of the politicians.

And at the head of the parade is a high-stepping drum major who shouts at the top of his lungs the mantra: "Yes we can!"

The pathetic truth is that many of us standing alongside the parade route know very well that these slogans and phrases are totally meaningless. At the same time, nobody is willing to step onto the street and challenge the demonstrators. Instead, most of us just scratch our heads and do nothing.

Our struggle is not new.

A quote attributed to Edmund Burke, an Irish philosopher and politician, stated: "All that is necessary for the triumph of evil is that good men do nothing."

His words hold as much meaning today as when they were spoken more than two hundred years ago.

Burke was not the first man to warn us about the evils resulting from a do-nothing society. This truth is as old as the Bible itself.

Yes, I sometimes quote the Bible. I was raised in an Irish Catholic home and was an altar boy at Our Lady Help of Christians for three years.

In the days of the Hebrew prophet Elijah, many of the people of Israel had permitted the evil of Ahab and Jezebel to dominate their land. They stood idly by and permitted the enemies of Israel to proclaim that an idol—one they called Baal—was the god that the people should worship. Elijah grew increasingly angry. To a large assembly of the Israelites gathered on Mount Carmel, the prophet boldly challenged his people with an ultimatum: "How long will you go limping with two different opinions? If the Lord be God, follow him, but if Baal is your god, then follow him." And the crowd remained silent.[1] They stood by and did nothing.

Later, Jesus, in his famous parable of the talents, described a servant who, along with others, was given some money by a wealthy landowner. While the rest of his friends invested the money or used it for worthy projects, this man elected to bury the cash into the ground. The land-owner returned a while later and praised those who made their money work for them. For the servant who buried his money, however, the landowner had nothing good to say. In fact, he fumed and referred to the servant as "wicked and slothful."[2]

Notice that the servant did not do anything evil such as stealing the landowner's money. But neither did he do anything good with it. He simply did nothing and, as a result, got nothing good accomplished.

Perhaps the most biting of all biblical condemnations of inactivity comes from the last book, when the church of Laodicea is rebuked for its do-nothing attitude. "I know your works," says Jesus. "You are nei-ther cold nor hot. Would that you were cold or hot. So, because you are lukewarm and neither cold nor hot, I will spew you out of my mouth."[3]

There's no way to mistake that message.

GETTING ACTIVE

Only those who dare to do make a difference.

As cited in John McCollister's *The Christian Book of Why*, a Roman Catholic cardinal named Leo Jozef Suenens (1904–1996) once wrote the pointed words: "Happy are those who dream dreams and are will-ing to pay the price to make them come true."

The same can be said of those of us who want to take back our coun-try. We dream to live in an America that once boasted of leaders who empowered its citizens to search for opportunities. We dream to live in an America that allows us to grow as far as our talents will allow.

Successful democracies are not easy to attain and even harder to maintain. Every generation had to produce its heroes willing to place causes ahead of personal comfort and pay the price to make them come true.

On December 1, 1955, for example, a forty-two-year-old African-American made history in Montgomery, Alabama, when she refused to give up her seat on a public bus to make room for a white passenger.

Rosa Parks was promptly arrested for her willful disregard for what were known as the Jim Crow laws.

Effective protests are dependent upon timing. Prior to the stand taken by Rosa Parks, other blacks had refused to surrender bus seats. Pioneers such as Irene Morgan in 1946, Sarah Louise Keys in 1955, and Claudette Colvin just nine months before Parks took her seat on bus number 2857 had challenged the practice. Their demonstrations yielded few results. Parks's actions, however, sparked the year-long Montgomery Bus Boycott and captured the support of enough Americans that a change of policy resulted.

Why did Rosa Parks take such a bold stand? In her autobiography, *My Story*, she revealed her motivation: "People always say that I didn't give up my seat because I was tired, but that isn't true. I was not tired physically, or no more tired than I usually was at the end of a working day. I was not old. . . . No, the only tired I was, was tired of giving in."[4]

Following her death at age ninety-two in 2005, Rosa Parks left a legacy that will, as President George W. Bush proclaimed, continue to lead all of us to commit ourselves to continue to struggle for justice for every American.

Another example comes from Major League Baseball—a sport that has traditionally been dubbed "America's pastime." One of the reasons for this label is that success in baseball is determined not by a person's height or weight. It's determined by his ability to hit a round ball with a round bat into fair territory and to run to first base quickly enough to beat a throw. Any kid in America can dream about donning a major league uniform and playing before thousands of fans in the stands and millions on television.

Of course, that wasn't true until 1947.

Before 1947, baseball endorsed an unwritten policy of not permitting "any person of color" to play in the majors. And so "America's pastime" wasn't really America's pastime. Not yet, anyway.

Several people worked hard to change that practice, but it wasn't easy by any stretch of the imagination. Even when they were victorious in their quest, the struggles continued.

Consider, for example, the trials endured by the first African-American ever to sign a major league contract.

Jack Roosevelt Robinson was a gifted twenty-seven-year-old graduate of UCLA who lettered in four sports his senior year. Any hope he may have had about becoming a player in the big leagues was thwarted because of the informal, but effective, ban on blacks.

One person who dared to step up for what was right was Wesley Branch Rickey, part-owner and general manager of the Brooklyn Dodgers. Rickey decided to buck the system and sign Robinson to a contract.

Prior to putting ink to paper, Rickey called the young Robinson into his office for a closed-door meeting.

"I need more than a great colored player," said Rickey. "I need a man to carry the flag for his race."

"Do you mean you want someone strong enough to fight back?" asked Robinson.

"No," said Rickey as he slammed his fist on his desk. "I want someone who is strong enough *not* to fight back. Even if a guy grabs you by your uniform and calls you a 'black son-of-a-bitch,' I want a man who will not be corrupted by human feelings."

After serving a year in the minors, Robinson was introduced to the hometown crowd prior to his first big league game on April 17, 1947. In spite of the fact that other ball clubs and even some of his own teammates threatened to boycott games if he played, Robinson and Rickey stood firm.

American history books might record that the civil rights movement in the nation began in 1965 with an organized march across the Edmund Pettus Bridge in Selma, Alabama. Not so. It started nearly two decades earlier on the red clay infield dirt around first base at a field called Ebbets in Brooklyn, New York.

The gamble paid off. Other teams accepted black players and the barrier was forever broken. Robinson himself was more than just a symbol. He developed into a premier player for the Dodgers, winning Rookie of the Year and Most Valuable Player honors.

Robinson spent ten years with the club and had plenty of opportunities to quit because of the racial slurs and taunting from opposing players and fans. He followed Rickey's advice, kept his cool, and eventually won the admiration and respect of all of baseball. He was elected to Baseball's Hall of Fame in 1962. His number has been retired throughout baseball.

INDEPENDENCE FOREVER!

If you're sick of being a pawn on the chessboard, protecting the kings (President Obama) and the queens (Nancy Pelosi), then stop being a pawn and *fight*. More than two hundred years ago, we fought to get rid of the kings and the queens; we fought to govern ourselves and our lives as individuals and families. Now that wretched royalty is back in another form—and we can't let them overturn the results of the American Revolution by governmental fiat.

And we won't let them do it. Not today. Americans still have that fire in their bellies; the ember still glows. We are the descendants of great men and women, and we will not let their triumphs be washed away by the soft flow of ever-increasing governmental encroachment.

We will say what John Paul Jones said when faced with the possibility of surrender to the British: "I have not yet begun to fight."

We will say what Nathan Hale said as he was being hanged by the British for spying for the fledgling United States: "I only regret that I have but one life to give my country."

We will say what Thomas Jefferson said on his deathbed: "Independence forever."

Independence *is* forever. But only if we find what we have lost: our guts, our principles, and our country.

IT'S TIME FOR AN "ALTAR CALL"

A tradition repeated in many fundamentalist churches today is the "altar call." It's a practice made popular by one of America's icons, evangelist Billy Graham. Graham ended each worship service with an invitation for those in the audience to leave their seats and come forward to show their willingness to devote their lives to Christ.

As Graham's audiences grew, so did the number of people who responded.

Did every one of them remain loyal to the church and to the cause of the faith? Certainly not. But plenty of them did. And it all began when they made their first move toward the front of the church or the arena in which Graham had just preached.

It's time for those of us who have been for too long standing along the side of the road watching the parade march by to speak out. It's time for us to rally others to the cause. And it's time to organize our own parades.

You don't have to conduct huge rallies under the cover of canvas tents. You can write editorials to your local newspaper. You can contribute a few dollars to a political candidate who reflects a solid sense of values. One pragmatic reporter suggested that the next time we go to the polls we merely vote every incumbent—Republican and Democrat—out of office. Question: would you seriously consider running for public office yourself?

These are just a few examples of how you can respond to America's call to arms to you.

Somebody might well ask: "What's the difference between Jerry Doyle's call to arms and the protests of the Timothy Learys and the Charles Mansons of the 1960s who urged us to tear down the walls of the establishment?"

The answer is simple: These people urged us to *destroy* and to *kill*; I am calling on Americans to *build* and to *give meaning to life.*

Think about it. Any shallow idiot can destroy; it takes a creative mind to build.

THIS IS YOUR CALL TO ARMS

Thomas Jefferson was right on target when he said: "Whenever any form of government becomes destructive, it is the right of the people to alter or abolish it, and to institute new government."

This is not your ordinary battle of ideas discussed at a local town meeting or over a beer in your neighborhood bar.

This, ladies and gentlemen, is a war. A righteous war.

Again, I call upon the wisdom of Thomas Jefferson: "We in America do not have a government by the majority. We have government by the majority who participate."

Granted, some of your friends and neighbors who read this book will choose to hit the snooze alarm and remain asleep in their cocoons of conformity, merely daydreaming about the hope of a better tomorrow.

It's up to the rest of us to jump out of bed, get dressed, venture out into the real world, and do whatever we can in order to make a difference.

The good news is that there is still time for you to join in America's call to arms.

This is your wake-up call, America.

If not you, who?

If not now, when?

As Todd Beamer put it on September 11, 2001, aboard hijacked United Flight 93, "Let's roll!"

NOTES

Chapter 1: Smoke for the Children

1. Campaign for Tobacco-Free Kids, http://www.tobaccofreekids.org.
2. "Pelosi SCHIP Bill: A Giant Step for America's Children," September 6, 2007, http://www.house.gov/Pelosi.
3. "Text of Nancy Pelosi's Speech," NewsNet5.com, January 4, 2007.
4. Audra Ang, "Pelosi Appeals for China's Help on Climate Change," Associated Press, May 28, 2009.
5. According to *America's Agenda Health Care for Kids,* "First Lady Hillary Clinton knew that focus on children would be politically popular and a 'Kids First' program had been envisioned as a backup plan during the original 1993 health reform effort," http://www.americasagenda-kidshealth.org/history.html.
6. Robert Pear, "Hatch Joins Kennedy to Back a Health Program," *New York Times,* March 14, 1997.
7. Jerry Gray, "Through Senate Alchemy, Tobacco Is Turned into Gold for Children's Health," *New York Times,* August 11, 1997.
8. Adam Clymer, "Child Insurance Bill Opposed as Threat to Cigarette Revenue," *New York Times,* May 21, 1997.
9. Jerry Gray, "Through Senate Alchemy, Tobacco Is Turned into Gold for Children's Health," *New York Times,* August 11, 1997.
10. Michael Abramowitz and Jonathan Weisman, "Bush Vetoes Health Mea-

sure," *Washington Post,* October 4, 2007; Martin Kady II, "As Expected, Bush Vetoes SCHIP Bill Again," Politico.com, December 12, 2007.

11. Robert Pear, "Obama Signs Children's Health Insurance Bill," *New York Times,* February 5, 2009.

12. Robert Pear, "Senators Approve Health Bill for Children," *New York Times,* January 30, 2009.

13. Robert Pear, "Children's Health Bill Dispute Turns to Income Limits," *New York Times,* October 17, 2007.

14. Robert Pear, "Senators Approve Health Bill for Children," *New York Times,* January 30, 2009.

15. U.S. Census Bureau, "Income, Poverty, and Health Insurance Coverage in the United States: 2007," Census.gov, August 2008, http://www.census .gov/prod/2008pubs/p60-235.pdf.

16. U.S. Census Bureau, "Historical Poverty Tables," Census.gov, http:// www.census.gov/hhes/www/poverty/histpov/hstpov13.html.

17. Sally C. Pipes, "Five Myths About Health Care," Forbes.com, November 1, 2008.

18. "Smoke or Not, You Cost Either Way," Associated Press, April 8, 2009.

19. Ross Kaminsky, "Why That 48 Million Uninsured Number Is Wrong," National Review Institute, April 2, 2009, http://nrinstitute.org/mediamal practice/?p=134.

20. Insure.com, "Know Your Emergency Room Rights," MSN.com, http:// articles.moneycentral.msn.com/Insurance/KnowYourRights/KnowYour EmergencyRoomRights.aspx.

21. Department of Health and Human Services, Nevada State Health Division, Bureau of Community Health, Tobacco Prevention and Educational Program, "Nevada Tobacco Profile," Healthy People 2010, http:// health.nv.gov/PDFs/Tobacco/04Data.pdf.

22. Marlene Naanes, "Cigarettes Jump Past $8 a Pack," Newsday.com, June 2, 2008.

23. "Congress: Don't Roll Your Own," Postandcourier.com, April 15, 2009.

24. "Instructions for TTB F 5000.28T09," Department of the Treasury: Alcohol and Tobacco Tax and Trade Bureau, http://www.ttb.gov/forms/ p500028t09.pdf.

25. Deborah Anderson, "The California Smoke-Free Workplace Law," Associated Content, January 31, 2007.

26. "Smoking Ban in California Bars Widely Ignored," CNN.com, January 23, 1998.

27. "Governor Signs into Law Measure to Outlaw Smoking in Cars with

Kids," Web site of State Senator Jenny Oropeza, October 10, 2007, http://dist28.casen.govoffice.com/index.asp?Type=B_PR&SEC=%7B15 8155BF-B41C-452C-A7E3-439790D3B207%7D&DE=%7B09B6D3B0-E9 A5-4B7B-B85C-A4B7CF99C73F%7D.

28. Jesse McKinley, "Smoking Ban Hits Home. Truly.," *New York Times,* January 26, 2009.

29. Ibid.

30. "El Cajon City Council Approves Smoking Ban," 10News.com, August 14, 2007.

31. John M. Broder, "Smoking Ban Takes Effect, Indoors and Out," *New York Times,* March 19, 2006.

32. Ibid.

33. Associated Press, "House Approves FDA Control over Tobacco," MSNBC.com, April 2, 2009.

34. Stephen Dinan, "Stimulus Bills Include STD Prevention," *Washington Times,* January 29, 2009.

35. TobaccoFreeAction.org.

36. "New York City Passes Trans Fat Ban," MSNBC.com, December 5, 2006.

37. Ibid.

38. Kelly D. Brownell, Ph.D., and Thomas R. Frieden, M.D., M.P.H., "Ounces of Prevention—The Public Policy Case for Taxes on Sugared Beverages," *New England Journal of Medicine,* April 30, 2009.

39. Ibid.

40. Anemona Hartocollis, "New York Health Official Calls for Tax on Drinks with Sugar," *New York Times,* April 8, 2009.

41. Ibid.

42. David N. Bass, "Pelosi's Children," Spectator.org, February 6, 2009.

43. "Obama Getting Heat for Turning Up the Oval Office Thermostat," FoxNews.com, February 3, 2009.

44. *Jerry Doyle Show,* April 15, 2009.

Chapter 3: Rip That Sink Out

1. Dwight Schultz, "The Liberal Bastille," March 16, 2009, http://bigholly wood.breitbart.com/dschultz/2009/03/16/the-liberal-bastille/#more -78910.

Chapter 4: Economic Fascism: The Origins

1. Joe Curl, "Obama Makes Oval Office Call to Reporters," *Washington Times,* March 8, 2009.

2. Jonah Goldberg, "Obama's Fear-Mongering," *Los Angeles Times,* March 10, 2009.

3. Deroy Murdock, "Robama Hood's Tax 'Fairness,'" National Review Online, October 20, 2008.

4. "Obama Tells the Tax Truth," *New York Post,* October 15, 2008.

5. Associated Press, "Biden Calls Paying Higher Taxes a Patriotic Act," MSNBC.com, September 18, 2008.

6. http://www.Merriam-Webster.com/dictionary/Fascism.

7. Spencer Tucker and Priscilla Mary Roberts, *Encyclopedia of World War II* (Santa Barbara: ABC-CLIO, 2004), 1037.

8. Jeffrey Herbener, "The Vampire Economy: Italy, Germany, and the US," Ludwig von Mises Institute, October 13, 2005, http://www.mises.org/story/1935.

9. Thomas DiLorenzo, "Economic Fascism," *The Freeman,* Vol. 44, No. 6 (June 1994).

10. "After 25 Years: Memory of Two Dictators," *Time,* May 4, 1970.

11. Denis Mack Smith, *Mussolini* (New York: Alfred A. Knopf, 1982), 118.

12. William L. Shirer, *The Rise and Fall of the Third Reich* (New York: Simon & Schuster, 1960), 259–61.

13. Bill Koenig, "Ford Has $8.7 Billion Loss, Shifts Away from Trucks," Bloomberg.com, July 24, 2008.

14. Ibid.

15. "Timeline: Tracing Chrysler's History," NPR.org, May 14, 2007.

16. "Chrysler, Ford and GM in Trouble," WhatCar.com, November 10, 2008.

17. "Daimler, Cerberus Spar Over Chrysler," Reuters, November 26, 2008.

18. Jeffrey McCracken and John D. Stoll, "Bankruptcy Fears Rise as Chrysler, GM Seek Federal Aid," *Wall Street Journal,* October 27, 2008.

19. "Dissident Chrysler Group to Disband," *New York Times,* May 8, 2009.

20. McCracken and Stoll, "Bankruptcy Fears Rise."

21. Brian Ross and Joseph Rhee, "Big Three CEOs Flew Private Jets to Plead for Public Funds," ABCNews.com, November 19, 2008.

22. Josh Levs, "Big Three Auto CEOs Flew Private Jets to Ask for Taxpayer Money," CNN.com, November 19, 2008.

23. Rachel Balik, "Congress Under Fire for Travels During Recess," Finding Dulcinea.com, February 20, 2009.
24. Nelson Solomon, "Pelosi in Italy: Why Is This Better than Auto Executives Flying?," TheVistaOnline.com, February 24, 2009.
25. Ross and Rhee, "Big Three CEOs Flew Private Jets."
26. Jonathan Weisman and Shailagh Murray, "House Approves Broadest Ethics Bill Since '70s," *Washington Post,* January 5, 2007.
27. David D. Kirkpatrick, "Senate Passes Vast Ethics Overhaul," *New York Times,* January 19, 2007.
28. "GM: We Need $12 Billion to Stay in Business," MSNBC.com, December 3, 2008.
29. "$17.4 Billion Auto Bailout Has Strings Attached," MSNBC.com, December 19, 2008.
30. "Wagoner Is Ousted to Maintain GM's Lifeline," BusinessWeek.com, March 29, 2009.
31. "Exclusive: General Motors CEO Fritz Henderson," FoxNews.com, May 15, 2009.
32. Sheryl Gay Stolberg and Bill Vlasic, "President Gives a Short Lifeline to Carmakers," *New York Times,* March 30, 2009.
33. "Mich. Gov. Says Wagoner Was 'Sacrificial Lamb,'" Associated Press, March 30, 2009.
34. John D. Stoll and Sharon Terlep, "GM Offers US a Majority Stake," *Wall Street Journal,* April 28, 2009.
35. "Gettelfinger Motors," *Wall Street Journal,* May 4, 2009.
36. Stolberg and Vlasic, "President Gives a Short Lifeline." *New York Times,* March 30, 2009.
37. Stephanie Condon, "Obama: 'I Don't Want to Run Auto Companies,'" CBSNews.com, April 29, 2009.
38. "Obama Announces Chrysler Bankruptcy Plan," NYTimes.com, April 30, 2009.
39. "UAW Leaders Recommend Chrysler Concessions; Union Trust to Own 55 Percent of Company," Associated Press, April 28, 2009.
40. "Dissident Chrysler Group to Disband," NYTimes.com, May 8, 2009.
41. "Obama Announces Chrysler Bankruptcy Plan," NYTimes.com, April 30, 2009.
42. "Remarks by the President on the Auto Industry," The White House, April 30, 2009, http://www.whitehouse.gov/the_press_office/Remarks-by-the-President-on-the-Auto-Industry/.

43. Ben Shapiro, "If You Disagree with Obama, Are You Anti-American?," Creators Syndicate, May 13, 2009.

44. "Statement from Non-Tarp Lenders of Chrysler," *Wall Street Journal,* April 30, 2009.

45. Jake Tapper, "White House Denies Charge by Attorney That Administration Threatened to Destroy Investment Firm's Reputation," ABC News.com, May 2, 2009.

46. Sharon Terlep, "GM, Segway to Make Vehicle," WSJ.com, April 7, 2009.

47. Josie Garthwaite, "What the Chrysler-Fiat Deal Means for Green Car Battery Startups," Earth2Tech, May 1, 2009.

48. Wendell Goler, "President Obama Announces Gas Mileage Standards," FoxNews.com, May 19, 2009.

49. David Kiley, "Cash-for-Clunkers Proposals Gain Popular Traction," *BusinessWeek,* April 1, 2009.

50. David Kiley, "Autos: Cash for Clunkers Advances," *BusinessWeek,* May 5, 2009.

51. Michael E. Telzrow, "UAW, Feds Gain Control of Chrysler," The NewAmerican.com, May 5, 2009.

52. Ben Shapiro, "Unions Fight to End American Capitalism," Creators Syndicate, November 26, 2008.

Chapter 5: Financial Incest

1. "Bush's Speech on the Financial Crisis, September 2008," CFR.org, September 19, 2008.

2. "JPMorgan to Buy Bear Stearns for $2 a Share," Reuters, March 17, 2008.

3. "Bear Stearns Rescue Defended," USAToday.com, April 3, 2008.

4. Ibid.

5. Elizabeth MacDonald, "Did the SEC Miss Warning Signs at Bear Stearns?," FoxBusiness.com, June 23, 2008.

6. "Bear Stearns CEO: No Liquidity Crisis for Firm," CNBC.com, March 12, 2008.

7. "Bernanke Says Bear Stearns Rescue Was 'Necessary,'" PBS.org transcript, *Online NewsHour,* April 3, 2008, http://www.pbs.org/newshour/bb/business/jan-june08/fed_04-03.html.

8. A. Craig Copetas, "'Out of Control' CEOs Spurned Davos Warnings on Risk," Bloomberg.com, October 24, 2008.

9. Tim Weber, "Market Turmoil in Focus for Davos," BBCNews.com, January 22, 2008.

10. Copetas, " 'Out of Control' CEOs."

11. Ibid.

12. Ibid.

13. Mark Pittman, Elliot Blair Smith, and Jesse Westbrook, "Cox's SEC Censors Report on Bear Stearns Collapse," Bloomberg.com, October 7, 2008.

14. Michael Siconolfi, "Did Authorities Miss a Chance to Ease Crunch?—SEC, Spitzer Probed Bear CDO Pricing in '05, Before Backing Away," *Wall Street Journal,* December 10, 2007.

15. Elizabeth MacDonald, "Did the SEC Miss Warning Signs at Bear Stearns?"

16. Stephen Labaton, "New Agency Proposed to Oversee Freddie Mac and Fannie Mae," *New York Times,* September 11, 2003.

17. "Federal Housing Enterprise Regulatory Reform Act of 2005," Gov Track.us, May 25, 2006.

18. Ann Coulter, "They Gave Your Mortgage to a Less Qualified Minority," Universal Press Syndicate, September 24, 2008.

19. Steven Malanga, "Feds Re-Impose Loan Standards They Helped Undermine," Manhattan Institute, February 18, 2009.

20. Stephen Labaton and Steven Weisman, "US Weighs Takeover of Two Mortgage Giants," NYTimes.com, July 11, 2008.

21. Ashley Seager and Phillip Inman, "US Housing Crisis: Freddie and Fannie Are Nationalised," *The Guardian,* September 8, 2008.

22. "Fannie Mae Seeks $15.2B After $25.2B 4Q Loss," Associated Press, February 26, 2009.

23. Ryan Grim, "Dems Investigating Bush Administration Role in AIG Collapse," HuffingtonPost.com, April 1, 2009.

24. Matthew Karnitschnig, Deborah Solomon, Liam Pleven, and Jon E. Hilsenrath, "U.S. to Take Over AIG in $85 Billion Bailout," *Wall Street Journal,* September 16, 2008.

25. Lisa Lerer, "Fannie, Freddie Spent $200M to Buy Influence," Politico.com, July 16, 2008.

26. Seager and Inman, "US Housing Crisis."

27. "President Bush Promotes Compassionate Conservatism," National Education Association Health Information Network, April 30, 2002, http://www.neahin.org/programs/schoolsafety/september11/vpvtbush april.htm.

28. George Will, "Freedom vs. Equality," Townhall.com, February 1, 2004.

29. "Bush Says Sacrificed Free-Market Principles to Save Economy," Associated Press, December 16, 2008.

30. "Despite 'Regret,' US to Pour Money into Banks," Associated Press, October 14, 2008.
31. "Judicial Watch Forces Release of Bank Bailout Documents," Judicial Watch.org, May 13, 2009.
32. Damian Paletta, Jon Hilsenrath, and Deborah Solomon, "At Moment of Truth, U.S. Forced Big Bankers to Blink," *Wall Street Journal,* October 15, 2008.
33. Ben Shapiro, "If You Play Ball with the Government, Expect to Strike Out," Creators Syndicate, March 4, 2009.
34. Dan Fitzpatrick, Susanne Craig, and Deborah Solomon, "In Merrill Deal, U.S. Played Hardball," *Wall Street Journal,* February 5, 2009.
35. "Busting Bank of America," *Wall Street Journal,* April 28, 2009.
36. Ibid.
37. Ivea M. Augstums and Mitch Weiss, "Ken Lewis Fired as BOA Chairman, to Remain as CEO," Associated Press, April 29, 2009.
38. "Citigroup Bailout: Feds Offer Massive Rescue Package to Financial Giant," HuffingtonPost.com, November 23, 2008.
39. Chris Isidore, "Feds Step Deeper into Citi Bailout," CNN.com, February 27, 2009.
40. "Obama Sets Executive Pay Limits," CNN.com, February 4, 2009.
41. "New Rules," WhiteHouse.gov, February 4, 2009.
42. Heidi N. Moore, "Citigroup: The Struggle to Keep Phibro Happy," WSJ.com, April 29, 2009.
43. Joseph Woelfel, "Morgan May Spin Off Proprietary Trade Desk," The Street.com, April 24, 2009.
44. Jackie Calmes, "Geithner Opposes Caps on Executive Pay," NYTimes.com, May 18, 2009.
45. Stuart Varney, "Barack Obama Maintains Control Over Banks by Refusing to Accept Repayment of TARP Money," WSJ.com, April 4, 2009.
46. Jim Puzzanghera and E. Scott Reckard, "Big Banks' 'Stress Test' Results to Be Reassuring, Geithner Says," *Los Angeles Times,* May 7, 2009.
47. David Enzrich, Dan Fitzpatrick, and Marshall Eckblad, "Banks Won Concessions on Tests," *Wall Street Journal,* May 9, 2009.
48. Jeff Poor, "Media Mum on Barney Frank's Fannie Mae Love Connection," Business & Media Institute, September 24, 2008.
49. Damian Paletta and David Enrich, "Political Interference Seen in Bank Bailout Decisions," *Wall Street Journal,* January 22, 2009.

Chapter 6: Timothy Leary Is Not Dead

1. Jake Tapper, "Obama and McCain Yuk It Up at Al Smith Dinner," ABC News.com, October 16, 2008.
2. Barack Obama, *The Audacity of Hope* (New York: Crown, 2006), 36–37.
3. Michelle Malkin, "Barack Obama: Soul-fixer," MichelleMalkin.com, February 16, 2008.
4. Laura Mansnerus, "Timothy Leary, Pied Piper of Psychedelic 60's, Dies at 75," *New York Times,* June 1, 1996.
5. Martin Torgoff, *Can't Find My Way Home* (New York: Simon & Schuster, 2003), 209.
6. Mansnerus, "Timothy Leary."
7. Audio Cassette, "Timothy Leary Live at Starwood," Association for Consciousness Exploration (1992).
8. Timothy Leary, *The Politics of Ecstasy* (Berkeley: Ronin, 1998), 134.
9. Timothy Leary, *How to Operate Your Brain* (video, 1993).
10. Timothy Leary, *Timothy Leary's Last Trip* (video, 1997).
11. Leary, *The Politics of Ecstasy,* 43.
12. Martin Higgins, *The Nastiest Things Ever Said About Republicans* (Guilford, CT: Globe Pequot Press, 2006), 130.
13. Timothy Leary, *The Politics of Ecstasy,* 168.
14. Ibid., 169.
15. Ibid., 168.
16. Ibid., 172.
17. Ibid., 168–71.
18. Jim Miller, *Democracy Is in the Streets* (Cambridge: Harvard University Press, 1995), 29.
19. Tom Hayden, *The Port Huron Statement* (New York: Thunder's Mouth Press, 2005).
20. Students for a Democratic Society, "Port Huron Statement," 1962, http://coursesa.matrix.msu.edu/~hst306/documents/huron.html.
21. Ibid.
22. Ibid.
23. Ibid.
24. Ibid.
25. Ibid.
26. Jama Lazerow and Yohuru Williams, *In Search of the Black Panther Party* (Durham, NC: Duke University Press, 2006), 227.
27. Robert Vincent Daniels, *Year of the Heroic Guerrilla* (Cambridge: Harvard University Press, 1996), 146.

28. Barber, *A Hard Rain Fell* (Jackson: University Press of Mississippi, 2008), 210.

29. Klaus P. Fischer, *America in White, Black and Gray* (New York: Continuum International Publishing Group, 2006), 278.

30. Barber, *A Hard Rain Fell,* note 27, 211.

31. Alan Wang, "Ayers' Speech Interrupted by Protesters," ABCLocal.go .com, January 28, 2009.

32. Dinitia Smith, "No Regrets for a Love of Explosives; In a Memoir of Sorts, a War Protestor Talks of Life with the Weathermen," *New York Times,* September 11, 2001.

33. Jeremy Varon, *Bringing the War Home* (Berkeley: University of California Press, 2004), 151.

34. Ibid., 153.

35. Smith, "No Regrets for a Love of Explosives."

36. "The Black Panther Party Platform," October 1966, http://history .hanover.edu/courses/excerpts/111bppp.html.

37. Danny Westneat, "Reunion of Black Panthers Stirs Memories of Aggression, Activism," *Seattle Times,* June 1, 2005.

38. Kate Coleman, "Souled Out," *New West Magazine,* May 19, 1980.

39. "Justice: A Bad Week for the Good Guys," *Time,* August 17, 1970.

40. "Arrest in Murder of Huey Newton," *New York Times,* August 26, 1989.

41. Earl Caldwell, "Angela Davis Acquitted on All Charges," *New York Times,* June 5, 1972.

42. Aleksandr Solzhenitsyn, *Warning to the West* (New York: Macmillan, 1986), 61.

43. Tom Wolfe, *The Purple Decades* (New York: Farrar, Straus, & Giroux, 1982), 183.

44. Jerry M. Lewis and Thomas R. Hensley, "The May 4 Shootings at Kent State University: The Search for Historical Accuracy," Department of Sociology, Kent State, http://dept.kent.edu/sociology/lewis/lewihen.htm.

45. "Kent State University," *Weekly Compilation of Presidential Documents,* Vol. 6, No. 19 (May 11, 1970) (Washington, D.C.: U.S. Government Printing Office, 1970), 613.

46. Ron Grossman, "Family Ties Proved Ayers' Point," *Chicago Tribune,* May 18, 2008.

47. Guy Benson and Bernardine Dohrn, "A Terrorist Law Professor," Front PageMagazine.com, April 19, 2005.

48. "The Weather Underground: Exclusive Interview: Bernardine Dohrn and Bill Ayers," PBS.org, January 2004.

49. Ibid.

50. Smith, "No Regrets for a Love of Explosives."

51. Stanley Kurtz, "Obama and Ayers Pushed Radicalism on Schools," *Wall Street Journal,* September 23, 2008.

52. Solzhenitsyn, *Warning to the West,* 61.

53. "Faculty, History of Consciousness, University of California, Santa Cruz," Histcon.UCSC.edu, http://histcon.ucsc.edu/faculty/davis.html.

54. "Angela Davis," DiscoverTheNetworks.org, http://www.discoverthenet works.org/individualProfile.asp?indid=1303.

55. Ibid.

56. Kevin Flynn, "Special Report: The Churchill File," *Rocky Mountain News,* June 9, 2005.

57. Ward Churchill, "Some People Push Back: On the Justice of Roosting Chickens," *Kersplebedeb Revolutionary Writings,* http://www.kersplebe deb.com/mystuff/s11/churchill.html.

58. Katherine Mangu-Ward, "A Radical Takes the Stand," *Wall Street Journal,* March 26, 2009.

59. Associated Press, "Ayers: Churchill Was Fired from University in 'Witch Hunt,'" FoxNews.com, March 6, 2009.

60. Katherine Mangu-Ward, "A Radical Takes the Stand," *Wall Street Journal,* March 26, 2009.

61. Chris Hedges, "Why I Am a Socialist," TruthDig.org, December 29, 2008, http://www.truthdig.com/report/item/20081229_why_i_am_a _socialist/.

62. "Transcript: Bill Moyers Talks with Chris Hedges," PBS.org, March 7, 2003.

63. Tony Blankley, "Obama's 'Blank Screen,'" *Washington Times,* January 27, 2009.

64. Stanley Kurtz, "NYT's Ayers-Obama Whitewash," NationalReview.com, October 4, 2008.

65. Jack Cashill, "Who Wrote *Dream from My Father?*," AmericanThinker .com, October 9, 2008.

66. "Transcript of Obama's Wesleyan Commencement Address," WFSB .com, May 5, 2008.

67. "Obama ASU Speech: Full Text," HuffingtonPost.com, May 13, 2009.

Chapter 7: Where's My Pony?

1. Adam Lerrick, "Obama and the Tax Tipping Point," *Wall Street Journal,* October 22, 2008.

2. Amber Ellis, " 'Tea Party': Stimulus Bill Too Steep," *Cincinnati Enquirer,* March 16, 2009.

3. Michelle Malkin, "And the Winner Is . . . Peggy the Moocher," Creators Syndicate, November 5, 2008.

4. Robert DiClerico, *Voting in America* (Santa Barbara: ABC-CLIO, 2004), 2–3.

5. Alexander Keyssar, *The Right to Vote* (New York: Basic Books, 2001), 23.

6. Philip B. Kurland and Ralph Lerner, ed., *The Founders' Constitution* (Chicago: University of Chicago Press, 1987), 396.

7. Ibid., 650.

8. Woodrow Wilson, "Socialism and Democracy," http://teachingameri canhistory.org/library/index.asp?document=2208.

9. Neal Boortz and John Linder, *The FairTax Book* (New York: Harper-Collins, 2006), 23.

10. Joe Lauria, "Wall Street Hated FDR Too," HuffingtonPost.com, February 4, 2009.

11. John Fund, "Above All, Try Something," *Wall Street Journal,* March 14, 2005.

12. Neal Boortz and John Linder, *The FairTax Book* (New York: Harper-Collins, 2006), 25–26.

13. Christina Hoff Summers and Sally Satel, M.D., *One Nation Under Therapy* (New York: St. Martin's, 2005), 68–71.

14. Ibid.

15. Ibid., 27.

16. Anita Vogel, "School Says Game of Tag Is Out," FoxNews.com, June 20, 2002.

17. "Grade Inflation Seen Rising," Inside Higher Ed, March 12, 2009, http://www.insidehighered.com/news/2009/03/12/grades.

18. Bruce Cole, "Interview with Harvey Mansfield," NEH.gov, http://www.neh.gov/whoweare/mansfield/HMinterview.html.

19. Steve Salerno, "Overdosing on Oprah," NationalReview.com, May 12, 2005.

20. Lyndon Baines Johnson, "The Great Society," May 22, 1964, http://www.americanrhetoric.com/speeches/lbjthegreatsociety.htm.

21. 397 U.S. 254 (1970).

22. 457 U.S. 202 (1982).

23. "Reparations," JohnConyers.com, http://www.johnconyers.com/issues/reparations.

24. "Obama Suggests Reparations to Blacks, Native Americans," WorldNet Daily.com, July 30, 2008.

25. "It's Easier than Ever to Find Out if You Qualify for EITC," IRS.gov, http://www.irs.gov/individuals/article/0,,id=96406,00.html.

26. "EITC Eligibility Rules Outlined," IRS.gov, http://www.irs.gov/news room/article/0,,id=203139,00.html.

27. Laurence Vance, "Tax Credit or Income Transfer?," LewRockwell.com, April 14, 2004, http://www.lewrockwell.com/vance/vance11.html.

28. "EITC Eligibility Rules Outlined," IRS.gov, http://www.irs.gov/news room/article/0,,id=203139,00.html.

29. "FNS Supplemental Nutrition Assistance Program (SNAP)," USDA.gov, October 1, 2008, http://www.fns.usda.gov/FSP/

30. "Obama's 95% Illusion," *Wall Street Journal,* October 13, 2008.

31. Ibid.

32. "House Approves 'Cash for Clunkers' Plan," Associated Press, June 9, 2009.

33. Ann Coulter, "They Gave Your Mortgage to a Less Qualified Minority," Universal Press Syndicate, September 24, 2008.

34. Thomas J. DiLorenzo, "The CRA Scam and Its Defendants," Mises.org, April 30, 2008.

35. Stan Liebowitz, "The Real Scandal," *New York Post,* February 5, 2008.

36. Steven Malanga, "Feds Re-Impose Loan Standards They Helped Undermine," Manhattan Institute, February 18, 2009.

37. Ibid.

38. Ibid.

39. Shailagh Murray, "Student-Loan Overhaul Key to Obama's Goals," *Washington Post,* May 5, 2009.

40. Lisa Mascaro, "How Obama's Mortgage Relief Plan Pencils Out," *Las Vegas Sun,* February 21, 2009.

41. Ibid.

42. Ibid.

43. Michael Kelly, "The 1992 Campaign: The Democrats; Clinton Says Bush Imperils Elderly," *New York Times,* September 2, 1992.

44. Adam Nagourney, "Democrats' Ad Has Bush Mistreating Elderly," *New York Times,* October 4, 2002.

45. Brooks Jackson, "Obama's False Medicare Accusation," FactCheck.org, October 20, 2008, http://www.newsweek.com/id/164796.

46. Jim Malone, "Obama, McCain Joust Over Economic Issues," VOANews .com, July 30, 2008.

47. 545 U.S. 469 (2005).
48. Ibid.

Chapter 8: Grapefruit, Anyone?

1. Lenore Skenazy, "Why I Let My 9-Year-Old Ride the Subway Alone," *New York Sun,* April 1, 2008.
2. Lenore Skenazy, "The Last Word: Advice from 'America's Worst Mom,'" TheWeek.com, May 8, 2009.
3. Lenore Skenazy, "America's Worst Mom?," *New York Sun,* April 8, 2008.
4. Al Baker, "City Homicides Still Dropping, to Under 500," *New York Times,* November 23, 2007.
5. Joe Barton, "Sending Us Back to 1875," *Washington Times,* May 10, 2009.
6. Ibid.
7. "Committee on Oversight and Government Reform," Oversight and Government Reform—Republicans, April 28, 2009, http://republicans .oversight.house.gov/news/PRArticle.aspx?NewsID=519.
8. Japhy Grant, "Perez Hilton's Gay Witch Hunt," Salon.com, December 15, 2006.
9. Ibid.
10. "Perez Hilton Calls Miss California a 'Dumb Bitch,'" YouTube, April 21, 2009, http://www.youtube.com/watch?v=NMYP9opfMfI.
11. Michelle Healy, "'Katie Couric Effect' Boosts Colonoscopy Rates," *USA Today,* July 14, 2003.
12. Katie Couric, "Katie Couric: I Must Share This Vital Information," MSNBC.com, March 31, 2004.
13. Michelle Healy, "'Katie Couric Effect' Boosts Colonoscopy Rates."
14. Bayard Webster, "Experts Theorize About 'Copycat Syndrome,'" NY Times.com, October 30, 1982.
15. Adam Cohen, "Criminals as Copycats," Time.com, May 31, 1999.
16. Mick Sinclair, *San Francisco* (Oxford: Signal, 2004), 121.
17. Alex Johnson, "Sex Scandal? We've Been Here Before," MSNBC.com, March 1, 2005.
18. David Margolick, "Judge in Simpson Trial Allows TV Camera in Courtroom," *New York Times,* November 8, 1994.
19. "Martha Stewart Released from Prison," FoxNews.com, March 5, 2005.
20. "Durbin Cashed Out During Big Stock Collapse," *Chicago Sun-Times,* June 13, 2009.

21. "1993: Michael Jackson Accused of Child Abuse," BBC.co.uk, August 24, 1993.

22. Michael Levenson and Jonathan Saltzman, "At Harvard Law, a Unifying Voice," *Boston Globe,* January 28, 2007.

23. Paul Watkins, "A Promise of Redemption," *New York Times,* August 6, 1995.

24. Paul Ruffin, "Dreams from My Father: A Story of Race and Inheritance," *Washington Post,* August 20, 1995.

25. Scott Malcomson, "The Nation; An Appeal Beyond Race," *New York Times,* August 1, 2004.

26. "Barack Obama Dazzles Hollywood," Associated Press, February 20, 2007.

27. Ben Shapiro, "Obama's Hollywood: Backing Evil from Moscow to Tehran," Creators Syndicate, March 11, 2009.

28. "George Clooney Denies Advising Barack Obama," *Daily Mail* (U.K.), August 14, 2008.

29. *Hardball with Chris Matthews,* June 8, 2007.

30. http://marcambinder.theatlantic.com/Important%20memo%20from%20Walter%20Shorenstein%20on%20Press%20and%20the%20Presidential%20Campaign.pdf.

31. Ibid.

32. "Helen Thomas: Not Even Nixon Tried to Control the Media like Obama," CNSNews.com, July 1, 2009.

33. Daniel Kurtzman, "President Obama's Best Jokes from the Radio and TV Correspondents Dinner," About.com.

34. "ABC News Health Care Special Draws Fire," THRFeed.com, June 16, 2009.

35. Kurtzman, "President Obama's Best Jokes."

36. Jeff Gerth and Brady Dennis, "How a Loophole Benefits GE in Bank Rescue," *Washington Post,* June 29, 2009.

37. Greg Braxton, "Funny Thing About Obama . . ." *Los Angeles Times,* May 4, 2009.

Chapter 9: Drain the Political Swamp

1. David McCullough, *John Adams* (New York: Simon & Schuster, 2001), 542.

2. Ibid., 553.

3. David Espo, "Pelosi Says She Would Drain GOP 'Swamp,' " *Washington Post,* October 6, 2006.

4. Senator Harry Reid, "Excerpt from *The Good Fight*," HuffingtonPost .com, April 30, 2008.

5. Susan Schmidt and James V. Grimaldi, "Abramoff Pleads Guilty to 3 Counts," *Washington Post,* January 4, 2006.

6. Michael Crowley, "A Lobbyist in Full," *New York Times,* May 1, 2005.

7. Tim Wheeler, "'Put the Hammer in the Slammer': DeLay Linked to Swindle of Indian Tribes," PWW.org, April 23, 2005.

8. Crowley, "A Lobbyist in Full."

9. Ibid.

10. Deborah White, "Sen. Harry Reid Decries Republican 'Organized Crime,'" About.com, January 18, 2006.

11. "Reid Aided Abramoff Clients, Records Show," Associated Press, February 9, 2006.

12. "Abramoff Tribes Donated Funds to Lawmakers," Associated Press, November 17, 2009.

13. "Reid Aided Abramoff Clients, Records Show," Associated Press, February 9, 2006.

14. Chris Isadore, "Countrywide: $1.2 Billion Loss, but Forecasts Profit in 4Q," Money.cnn.com, October 26, 2007.

15. David Scheer and Karen Gullo, "Countrywide's Mozilo, Two Ex-Executives Accused by SEC of Fraud," Bloomberg.com, June 4, 2009.

16. Daniel Golden, "Countrywide's Many 'Friends,'" *Portfolio,* June 12, 2008.

17. "Dodd's Peek-a-Boo Disclosure," WSJ.com, February 3, 2009.

18. Al Hubbard and Noam Neusner, "Where Was Sen. Dodd?," *Washington Post,* September 12, 2008.

19. Jake Lansburgh, "Dodd on Fannie, Freddie: They Are 'Sound,'" CNN .com, July 13, 2008.

20. Kevin Hassett, "How the Democrats Created the Financial Crisis," Bloomberg.com, September 22, 2008.

21. Hubbard and Neusner, "Where Was Sen. Dodd?"

22. Alison Vekshin, "Dodd Plans Senate Hearing on Fannie, Freddie Take-over," Bloomberg.com, September 8, 2008.

23. Ibid.

24. Michael D. Shear and Paul Kane, "Anger Over Firm Depletes Obama's Political Capital," *Washington Post,* March 17, 2009.

25. "Dodd Defends Actions as an AIG Exec Returns $6 Million Bonus," CNN.com, March 20, 2009.

26. "Dodd's AIG Problem," USAToday.com, March 19, 2009.

27. "AIG: All Recipients," OpenSecrets.org, http://www.opensecrets.org/orgs/recips.php?id=D000000123&type=P&state=&sort=A&cycle=A.

28. Judson Berger, "Congress Invites Court Challenge with AIG Taxation Plan," FoxNews.com, March 18, 2009.

29. Ibid.

30. Greg Hitt, "Pelosi Presses for 'Truth Commission,'" WSJ.com, April 22, 2009.

31. "What Congress Knew," WSJ.com, May 11, 2009.

32. Ibid.

33. Deirdre Walsh and Pam Benson, "CIA Says Pelosi Knew About Waterboarding; She Says No," CNN.com, May 8, 2009.

34. Sam Youngman, "CIA Director Says Pelosi Received the Truth," The Hill.com, May 15, 2009.

35. Mike Soraghan and Jared Allen, "Pelosi: CIA Lied to Me About Waterboarding," Politico.com, May 14, 2009.

36. Kara Rowland, "Pelosi Refuses Queries on CIA Dispute," *Washington Times,* May 23, 2009.

37. John Hawkins, "If the Bush Administration Lied About WMD, So Did These People—Version 3.0," RightWingNews.com http://www.rightwingnews.com/quotes/demsonwmds.php.

38. Ibid.

39. Audra Ang, "Pelosi Appeals for China's Help on Climate Change," Associated Press, May 27, 2009.

40. David S. Morgan, "When Diplomacy Doesn't Work," CBSNews.com, March 30, 2007.

41. Hawkins, "If the Bush Administration Lied About WMD."

42. Ibid.

43. "Words of Mass Destruction," Snopes.com http://www.snopes.com/politics/war/wmdquotes.asp.

44. Glenn Kessler, "Clinton: Cheney Not a Reliable Source," Washington Post.com, April 22, 2009.

45. "Hillary Clinton Says She Wouldn't Have Voted for Iraq War," ABC News.com, December 18, 2006.

46. Bill Dedman, "TV Movie Led to Prostitute's Disclosures," *Washington Post,* August 27, 1989.

47. Jeff Poor, "Media Mum on Barney Frank's Fannie Mae Love Connection," Business & Media Institute, September 24, 2008.

48. Beth Healy, "Frank: Lack of Government Regulation Led to Troubles Plaguing Wall Street," *Boston Globe,* September 18, 2008.

49. "Barney the Underwriter," *Wall Street Journal,* June 24, 2009.

50. Chuck Neubauer, "Senator's Way to Wealth Was Paved with Favors," *Los Angeles Times,* December 17, 2003.

51. Ibid.

52. "Alaska Senator on Charges: 'I Am Innocent,'" CNN.com, July 29, 2008.

53. Matt Apuzzo and Jesse J. Holland, "Stevens Convicted on All Counts," Associated Press, October 27, 2008.

54. "Ted Stevens Conviction Overturned," BBCNews.com, April 7, 2009.

55. "Nevada Dem Skips Katrina Vote to Have Neck Lift," DrudgeReport .com, February 27, 2006.

56. Robert W. Greene, *The Sting Man: Inside Abscam* (New York: E. P. Dutton, 1981).

57. Ibid.

58. Ibid. 254.

59. Ibid.

60. "Lawmaker: Marines Killed Iraqis 'in Cold Blood,'" MSNBC.com, May 17, 2006.

61. Dennis B. Roddy, "Critics Claim John Murtha Is Capitalizing on a Corrupt System, but He's Not Apologizing," Post-Gazette.com, March 29, 2009.

62. "Lawyers/Law Firms: Top Recipients: 2008," OpenSecrets.org.

63. "Educators: Top Recipients: 2008," OpenSecrets.org.

64. "Hedge Funds: Top Recipients: 2008," OpenSecrets.org.

65. Mike Viquera, "A Do-Nothing Congress?," MSNBC.com, April 29, 2008.

66. H. Res. 274, March 23, 2009.

67. H. Res. 255, March 17, 2009.

68. H. Res. 263, March 18, 2009.

69. H. Res. 459, May 19, 2009.

70. H. Res. 191, February 25, 2009.

71. H. Res. 193, February 25, 2009.

72. S. Res. 86, March 26, 2009.

73. S. Res. 113, April 23, 2009.

74. H. Res. 388, May 12, 2009.

75. H. Res. 438, May 14, 2009.

76. "About," Committee on Standards of Official Conduct, http://ethics .house.gov/About/Default.aspx?Section=7.

77. "Affidavit: $90,000 Found in Congressman's Freezer," CNN.com, May 22, 2006.

78. Daphne Retter, "Rangel Faces Another Ethics Inquiry: Report," *New York Post,* June 2, 2009.

79. "First on CNBC: CNBC Transcript: CNBC's Erin Burnett and Mark Haines Interview Congressman Charles Rangel, Chairman of the House Ways and Means Committee, Today on 'Squawk on the Street,'" CNBC .com, March 19, 2009.

80. Jonathan Weisman, "Hastert Aides Interest Ethics Panel," *Washington Post,* October 12, 2006.

81. John Fund, "Meet the New Boss," OpinionJournal.com, November 15, 2006.

82. Mike Allen, "House GOP Leaders Name Loyalist to Replace Ethics Chief," *Washington Post,* February 3, 2005.

83. "Text of Draft Proposal for Bailout Plan," NYTimes.com, September 20, 2008.

84. Connie Hair, "SURPRISE! Dems Break Promise: Stimulus Bill to Floor Friday," HumanEvents.com, February 12, 2009.

85. Jared Allen, "House Passes $787B Economic Stimulus Bill," TheHill .com, February 13, 2009.

86. "Reelection Rates Over the Years," OpenSecrets.org, http://www.open secrets.org/bigpicture/reelect.php.

87. Alexander Hamilton, *Federalist No. 57.*

Chapter 10: The Right Stuff

1. "75% Have Favorable Opinion of U.S. Military This Memorial Day," RasmussenReports.com, May 24, 2009.

2. Lydia Saad, "Americans' Confidence in Military Up, Banks Down," Gallup.com, June 24, 2009.

3. Humphrey Taylor, "Changing Attitudes to the Police," Harris Poll, April 7, 1999.

4. Tom Wolfe, *The Right Stuff* (New York: Bantam, 1983), 19.

5. Mark Murray, "Obama: Buchenwald, Not Auschwitz," MSNBC.com, May 28, 2008.

6. Larry Gelbart, *Laughing Matters* (New York: Random House, 1998), 44.

7. Heather Huntington, "John Cusack on *Grace Is Gone*," ReelzChannel .com, December 7, 2007.

8. Tim Kane, "Who Bears the Burden? Demographic Characteristics of

U.S. Military Recruits Before and After 9/11," Heritage.org, November 7, 2005.

9. Stone Martindale, "Matt Damon Thinks the Bush Twins Can Serve Too," MonstersandCritics.com, December 17, 2006.

10. Bob Herbert, "Blood Runs Red, Not Blue," *New York Times,* August 18, 2005.

11. Kane, "Who Bears the Burden?"

12. Shanea Watkins, Ph.D., and James Sherk, "Who Serves in the U.S. Military? The Demographics of Enlisted Troops and Officers," Heritage.org, August 21, 2008.

13. Erika Hayasaki, "Military Recruiters Targeting Minority Teens," *Los Angeles Times,* April 5, 2005.

14. Deborah Sontag and Lizette Alvarez, "Across America, Deadly Echoes of Foreign Battles," *New York Times,* January 13, 2009.

15. Ann Coulter, "Murder Spree by People Who Refuse to Ask for Directions," AnnCoulter.com, January 14, 2009.

16. "Homeland Security Chief Apologizes to Veterans Groups," CNN.com, April 16, 2009.

17. Patrik Jonsson, "Shooting of Two Soldiers in Little Rock Puts Focus on 'Lone Wolf' Islamic Extremists," CSMonitor.com, June 10, 2009.

18. "Military Suicide Rate," ChicagoTribune.com, May 29, 2008.

19. Al Pessin, "US Army Suicide Rate Continues to Rise," VOANews.com, May 29, 2008.

20. John Larson, "Behind the Death of Timothy Thomas," *Dateline NBC,* April 9, 2004.

21. Mara H. Gottfried, "Sharpton: Police Need Federal-Level Oversight," Enquirer.com, April 16, 2001.

22. John Ridley, "The Manifesto of Ascendancy for the Modern American Nigger," Esquire.com, November 30, 2006.

23. Lou Cannon, "American Travesty: How Justice Failed the Rodney King Cops," *National Review,* August 30, 1999.

24. Seth Mydans, "The Police Verdict," *New York Times,* April 30, 1992.

25. Jim Crogan, "The L.A. 53," LA Weekly.com, May 2, 2002.

26. "The L.A. Riots: 15 Years After Rodney King," Time.com, http://www.time .com/time/specials/2007/article/0,28804,1614117_1614084_1614511,00 .html.

27. "The Arrest Record of Rodney King," University of Missouri-Kansas City School of Law, http://www.law.umkc.edu/faculty/projects/ftrials/ lapd/kingarrests.html.

Chapter 11: A Call to Arms

1. 1 Kings 18:21.
2. Matthew 25:26.
3. Revelation 3:15–16.
4. Rosa Parks and Jim Haskins, *Rosa Parks: My Story* (New York: Dial, 1992), 116.